OUTPACING THE PROs

OUTPACING
THE PROs

Using Indexes to Beat Wall Street's Savviest Money Managers

David M. Blitzer

McGraw-Hill

New York   San Francisco   Washington, D.C.   Auckland   Bogotá
Caracas   Lisbon   London   Madrid   Mexico City   Milan
Montreal   New Delhi   San Juan   Singapore
Sydney   Tokyo   Toronto

Library of Congress Cataloging-in-Publication Data

Blitzer, David M.
    Outpacing the pros : using indexes to beat Wall Street's savviest money managers / by David M. Blitzer.
        p.   cm.
    Includes bibliographical references.
    ISBN 0-07-135586-3
    1. Stock price indexes. 2. Stock price forecasting. 3. Speculation. I. Title.
HG4636.B56   2000
332.63'22—dc21   00-062223

McGraw-Hill

*A Division of The **McGraw-Hill** Companies*

1 2 3 4 5 6 7 8 9 0   AGM/AGM   0 9 8 7 6 5 4 3 2 1 0

ISBN 0-07-135586-3

This book was set in Times Roman by Matrix Publishing Services.
Printed and bound by Quebecor World/Martinsburg.

This publication is designed to provide accurate and authoritative information in regard to the subject matter covered. It is sold with the understanding that neither the author nor the publisher is engaged in rendering legal, accounting, futures/securities trading, or other professional service. If legal advice or other expert assistance is required, the services of a competent professional person should be sought.

      —From a Declaration of Principles jointly adopted by a Committee
        of the American Bar Association and a Committee of Publishers.

This book is printed on acid-free paper.

Contents

v

close, we are enjoying the bull market of the 1990s—the strongest bull market of the century.

The bull market of the 1990s saw a range of old and new investment ideas, strategies, and tools tried. Day trading—an idea that combined computer technology, hyperactive trading, and eternal hope to try and beat the markets—flourished as some people gave up their nine-to-five jobs to rent a seat in front of a computer and trade away fortunes. Though far removed by technology from the scalpers and bucket shop denizens of a century earlier, their results were equally forgettable. At the other extreme, the 1990s saw the continued rise and wider recognition of stock indexes as a tool to track investing results, a way to choose investments and—most of all—as a successful investment strategy.

An index, such as the S&P 500 or the Dow Jones Industrials, is a portfolio of stocks designed to match either the overall market or a particular part of the market. It consists of a list of stocks, some plan to update the list, if necessary, and a way to turn the list into a portfolio. The most widely used index among investors in the United States is the S&P 500. In 1976 The Vanguard Group introduced the first publicly available index mutual fund, the Vanguard 500 Index Fund. The fund holds the same stocks as those in the S&P 500 in the same proportions as the index. The fund's performance would seek to mimic the performance of the index as closely as possible.

In the early days the idea of index funds was derided; index funds were for investors who wouldn't, or couldn't, think for themselves. They were for people who would settle for being merely average rather than seeking to do better. They were a sure way to mediocre investment results. History has proven otherwise. From September 1976 to the end of 1999, the Vanguard 500 Index Trust has provided an annual total return of 15.85 percent, closely matching the 16.22 percent return of the S&P 500 for the same time period.[1] The number of investors who have beaten that return over the entire time period is minimal. Some have done better than the index for a number of years, but possibly only Warren Buffett can claim a better compound return over those 24 years.[2] If popularity is any measure of success, one should note that currently the Vanguard 500 Index Trust is the second largest mutual fund in the country. Further, if one combines all the money indexed to the S&P 500, one gets a figure between 5 percent and 10 percent of the total stock market.

It is hard to say exactly what percentage of money managers beat or fail to beat the S&P 500. For one thing, it is not always easy to identify all the money managers and gauge their performance. Further, some will argue that they are playing a different game and are not really competing with the index. (Others argue that the different-game argument is a poor excuse for poor results.) However, it seems generally accepted that about two-thirds of all money managers do not outperform the index over any reasonable time, say a few years or more. Who wins or loses over a week or a month is of little interest, since this is a long-term game. There are some years when the money managers do better and two-thirds beat the index—but there are also some years when they do terribly and only 10 percent or less beat the index. So, settling for an index is not settling for mediocre performance. In the long run it has proven to be a winning strategy. Moreover, in a typical mutual fund, that money manager costs three to five times more than the index fund.

This book is about investing and making money with stock indexes. Whether you want to buy an index fund and sit back and count the results or choose a portfolio of stocks to beat the market—beat the index—you need to understand indexes. Indexes are the guideposts, direction signs, and road maps to investing. On any car trip—from a short excursion to a long drive of several days—knowing the signs and the maps is a big help. Yes, some people do get to their destination with little more than a lucky guess, a hunch, and some luck; but a lot of others get lost. In investing, getting lost usually costs both time and money.

The book is divided into four parts. First, we look at stock indexes and investing overall. If you're an active investor who can quote the market's results daily and weekly, some of this will be very familiar. But even for those of us in the day-to-day swirl of the markets, a little perspective is useful at times. Part I also reviews the history of the 1990s bull market and points to some reasons why we've been so lucky in recent years. Part II is for people who want to use indexes to invest. We look at how indexes have done before. Then we will consider different indexes and different ways to use them to make money. Some indexes do better than others and some index-based products are better for certain investors than others. This is where the believers can figure out how to put their money to work.

Of course, not everyone wants to own index funds. Even among those that do own index funds, some of their money may not be in the funds. For all these people, Part III shows how indexes are a very good tool for evaluating stocks and judging investments. Indexes pack a lot of information about the market and its performance. Exploiting this information is critical to choosing good stocks. Part IV is about how to take a step from reading theories and understanding history to putting it all to work. We will take a step-by-step approach to building a series of portfolios using indexes to give some real directions for using the index road map to investing.

Once upon a time people figured any book that made its way to two nice-looking covers was probably worth reading. Nowadays readers usually want to know where the book came from and who the author is. In the case of this book, you (the reader) should know some of these facts, since I (the author) work for a company deeply involved in the stock market and in indexes. I am the Chief Investment Strategist and Director of Quantitative Services for Standard & Poor's (or "S&P"). I am also the chairman of the Index Committee, the group that manages Standard & Poor's indexes, including the S&P 500. Do we like the index to do well? Yes. Do we like people to think well of the index? Yes. Do we want people to invest using the S&P 500? Yes. Is the S&P 500 the only index? Definitely not. We will talk about the Dow and about other indexes. We'll also talk about markets where Standard & Poor's indexes are not the most widely used or where S&P doesn't even have an index. Naturally, being involved in the indexes and the S&P 500 all the time, I have some opinions about it. But more important, I know a lot about it, how it works, and why it works. Both the opinions and the understanding will find their way into the chapters that follow. One more item of disclosure. Standard & Poor's is a division of The McGraw-Hill Companies, Inc. The publisher of this book is also a division of The McGraw-Hill Companies.

David M. Blitzer

I

STOCK INDEXES: THE KEY TO SUCCESSFUL INVESTING

Unless an investor slept through the last half of the 1990s, they know that both the U.S. economy and the U.S. stock market turned in stellar performances. Whether it is cheering the new economy or the Great Bull Market, the numbers were wonderful and the results spelled investment success and newfound wealth. At the same time, many of us who were slightly interested bystanders rather than investors 10 years ago became investors in recent years. Some of us were drawn in by the market's results; others were pushed in as we began to manage our 401(k) accounts, our retirement plans, and our financial future.

Part I of *Outpacing the Pros* begins with some of the background to our experiences in the market. We start by looking at how the stock market did in the end of the 1990s, where it came from, and how it is poised at the beginning of the millennium. One big question about the market is whether it is unprecedented. By and large, today's market is not without precedent, but every bull market is a bit different. We look at two other famous market advances in the 1920s and the 1960s. Then we turn to the more difficult and compelling questions—why did the bull market happen and what to do when it ends. These concerns lead to some discussions of how to consider and even control the risks of investing.

Any kind of history, and certainly all kinds of investing, are easier when we can measure the results. This is where indexes come in. Indexes are the key tools to measure the market's speed and directions, determine how successful investments are, and ultimately to do the investments. Toward the end of Part I we introduce indexes and discuss how they can be used to gauge the market. At the end of Part I, the last chapter offers a brief Who's Who of indexes.

1
C H A P T E R

WELCOME TO THE GREAT BULL MARKET
We're All Investors Now

THE LAST FOUR YEARS AND THE LAST 20 YEARS—INCREDIBLE GAINS
For anyone under the age of 40, just about all of their investing life has
been since 1982. For these folks, the bull market of the last two decades
certainly seems natural—it is the only thing they've known firsthand. For
people with longer memories or for investors who have wondered enough
about patterns to look into the past, these last two decades are nothing short
of incredible. Over most of modern history (1926–1999), stocks have returned an average of 13 percent per year. Over 1982–1999, stocks did even
better—an average annual return of 18 percent. In the five years from 1995
to 1999, stocks returned 29 percent. The last is the best consecutive five
years on record and is also a big reason why all these numbers are so high.
Further, none are adjusted for inflation, which has averaged about 5 percent in the last 30 years.

The best time to buy stocks is when they are very cheap, not when
everyone is clamoring that you must be in the market. Of course, it is hard
to know in advance if stocks at today's prices will look cheap tomorrow.
History confirms that the summer of 1982 was one of the half-dozen best
times to buy stocks in the twentieth century. In the summer of 1999, the
Dow Jones Industrials were trading around 11,000, and the S&P 500 was
trading around 1350. As of July 30, 1982, the Dow was 808.6, and the S&P
500 was 107.09—figures that today seem so small they sound like the

3

wrong index. It's no wonder that this fantastic bull run has made us all into investors and believers.

If one had invested beginning in 1926, that person's average annual return through 1999 would be 13.7 percent, after removing the effects of inflation. However, from 1926 to 1981, the investor would have made 11.5 percent; from 1982 to 1999, the investor would have earned 18.5 percent. The last 20 years stand out as incredible; the last four or five as doubly incredible. From 1926 to 1999, the market lost money a bit more than one year in every three. From 1982 to 1999, there was only one losing year—1990. Not even the year of the 1987 crash was a money loser. We are in one of the great bull markets of all time.

Moreover, in recent years this market has even accelerated. If one looks for the best returns over a string of five years, there is actually one that does a bit better—1995–1999 has a total return of 28.5 percent annually. The five years from June 1932 offered a return of 36.2 percent, but then that was coming off the worst year of the Great Depression, 1932, and a cumulative decline in stocks of about 80 percent after the 1929 crash. The last five years are also the only time when the market saw five consecutive years with returns better than 20 percent, actually better than 23 percent. Look at Figure 1-1, which shows the annual returns to the S&P 500 since 1926. The only time we've had five years better than 20 percent in a row is 1995–1999. We did almost that well in the 1940s, and we did have two out of three years in the early 1930s above 40 percent—but that cost us a war and the Great Depression. In short, the late 1990s have been one hell of a bull market.

FIGURE 1-1   Annual Returns to the S&P 500, 1926–1999

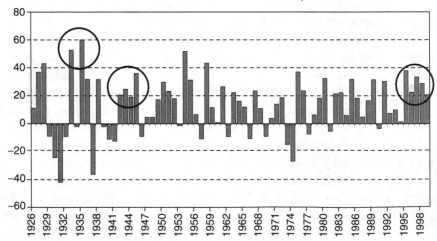

Of course, the 1990s are the past and investing means looking to the future. Further, we all know that nothing lasts forever, not even this bull market. However, there are some aspects of the current market and economy that should be considered lest we all decide we missed the boat and should forget about investing, owning stocks, or investing and making money. This bull market has been declared dead and buried several times over. In 1987 the market crashed, comparisons with 1929 appeared in the newspapers, and everyone nervously looked over their shoulders. Those who hung on to their stocks were vindicated by mid-1988 as the market rolled on. In December 1996, Fed Chairman Alan Greenspan declared that stock prices were too high and investors were "irrationally exuberant." Wall Street worried for a bit, but since then stock prices have more than doubled. Of course, a series of mistaken predictions of demise don't guarantee that the bull market will continue.

Rising stock prices aren't the only legacy of the 1990s. A far bigger legacy for the economy is the rise of the Internet and information technology. This combination has been dubbed the "new economy" with promises of everlasting riches around the corner. Certainly not all the claims of what the Internet can do for us will come true, but it is already making some big differences in our economy. One of the key factors in the long bull market and the long economic expansion is the growing role for information technology. This is not about to change overnight or even over a decade.

Sometimes bull markets end with disasters and horrendous bear markets. The most infamous is the bull market of the 1920s; it was followed by the Great Depression and stocks fell 80 percent from their 1929 peak. The "Go-Go" years of the 1960s were followed by the 1973–1975 bear market and oil crisis, and stocks fell 37 percent from December 1972 to December 1974. Really bad bear markets seem to need two things to get them started—very high stock prices and a collapse in the economy. In 1929–1932 the economy crumbled and unemployment topped 25 percent. In 1973–1975, oil prices surged, production shrunk, and unemployment climbed to the highest levels since the 1930s. So, if you think it is too late in this bull market cycle to invest, you should not only argue that stock prices are too high, you should also argue that the economy is about to fall apart.

However, the biggest reason for looking at investing now is not the bull market at all. After all, we've already said that the best time to have bought stocks was 1982, not 1998. The reason for investing now is that waiting is almost always a mistake. Maybe the worst time to have invested was August 1929. (Stocks fell in September and the crash was in October 1929.) It would have been a long haul—$1000 in August 1929 would have withered to only $175 in June 1932. By June 1944 it would be back to $1000, and finally in July 1951 your investment would have surpassed bonds. (All of this assumes reinvesting the dividends.) But on the eve of the Great Bull Market, in July 1982, your $1000 would be $43,000, while $1000 invested in bonds in August 1929 would be only about $5200. And at the end of 1998? The mistakenly invested $1000 from 1929 would be almost $841,000, while the bonds would be about $47,000—barely more than what the stocks were worth in 1982.

Another example of dismal results might be investing at the end of the "Go-Go" 1960s before the 1974–1975 bear market. A $1000 investment in December 1972 would have shrunk to about $574 in September 1974. By June 1976 it was back at $1000. In December 1982—10 years later—it was $1900, and by 1998 it was $27,700. So, even in the worst of times, stocks made out alright after a very difficult wait. But, before you leave these dismal stories there is one other aspect—bonds didn't do too well either. Of course, they lost less than stocks at the worst moment, but in June 1976, when stocks were back to even, $1000 in bonds would have been only up to about $1125. In February 1983, when stocks had doubled one's money, bonds were behind, having turned $1000 into only $1600.

So, even if one had invested at the worst possible moments, stocks would have won out after a long, long wait. Fortunately, dumb luck assures that most of us will miss investing at the worst possible moment. Moreover, how long we stay invested is up to us to decide and the how long matters a whole lot. In simple terms, stocks do better on average than bonds, so if you stay in long enough, stocks will get you that average and you will do better. To give you an idea, look at Table 1-1, which shows periods of 1 year, 5 years, 10 years, and 20 years to see what you would have made in stocks or bonds and how often stocks would have beaten bonds.

Table 1-1 shows average annualized returns using data from 1945 to 1999 for the S&P 500 and AAA bonds and the percentage of time periods when stocks did better than bonds.

TABLE 1-1   Average Annualized Returns for S&P 500 and AAA Bonds, 1945–1999

	1 Year	5 Years	10 Years	20 Years
Stocks	14.5%	13.2%	12.2%	11.1%
Bonds	6.0%	5.7%	5.4%	4.7%
Stocks Beat Bonds	65.0%	80.0%	91.0%	98.0%

After you look at this data you are likely to conclude that:

- if you wait long enough, stocks beat bonds,
- the longer you wait, the more likely it is that stocks beat bonds, or
- if you wait long enough, stocks almost always beat bonds.

Of course, if you knew in advance when that really bad moment was coming or if the great bull market of the 1990s will keep going or when the next bull market will begin, it would be a lot easier. No one does know. (Sorry, but that's the truth.) However, there are two things you can do to stack the odds in your favor a bit. First, you can look at what is happening in the markets and the rest of the world and make an educated guess on the odds of hitting the next bull, or bear, market right away. Second, you can mix stocks and bonds and trade away a lot of risk at the cost of only a little return.

WE'RE ALL INVESTORS NOW

Most of us are old enough to have seen at least some fads come and go. We can all remember television shows, dance steps, or popular books that have long since faded away. After almost 20 years of rising volume about investing and the stock market, some of us are probably ready to label investing as the next fad about to go away.

Wait a moment. Unlike most of the other fads, you have a very big stake in this one right here and now. Chances are that you are in the middle of it whether you know it or not. Moreover, if you want to live well in the future, learning a bit about investing before you get to the future would be a very good idea. Why? The time when working for a good company and doing a good job meant that the company would return the favor and take care of you in retirement is gone. It's not that companies are mean or nasty—certainly no more than people are mean to companies when they switch jobs and leave their retirement benefits behind at their old company. Rather, in the last 20 years there have been some large shifts in the way pensions and retirement planning work in the United States. Moreover, the United States is likely to be seen as an example by many other countries as well.

The first change may be the way we think about social security. It is still one of the most sacred or scared cows in Washington politics. But, it is now thought of as a safety net to keep people out of poverty, not to keep them in wealth. No one objects to arguments that social security will not pay enough to allow you to retire to Tahiti or the south of France or whatever your private idea of paradise on earth may be. Yes, social security should make it possible to pay some rent and eat three meals a day, but not at the Ritz. So, if social security was your secret to retirement, think again.

Second, company pension plans are changing and shifting. Twenty years ago many companies offered—often with great pride—a defined benefit plan. The plan got its name because the benefit or payout you got was defined by how much you earned near the end of your working life. Typically, the plan might pay 60 percent or 75 percent or the average salary earned during one's last five years on the job. If you worked for the company until regular retirement, you got the pension. The company, or probably professional money managers it hired, took care of all the investing and planning. In many cases employees made contributions, but they didn't need to worry about how to invest the money. The pros took care of that. Most importantly, the company promised you the pension and if the investment pros messed up and there was no money in the fund, it was up to the company to pay up.

Those days are fading away. Some companies continue to offer defined benefit plans and many people now approaching, or in, retirement are major beneficiaries of these plans. But, defined benefit plans do not look like the wave of the future. Rather, it is defined contribution plans. In these plans, what you get out depends on the contribution you put in and *on how well it is managed*. The last part is the key—how well it is managed. Take a very simple example. If you put in $10,000 per year and invested it at 4 percent in the money market fund, after 40 years you would have almost $1 million. But, if it earned 9 percent—about what one might expect in mostly stocks and some bonds—you would have $3.6 million. That is the difference between a retirement income you can count on of about $40,000 per year or an income of about $148,000 per year.

The most common kind of defined contribution plan is the 401(k) plan. The name comes from the section of the Internal Revenue Code that provides for tax-free investing for these plans. There are other, similar, plans such as 403(b) or 457 plans for some public employees or union employees. The key is that you are both the investor and the money manager. So, we're all investors now. As a group we've become fairly significant investors. There is currently over a trillion dollars in equities in defined contribution plans. As of 1999, they were bigger than the more traditional defined benefit plans.[3]

These plans are expanding rapidly. A survey by the Profit Sharing Council of America found that 72 percent of the companies with 100 or more workers, some 55,000 companies, offered 401(k) plans as of 1998.[4] 401(k) plans, and similar plans, allow individuals to direct how their money is invested. Collectively, these are called defined contribution plans. They differ from defined benefit plans where the employer is responsible for

WHAT'S YOUR 401(K) WORTH?

All over the World Wide Web and in numerous books, you can find projections of what your 401(k) fund is worth. To save you a few minutes of hunting, we have added a convenient table. Table 1-2 shows how much you would accumulate if you saved $7500 each year in your 401(k). The returns assumed (across the top) are excluding inflation. Over the last seven decades the stock market's real return is about 6 percent. Over the last five years it is about 20 percent. The "analysis" behind this table is very simple—you can probably create it with a calculator used in a junior high school math class. All it is is a little compounded interest on your investment of $7500 each year. $7500 is less than the statutory maximum for 401(k) plans, but it does represent a healthy 7.5 percent of your salary if you make $100,000 per year. In short, this is not some software mogul's plan, but it is also not a fast food hamburger flipper's plan. Nevertheless, it can tell us some important things. In these days of low inflation, many of us tend to ignore it. However, over the last century, inflation was a major concern. It averaged about 4 percent during the 1948–1998 period and the market's average return including inflation is about 13 percent for a real return of about 10 percent.

TABLE 1-2   What You Can Accumulate If You Invest $7500 a Year

Age	Years to 65	2%	4%	6%	8%	10%	20%
60	5	$39,030	$40,622	$42,278	$44,000	$45,788	$55,812
55	10	$82,123	$90,046	$98,856	$108,649	$119,531	$194,690
50	15	$129,701	$150,177	$174,570	$203,641	$238,294	$540,263
45	20	$182,230	$223,336	$275,892	$343,215	$429,562	$1,400,160
40	25	$240,227	$312,344	$411,484	$548,295	$737,603	$3,539,858
35	30	$304,261	$420,637	$592,936	$849,624	$1,233,705	$8,864,112
30	35	$374,959	$552,392	$835,761	$1,292,376	$2,032,683	$22,112,559

(Real Returns across the top.)

First, time is a critical element in all this. Even at a 20 percent return, you don't get much of a nest egg in only five years. Starting early is crucial. Think about what this means. If you have a 401(k), join it now. If you play the market for fun and entertainment and you make some big gains, don't assume the easy money is always there. Rather, take a chunk of the Internet stock wonder money and put it into something boring, reliable, and consistent—like an index fund—and leave it there. (Hopefully you can do this in a tax-protected account.) Now, when you go back to entertainment investing,

(continued)

the other will keep growing with the market. There is another side to the time element. If you do have the time, there is a good chance you can have a million dollars set aside when you retire and do it with little difficulty. If you work at it, it could be a lot more.

Returns matter a lot too. Table 1-2 indicates time seems more important than return. While a clear comparison is hard to make, time should be considered first. Don't wait around for the market to pull back or until you find the next hot stock—put some money to work in an index fund now. Returns should also be considered in light of the risks involved. We will return to this in Part IV when we talk about building portfolios.

Of course, you can't sit at this table and retire—you need to figure out how to spend the money. It turns out that this problem is trickier than one might think. When you're saving and investing, especially if you have a lot of time, one can argue that the good years and the bad years tend to average out. However, on the spending side, a few bad years can leave you in bad shape for the future since there is no new money coming in. Simply put, it takes a big nest egg to live well. As a quick rule of thumb, you need 25 times your hoped for annual income if you are planning to live for a while or want to leave something for your children. If you want to retire on $100,000 a year,

FIGURE 1-2   How Fast the Money Runs Out with a $2.5 Million Nest Egg Withdrawing $100,000 Each Year

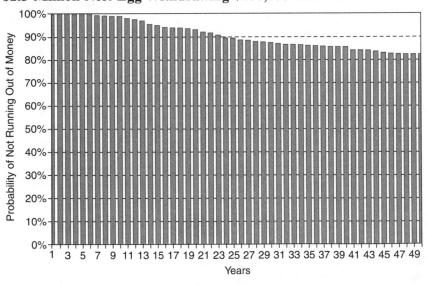

(continued)

plan for a $2.5 *million* 401(k) plan at retirement. That is, you can comfortably take out 4 percent of the nest egg's starting amount each year and not have to worry too much about a really bad year or a market crash.

A simulation model can give a more detailed look at how much one can safely spend in retirement and not run out of money. This model assumes that the unspent money is invested in a portfolio with an expected return and expected risks (or variation in the return). For instance, the return may be 10 percent annually, close to the real return of the last 50 years with a risk (measured as the standard deviation) of 20 percent. Roughly two-thirds of the time the market return would be between −5 percent and +25 percent. We assume one starts with $2.5 million and plans to withdraw $100,000 each year for living expenses. Figure 1-2 shows the probability that you will have at least $200,000—two years of income—left at the end of each year. In the early going you are assured of this. As shown in Figure 1-2, after 25 years, there is a 90 percent chance you would have at least $200,000 left.

No doubt some readers still think that $2.5 million is far more than they need to retire comfortably on $100,000 a year. Table 1-3 shows when you would have "only" a 90 percent chance of having two years of income left for three different assumptions about investment returns and four possible nest eggs. Table 1-3 was constructed with the same model used for Figure 1-2.

TABLE 1-3   How Many Years to Only a 90 Percent Chance of $200,000 Left

	$500,000	$1 million	$2.5 million	$5 million
5% return	2	5	14	23
10% return	3	7	25	>50
15% return	3	10	>50	>50

managing retirement assets and promises a pension based on the employee's salary and length of service. The employer, as the sponsor of a 401(k) plan, offers a menu of investment choices. Usually the choices include mutual funds or similar funds provided by institutional money managers. The rise in 401(k) and other defined contribution plans can be seen in the money totals as well. At the end of 1999, defined contribution plan assets totaled $2.5 trillion, exceeding defined benefit plans for the first time in several years.[5]

In case trillions of dollars in defined contribution plans doesn't sound big, realize that a lot of us are investors—at least according to our tax returns. In 1996 slightly over 100 million people filed tax returns that showed some adjusted gross income. Some 26 million returns included some dividend income and about 18 million included pension income. (Some of the 18 million were probably the same returns as some of the 26 million.) So about one in every four taxpayers is reporting some investment income to the IRS. Maybe not all of us are investors, but most of us are. All those tax returns suggest that as a group, Americans own a lot of stock. We do. As of December 1999, according to the Federal Reserve, household holding of stocks were some $8.5 trillion. In addition, there was another $3.2 trillion in mutual funds. That is in addition to the trillion dollars in defined contribution plans.[6] Even though you may not have all of these types of holdings yourself, you probably have enough to take notice.

AND WE'RE THE ONES RESPONSIBLE FOR HOW WE DO

Go back to the example above of $10,000 per year for 40 years and the difference between retiring on $40,000 or $148,000. Who makes the decisions that make that difference? Each of us does.

There are two players in the investment game—you and the market. Obviously what the market does makes a big difference, but what you do can make as big a difference. The New York State Lottery—which is a much, much less successful road to wealth and riches than the stock market—used to run advertisements showing people sailing on their new yachts, driving their new imported sports cars, or boarding their new private jets with the tag line, "Hey, you never know. . . ." Well, if you don't play, you won't win. And, in investments (though probably not in the lottery), how you play has a big impact on what you win.

Investing isn't as simple as the lottery, which is one reason why investing is a much better bet than the lottery. Investing requires some understanding, some knowledge, and some work—but nothing most of us can't handle. Probably the biggest step is realizing that it is our decisions that do matter and do make a difference. If all you do is join your company's 401(k) and never pay any attention to where your money goes, you won't end up with as much money as you would like. More importantly, you won't have as much money as you could have with a little effort. Our goal is to give you some tools to play the investment game and profit from it. It may even turn out to be fun.

A moment ago I mentioned that there are two players in the investment game—you and the market. A lot of investors forget about the first of these players. Yes, knowing about the market is important and understanding all kinds of things about the economy, the Federal Reserve, interest rates, why we should worry about oil prices and Malaysia, and so on all make a difference. But, let's begin with the investment player you know a lot about: You.

You know a lot about yourself and investing—and certainly you know more about yourself than other people, including brokers, planners, and financial advisers, do. You know so much about yourself that this book is not going to tell you much more. It will suggest a few things to consider, though. First, when do you expect to need, or spend, all the money you're accumulating in your investments? Maybe the answer is hopefully never— if you live long and die rich, a lot of your money will go to your heirs, some charity or foundation you choose, or (if you don't choose well) Uncle Sam's tax man. More likely though you do plan to spend some of it. Time is very important in investments, so having some idea of how much time you're planning for is important.

Another big item in investing is risk. In the lottery risk is simple—you buy a ticket and almost every time, nothing happens and you lost the price of the ticket. Investing is a bit more complicated and more fun—you put your money to work and can watch it. Often it grows, but sometimes it takes a bit of a detour. Moreover, as it grows, your sense of how much is at risk changes. Suppose you invest $10,000 in the stock market. A few years later it has grown to $14,000. Then we suffer a "correction" and the $14,000 drops to $12,000. Did you just lose $2000? Or have you made $2000 from the original $10,000?

To be a reasonable investor, you should have some idea of the time frame—how long until you're going to be spending the money. You should be able to keep score—know how much you have, how much you've made, and how much better or worse you would have done if you'd gotten the exact same results as the market. Believe it or not, in 1995 through 1998, someone who was willing to take some substantial risks and doubled his or her money didn't really do very well. From the end of 1994 to October 1999, an S&P 500 index fund would have tripled your money. You should also have an idea of how much risk you can take, how much investing will keep you up at night, and if you're willing to let it keep you up at night. Most of the next several chapters will focus on the part of investing you know less well—the market. But, at the end we will come back to the "you" part and talk about building some portfolios. Which one is right will depend on who you are.

Making investment decisions isn't always easy—but it doesn't have to be difficult either. Moreover, most of the decisions about money and how to invest it shouldn't be that hard to make with a little help. Here are some things you need to know.

KEEPING SCORE

There are at least two kinds of investing and at least two ways to keep score. Most of us use both approaches without realizing it. One approach is systematic, directed, and goal-driven—and needs a scorecard. The other is more opportunistic and is rewarded in the stories we tell and the bragging rights we claim more than in some dusty scorecard.

If we are looking at mutual funds, we usually compare the fund's results to a benchmark like the S&P 500. We want to know how well the fund did compared to some independent fair measure of investment success. However, if you buy stocks based on your own research, the measure of success is more likely to lead to bragging rights when your neighbor or brother-in-law asks you about the market. Even when people use computer-based or Web-based portfolio tracking programs, very few of us really check to see how we're doing. Are we all investing with split personalities? No, but there are different goals in investing and we should keep a clear eye on them.

In this new world where we must depend on ourselves rather than let some corporate pension plan take care of us, we should look at investing as a job we should do. We should have some clear goals and guidelines and a strong idea of how to get there. For this kind of investing, we need a way to keep score. Indexes and market history are the way we keep score. In baseball, a .300 batting average is an achievement; in football, rushing for 1000 yards in a season is an achievement. Why? Because the history of either game tells us that these are achievable, but quite difficult. The economics of the games tells us that teams will pay up for players who can meet these goals. In investing, there are also goals. Beating the S&P 500 is something like being a .300 hitter in baseball—it's done every year, but only by a few. Moreover, just as consistent .300 hitters are rare, so are fund managers who consistently beat the index.

In a bull market it is easy to think that everything always goes up and that we are all already very rich. There is no question that bull markets are wonderful. There is also no question that they don't happen all the time. A glance at the scorecard will tell us how good this one is, and warn us about the other times. It may also remind us how smart, or less than smart, we are. From the start of 1995 to the end of 1999, the stock market (measured by the S&P 500) rose 320 percent without including reinvested dividends. That is also the best five-year run in modern history. Look at the figure again and think about how you did—in your 401(k), your investment portfolio, or the cookie jar. To some extent the comparison isn't completely fair since there are no taxes being paid on the S&P 500 and you may have more, or less, risk in your own investing. Either way, the numbers and the index tells you at least two things—how well your own investing is doing and how rare the last five years are. If your own stocks did two or three times better than the index and if you consistently, over several years, get the kind of results the S&P 500 got in 1995–1999, you are a rare—no, very, very rare—investor. If not, don't worry: you're one of us human investors who can get rich with stock indexes and some time.

There is a bit of a conflict buried here as well. On the one hand we are keeping score and suggesting that we are not all .300 hitters in investments; on the other, we are seeking bragging rights. For many of us, investing is not just a means to an end of financial security. It is also entertainment, excitement, and fun. There is absolutely nothing wrong with this—having fun while doing something you have to do is a big plus, as long as you don't completely lose sight of what's going on. With market indexes you can track the performance and gauge the risks of your investments. Further, you have a measure to tell you how financially comfortable you are today and will probably be tomorrow. And, if you ignore the scorecard, a lot of that financial comfort is not going to be there tomorrow.

Keeping score and staying on track is important. So is having fun and winning some games. For many of us one of the big returns from investing is the stories we can tell, the bragging rights we can claim, about our own experience. In this bull market, investing has become entertainment and excitement for a lot of people. There is nothing wrong with this—we can all think of many less socially acceptable pursuits than the stock market. The same probably happens in any bull market. One common complaint about index funds and index investing is that they are dull and boring. Maybe so, but the bragging rights and the financial rewards can be quite substantial.

2

DID IT EVER HAPPEN BEFORE?

BULLS MARKETS ARE DIFFERENT

The 1990s bull market is not the first, nor is it likely to prove to be the last. It has certainly reminded us that bull markets are fun and, if you're invested, very profitable. One question not put to money managers often enough is whether their current (good) results come from brains or the bull market. In recent years it has not been that hard to make returns of 20 percent or more annually. But it has been very hard to beat the S&P 500, even with those kinds of gains. In 1995 through 1999, the average annual gain in the S&P 500 was 28.6 percent. The best year, 1995, saw the index return an impressive 37.6 percent. Of course, even bull markets have their disappointments. The S&P 500 slid about 20 percent in the summer of 1998 when Russia defaulted on its debt.

Bull markets are different. Different in the market psychology. Different in the balance of fear and greed. Different in what people expect from the market, what they look for, and how they think profits are made. The difficulty is that once you're in a bull market, it is easy to forget that it is not always like this and that stocks do not always go straight up. One reason for this forgetfulness is simply the impressive length of this market. As of late 1999, any investor who abandoned the stock market anytime after August 1982 made a mistake in getting out. Since then, the market has been rising and no pullback pushed it below the levels of that summer 19 years ago.

Most of the time, investors buy stocks because they believe the companies will perform unusually well, earn large profits, and grow. All these nice things mean more valuable companies paying larger dividends and, therefore, commanding higher prices in the stock market. Investors choose companies to own based on how well they are at managing their own businesses. Managers work to earn profits that will support higher stock prices. Bull markets are different. In bull markets investors buy stocks because they believe (or at least hope) that someone will buy the stocks from them at a higher price—not because earnings are rising or the company's business has improved; just because the price is higher and will keep going higher. Investors shift from studying the company's business to reviewing its stock price. They look for high momentum stocks—jargon for stocks where prices are rising rapidly. The idea is that the rich get richer. Or, more specifically, that the "Greater Fool Theory" will keep working. That is, that a greater fool will appear to buy the stock and keep pushing the price higher.

Why would someone pay 10 percent or 20 percent or 50 percent more than what you paid for a stock yesterday just because you bought it yesterday and now it is today? Other than some specific and relatively rare event, such as an announcement of a new discovery or a merger, there really isn't a rational reason for the price to jump. Yet, this is the kind of thinking that becomes common in bull markets. Stocks are chosen because they have "momentum," meaning their prices are rising. "You've got to own this stock!" is an oft-heard comment from brokers or the ever-growing crowd of financial commentators. In the process, stock prices often climb to levels that only a few weeks earlier would have been considered crazy. That is the essence of the bull market. Now, contrast this with normal or fundamental stock analyses.

The essence of normal investing is deciding what a stock is worth. If you know what the stock's value is, you know if the current price is fair, too high, or too low. How do you decide what a stock is worth? The tried-and-true idea is that the stock represents a share in a company—a share in the profits it earns and the dividends it might pay. Of course, profits will be earned over a period of years and a dollar today is worth more than a dollar promised in a few years. However, it is possible to calculate the value today of dollars to be earned in the future. So, if we know what the profits will be over the next several years, we can calculate what the stock is worth today. This idea—that a stock should sell for the present value of future dividends or earnings—is one of the older and more important building blocks of finance. One of its first formal presentations was in *The Theory of Investment Value* by John Burr Williams in 1938. For financial

types, it is embedded in a calculation called the *dividend discount model.*
This is simply the idea that a stock's price equals the discounted present
value of future dividends. Why not earnings or profits instead of dividends?
Because what isn't paid out as dividends is reinvested in the company
to produce more dividends later on. Therefore, we need only count the dividends that shareholders get, not the earnings that might promise future
dividends.

Another way to think of bull markets is the balance between fear and
greed, the two emotions that most believe rule the day in the market. Fear
of ruin, falling prices, and total collapse versus greed for more trading profits, higher prices, and bigger stories to tell to nervous people who don't
know enough to put all their money in the market. Whether these oppos-
ing forces are ever balanced for more than a fleeting moment is unclear. In
a bull market, greed carries the day.

THE 1960s BULL MARKET

For a few of today's investors, the bull market of the 1960s is a personal
memory; for many others it is history. Figure 2-1 shows the market in the
1960s. The line represents the value of an investment of $100 made on De-
cember 31, 1959. The bars show the monthly returns in the market. Both

FIGURE 2-1   The Bull Market of the 1960s

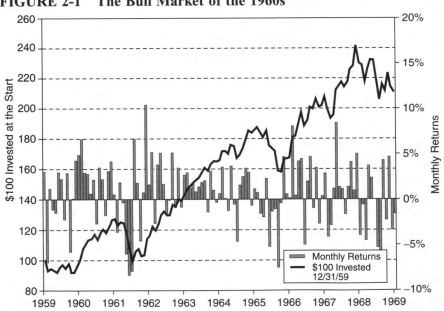

are based on the S&P 500 and are total returns—price change plus reinvested dividends. It was not straight up for the entire decade. In fact, the beginning of the 1960s was anything but positive for the stock market. However, once things got rolling there were some good years for the market and some notable years for the economy and the nation as well.

Most bull markets seem to be related to the tenor of their times. The 1960s was no exception. In 1961 John F. Kennedy became President, succeeding Dwight Eisenhower. The image of America—the nation, its people, and its government—began to change. The nation went from having a grandfatherly figure to a male sex symbol as President. Eisenhower came into office promising to settle the Korean War and manage the problems of the world. Kennedy timed his entry perfectly—inaugurated in January, and the recession of 1960–1961 ended in February. As if to prove he had both the imagination and the courage of the future, he pledged to put a man on the moon, and to bring him back, by the end of the decade. As important as this may have been to space travel, engineering, and technology, it was probably more important to people's hopes and aspirations. America, Kennedy seemed to declare, could and would do anything.

On Wall Street, the market had finally begun to shake off the fears of the Great Crash of 1929 and the Depression. During the 1950s the market had reached highs above the peaks of 1929 while the S&P 500 dividend yield (the dividend as a percentage of the price of the index) had fallen below the yields on most corporate bonds. Stocks had crossed a major barrier in the perception of risks and potential returns. Maybe most important of all, a generation of brokers and bankers was arising on Wall Street whose personal memories did not always include the heady days of 1927–1929 or the disastrous days of the Great Depression of the 1930s.

To be fair, the stock market and the President didn't always get along. In April 1962 Kennedy spoke out against price increases announced by a number of major steel companies. The steel industry was a focal point of the economy and big steel was used to being heard and having its way. Moreover, the idea that the government would tell companies how to set prices was seen as a throwback to wartime price controls, or something much worse. However, Kennedy's economic advisers felt that the price increases would lead to inflation and Kennedy decided to speak out. After a brief but tense period, one of the steel companies broke rank with the industry and rolled back its prices. Kennedy had won, but the stock market—shaken by the new President's aggressiveness—had tumbled.

Stocks did recover from the steel price debate. They recovered by finding a new idea and a new way to make it seem prices could rise forever—

conglomerates. The idea that companies with growing earnings should have growing stock prices was well accepted and well founded. It followed from the fundamental analysis of John Burr Williams and others, as noted previously. The market obviously liked companies with growing earnings better than those without them and rewarded such "growth" companies by giving them higher prices. One common way of comparing or evaluating stocks is to look at the ratio of the price to the earnings per share, the p–e. If the p–e is 20, you are paying a price equal to 20 times the company's annual earnings. If one company sells for a p–e of 20 and another for a p–e of 35, the market values the second one more highly. When one compares one stock to another, the higher p–e may reflect faster expected earnings growth; less risk that the earnings, and the company, will collapse; or that one industry is more exciting, appealing, and fashionable than another. Fashion does matter—utilities sound pretty mundane while telecommunications is part of the Internet and hot. Of course, some of the telecommunications hot picks were yesterday's telephone utilities.

The 1960s market wasn't sparked by utilities, but by the conglomerates. Conglomerates were companies built by merging firms in completely different industries to create a new diversified company. Conglomerates had a number of appealing properties at the beginning of the 1960s. One was the merger aspect. Since the breakup of the Standard Oil Trust in 1911, the U.S. courts had made mergers more and more difficult. In the beginning of the century the courts eliminated horizontal mergers, such as those used to build Standard Oil. Simply put, companies were not supposed to buy up their competition. Next, in the 1920s and 1930s, the courts moved against vertical mergers and to prevent companies from buying their suppliers. (Of course, sometimes buying the suppliers was a good way to put the squeeze on competitors dependent on the same suppliers.)

Conglomerates offered other attractions too. Wall Street didn't like risks and didn't like companies where earnings bounced around all the time. One idea was to combine companies with different patterns of ups and downs to even out the earnings streams through diversification. Something like combining a company selling suntan lotion with one selling raincoats to even out earnings on sunny and rainy days. The idea was that the combination would diversify earnings, reduce risks, and earn higher p–e's, and higher stock prices, as a result. As conglomerates came into fashion when the 1960s began, they offered one other more important attribute for the markets—multiplication.

To see how this magic worked, suppose a hot conglomerate with a p–e of 20 bought some mundane single-product company with a p–e of 6. To make things simple, assume that each company has a million shares outstanding and earns a dollar a share. The conglomerate, called Diversitronics, is worth $20 million. The second company, call it Mono-line, is worth only $6 million because of its lower p–e. Diversitronics buys Mono-line for stock by offering a Diversitronics share ($20) for two Mono-line shares ($6 each or $12). The merged company, still called Diversitronics, now has a million and a half shares. Its earnings are the sum of the earnings of Mono-line and premerger Diversitronics, or $2 million. Earnings per share are $1.33 compared to $1 for either company before. Diversitronics is hot and commands a p–e of 20, so its stock price rises to $26.67 from $20. In fact, it has just gotten hotter—it has further diversified its earnings by acquiring Mono-line and its earnings per share have grown by one-third to $1.33 from $1. If it was worth a p–e of 20 before the merger, surely it should be worth a p–e of 25 after the deal is done. At a p–e of 25, the stock climbs to $33.33.

This all sounds pretty far-fetched, and certainly not the kind of thing to build a multiyear bull market on. Maybe so, but it happened and it worked. Among the more famous (infamous?) beneficiaries were Litton Industries, LTV (begun as Ling Electric, later Ling-Temco-Vought and then LTV), Gulf and Western (parodied as Engulf and Devour), and International Telephone and Telegraph or ITT. The use of initials for names, sometimes initials whose origins had been long since forgotten, added to the appeal of these companies.

The game went on and on, until January 1968 when Litton Industries stunned the market with the announcement that rather than rising, its earnings were about to collapse. The party was ending though the market managed to keep climbing until the following autumn. The conglomerate boom was interrupted in the first half of 1966. The Fed, becoming alarmed about inflation, tightened policy and pushed interest rates higher. The market and then the economy slowed in 1966 and 1967. However, the Fed managed to slow the economy without a recession and by 1967 growth had resumed for stocks as well as the nation. However, as inflation climbed further in 1968 and 1969, the Fed pushed interest rates ever higher, setting the stage for the short 1969–1970 recession that ended the decade. If there is a small lesson here for the current period, it is that fighting the Fed is usually a losing battle—it was in the 1960s.

The conglomerate mania is also an example of how bull markets develop and how growth and the greater fool theory take over. When it began, conglomerates seemed to make good sense. There really was some ability to diversify earnings streams and reduce the volatility of earnings—

and the risks tied to the stocks. Moreover, the lower risk should mean that the present discounted value of future earnings would be higher. Putting two companies together did really mean more earnings and a bigger, more valuable company. However, as the wonders of the multiplier began to pump up stock prices, the market began to believe in its own silliness. Apparent growth became as good as real growth in earnings per share and p–e ratios began to rise as quickly as earnings multiplied. Buying stocks for real value gave way to buying stocks to benefit from multiplying earnings into seemingly higher earnings to garner higher and higher p–e's. It all worked until the moment when Litton Industries was forced to remind everybody that it didn't work.

There was one more hurrah to the 1960s, although it leaked into the 1970s. It is worth mentioning because it also shows how sound fundamental financial analysis is converted into the madness of crowds in a bull market. Moreover, there are hints that this kind of madness is returning today. This hurrah is the "Nifty-Fifty." In the late 1960s professional money managers became enamored of a handful of about 50 growth stocks—large, well-established blue-chip companies that seemed to be able to grow their earnings forever. Unlike the conglomerates, most of these did not rely on mergers and multipliers. In December 1972, when the Nifty-Fifty game reached its peak, the p–e for the S&P 500 was about 18.9. The stocks in this favored group sported p–e's the low 20s to as high as 70 or more for a few. The group included some familiar names such as Walt Disney & Co., McDonald's, General Electric, and IBM.[7] With the coming of the oil crisis in 1973 and subsequent recession in 1973–1975, earnings and stock prices all collapsed and the Nifty-Fifty declined with the rest.

A recent analysis of the Nifty-Fifty by Jeremy Siegel concludes that looking back from 1997, these stocks turned out to have done reasonably well—a return only a touch less than the S&P 500 over the same period. This may be less of a positive epitaph for the Nifty Fifty than it is a reminder that indexing often works. The Nifty-Fifty as of 1972 was close to an index of 50 well-known, widely followed large-cap growth stocks. In some ways, not too different from what the Dow is today. Index funds, even when found in unusual spots, are often reasonable performers.

THE 1920s BULL RUN

The story of the 1920s may sound more modern than the story of the 1960s. If anything, the 1920s story is likely to give some investors a few worried moments as they wonder if it could be as much a prediction of the future as a report of the past. However, the question here is how the stock market boomed, not how the economy swooned. As one looks at the story of the 1920s, there are three questions that keep coming up: Why did the stock market soar so high in 1927–1929? Why did it crash in 1929? and, most of all, Why did the economy collapse completely in 1929–1933?

One number can remind people how deep the Depression of the 1930s was, and why it is worth wondering about: At the bottom in 1932–1933, the unemployment rate was 25 percent—one in four workers were out of a job. Yes, some of the old economic statistics may be inaccurate. If anything, the true unemployment rate was probably higher.

While the entire decade of the 1920s was successful for both the market and the economy, it was a series of short expansions and contractions, not one continuous boom. The decade began with a short-lived expansion linked to World War I, running from March 1919 to January 1920. This was followed by a steep recession from January 1920 to July 1921. There were two more recessions, from May 1923 to July 1924 and from October 1926 to November 1927. The recession of 1920–1921 was very deep with a sharp decline in prices. Subsequent pullbacks were more modest. Moreover, while the last two decades have left many believing recessions are simply brief interruptions in long periods of economic growth, that was neither the belief nor the experience as of the 1920s. From 1840 (when the business cycles dates begin) until 1919, over 40 percent of the time the United States was in a recession. Since 1945, recessions only account for about 20 percent of the time. And, in the 1990s, only 8 of 120 months saw the economy in a recession.

The stock market's results for the 1920s is shown in Figure 2-2. The data are from the Cowles Commission Stock Indexes, developed by Alfred Cowles as part of an analysis of the stock market after the 1929 crash.[8] In the first two-thirds of the decade, from the end of the 1920–1921 recession through March 1928, the stock market climbed with only a few interruptions, gaining about 165 percent. Over this 80-month period the average gain was almost a 16 percent annual rate of increase. This does not include dividends. While dividends were more significant in the 1920s than recently, ignoring dividends makes the comparisons to recent news reports easier. However, in March 1928, the markets accelerated and prices continued to climb until their peak in September 1929. Over those 18 months, prices rose 63 percent for an annual rate of increase of 38 percent. At the peak, stock prices were 4.3 times their 1921 level.

As wonderful as these figures are, the most arresting part of Figure 2-2 is the right-hand end, where prices collapsed. From the September 1929 peak to November of that year, stock prices fell about 33 percent. While

FIGURE 2-2   The 1920s Stock Market

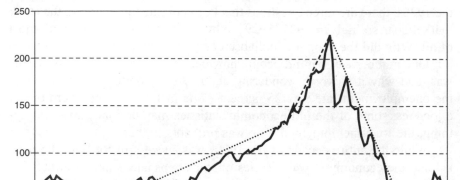

Cowles Commission Indexes—Stocks, 1926 = 100

there were some rebounds, the eventual bottom was in June 1932 for a total decline of 85 percent. (Eighty-five percent decline is not a typo.) The
June 1932 low was the lowest point since May 1897, 35 years earlier.

The 1920s was more than just an exciting period for the stock market.
The nation emerged from the Great War and saw its economy recover and
its industrial companies come into their own. The modern corporation ar-
rived in the economy and began to bring forth a wealth of products for the
common man. Ford introduced mass production and products for the
masses. General Motors organized itself and showed corporations how to
organize for a modern economy. Electric power was to the 1920s what computers and the Internet are to the 1990s. While electricity had been known
for decades and electric lighting was introduced by Edison in 1881 in New
York City, the 1920s saw electric power become almost universal in lighting, commercial use, and industry. The last was the important step for production and productivity.

The new industry though was radio. The new corporation formed to
exploit it was RCA. (Subsequently acquired by General Electric.) RCA was
lauded for leading the way to new technology and a new industry. Its research and development was widely praised. Although the stock did not
pay any dividends, it was considered a leading corporation and a blue chip
of the future. In many ways, RCA was the Microsoft of its era; along with

GM, it led the market higher and higher beginning in March 1928. It also suffered one of the larger retreats in late 1929.

GM and RCA were emblematic of the "new era" that was heralded in the 1920s and came to dominate the markets in 1928 and 1929. The stock market and talk about the market permeated almost everything, and it seemed as if almost everyone was in the market. The investment business discovered the idea that investment need not be limited to a wealthy few, but could reach out to the masses. Investment Trusts—the precursors of today's mutual funds—became more and more popular and made it possible for people of modest means to own diversified stock portfolios. The trusts, which began in the early part of the decade, mushroomed in the late 1920s.

The new-era idea reached into the press and stock indexes. In September 1928, Dow Jones expanded their industrial average from 20 to 30 stocks and added some new names. In the process, they recognized the new economy stocks of the 1920s. Six names were dropped. Some even sound old economy—American Car Foundry, American Locomotive, U.S. Rubber, and United Drug Co. Two others are more familiar, Western Union and American Telephone and Telegraph (AT&T). These were part of the new Dow Jones Utility Index launched at the start of 1929. AT&T was dropped from the Utility Index in 1938 and added back to the Industrials in 1939 where it replaced IBM. IBM later rejoined the Industrials. While some old ones came out, the new members of the expanded Industrials were a Who's Who of the 1920s new economy. They included such technology leaders as Radio Corporation of America (RCA) and the Victor Talking Machine Company along with retailers such as Sears Roebuck & Co.; wider representation of the auto industry with the addition of Chrysler Corporation and the Nash Motors Company (Ford was not publicly held at the time); and oil companies including Standard Oil Co. (New Jersey), later known as ExxonMobil and others. Indeed, the 1928 version of the Dow has a modern feel, the earlier version sounds more like history.

Two ideas floated through many of the contemporary discussions of the stock market as it rose higher and higher in 1928 and 1929. First, that the increases in stock prices were justified by the strong economy, strong earnings, and advancing technology. This had largely been true for the period from 1920 or 1921 through the beginning of 1928. The p–e rose from 8.8 times in 1923 (1921 and 1922 saw weak earnings and high p–e's in the aftermath of the 1920–1921 recession) to 13.7 times in 1928. While the 1928 p–e is certainly higher, the rise reflects rising hopes for stocks that seem justified by the increasing prices from 1923 to 1928. At the same time the dividend yield fell from 5.98 percent to 3.98 percent from 1923 to 1928.[9] Dividends, measured in dollars per share, rose; though not as fast as prices. Irving Fisher, probably the most widely recognized American economist of the time and a professor at Yale University, argued that prices were justified by dividend and earnings gains.

The second thought that echoed through Wall Street was that the economy of the 1920s, the advancing technology, the wonders of electricity, mass production, and radio were truly unprecedented and different from anything else seen before. The sense that the economy could only gain and advance was widespread, despite the history of periodic reversals and recessions. These ideas and the tenor of the times may have all come together in an interview in the *Ladies' Home Journal* with John J. Raskob, a senior executive of General Motors, titled "Everyone Ought to Be Rich." Roskob's investment advice and economic forecasting were no better than his timing—the article appeared days before the market reached its all-time high in September 1929. That peak would not be exceeded until 1954.

While the data suggest that the rise from 1921 to 1928 was within the realm of reason, there does not seem to be anything in the pattern of earnings, dividends, or the economy that can explain the acceleration in stock prices that began in March 1928 and continued to the fall of 1929. Almost anyone examining the market activity from early 1928 through mid-1932 comes to believe that it went up too far, too fast and then paid the ultimate price. Moreover, on the upswing, the stock market drove itself higher and pulled much of the economy and financial markets along with it. Credit for margin loans to buy and hold stock was readily available. But interest rates on these loans were climbing, a strong suggestion that the buoyant stock market drew funding into margin loans rather than easy money encouraged rampant speculation in the market. Likewise, shifts in bank lending and corporate finance during the 1920s may have helped to finance the stock market, but it was the market that was leading and the banks that were following. Initial public offerings also boomed. But here again, the rising market encouraged companies to go public rather than a sudden thirst for equity capital, sparking a speculative rise in the market. In short, it is hard to find some perpetrator to blame for the market's 16-month-long surge to higher and higher prices.

The downside is equally puzzling and also probably due to shifts in the market more than anything else. In a few short days in late October 1929, the market collapsed, losing about one-third of its value. There are comparable declines with the crashes of 1907 and 1987, the two that are closest. The crash of 1907 was a bigger drop by many measures.

What followed was spectacularly bad luck on numerous counts. While the New York Federal Reserve Bank did manage to contain the immediate damage in the stock market, monetary policy did not recognize how much fear and anxiety had been poured into the economy from the crash. As weeks turned into months, all willingness to invest or take any financial risks dried up and the economy withered with it. On top of that, difficulties overseas and efforts to maintain a gold-standard–based monetary system in many nations restricted efforts at stimulative economic policy. The result was a collapse that far, far exceeded anything that happened in the stock market.

There was a longer-term legacy, some of which we are only now beginning to come to terms with. Much of the current financial regulation and the current regulators were created in the wake of the market's 1929 crash. Investor protection, the SEC, regulations covering mutual funds, financial structures of banks, brokers, investment banks, and even electric utilities all emerged in legislation passed in the 1930s to prevent another market crash. The crash also left America with a generation scared of stocks and investing in them. Through the 1950s, the 1960s, and even into the 1970s, bonds were safe and stocks were seen as speculative, dangerous, or worse.

3

WHAT MADE THE BULL MARKET HAPPEN?

While the stock market's performance in 1995–1999 was incredible, the performance since 1982 has been very good. A couple of numbers serve to remind us how good the last two decades have been. From 1926 to 1999, one in every three years saw the market decline. In a similar vein, the compound annual return to stocks from August 1982 to December 1999 was 19.9 percent, substantially higher than the return for the entire period 1926 to 1999 of 11.3 percent and certainly higher than the period 1926 to July 1982 of 8.8 percent. Simply put, anyone who got out of the market anytime since August 1982 (through the end of 1999) regretted it. In this chapter we will look at what gave us the bull market that began in the summer of 1982 and has yet to end.

One way to understand the bull market is to look at various significant economic events in the last 20 or so years. However, wading through various encyclopedias or world almanacs doesn't seem too efficient. So, to bring some order to the puzzle, we will begin with some simple ideas of how the stock market works and what makes its values change. When you buy stocks—either individual stocks or a portfolio like the S&P 500—you are buying a share in the future earnings of these stocks. One way many people look at stock prices is by how much you pay for $1 of earnings, or the price–earnings ratio. (This is the price of a share divided by the earnings per share, abbreviated p–e.) When the p–e is low, the price for $1 of earnings is low and stocks appear to be cheap. When the p–e is high, the price for $1 of earnings is high and stocks appear to be high.

The p–e changes over time. Figure 3-1 shows the p–e for the S&P 500 over the last 20 years. It bounces around. Two related forces that affect the p–e are inflation and real interest rates. From experience we know that higher inflation rates tend to mean lower price–earnings ratios. High inflation seems to imply a lot of uncertainty about the future and a lot of stress on earnings, both of which point to lower stock prices and p–e's. Figure 3-2 shows a comparison of p–e's and inflation rates for the last 40 years. One can see that high inflation rates (the horizontal axis) tend to mean lower p–e's (the vertical axis). We do know that inflation has come down since 1982. In 1982 the inflation rate was 6.8 percent on the consumer price index, compared to 2.4 percent in 1999. This drop in inflation to about one-third of its former value should mean a higher p–e and higher stock prices. We can put some numbers on this relation by statistically fitting a curve to p–e's and the inflation rate. One such curve or relation is shown in Figure 3-2. As explained below, this can be used to estimate how much falling inflation could have boosted stocks by.

Stocks are also affected by interest rates. The p–e is related to interest rates because the earnings represent a return for buying the stock.

FIGURE 3-1   Price–Earnings Ratio for S&P 500, 1979–1999

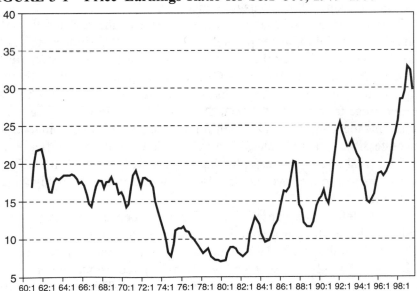

FIGURE 3-2   Comparison of Price–Earnings Ratios and Inflation Rates, 1959–1999

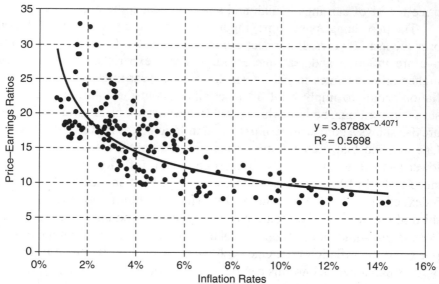

Figure 3-3 shows the relation between the real interest rate and p–e's, similar to Figure 3-2 for inflation and p–e's. In 1982, interest rates on 10-year treasury notes were about 14 percent; at the end of 1999, they were about 6 percent, a drop of 8 percentage points.

The combination of changes in the real rate of interest and the inflation rate both point to higher p–e's in 1999 than in 1982. Indeed, this is the case. In 1982 the p–e for the S&P 500 was about 8.7 times compared to about 32 times at the end of 1999. Of course, the p–e wasn't the only thing that affected stock prices. Earnings went up as well. From 1982 to 1999 earnings rose from $12.64 to about $50, a gain of almost four times. If we put all this together, we can account for a large part of the bull market, but not quite all as yet. In Table 3-1, we show how the drop in inflation and the lower real rate of interest, plus higher earnings, all point to a substantial rise in stock prices over the last 18 years—but not quite as high a gain as we got.

We are left with a gap of about 27 percent between the explained or predicted rise in stock prices and the actual rise in the S&P 500 from the end of 1982 to the end of 1999. One can argue that prices were depressed at the start of 1982—the economy was in a deep recession, unemployment was hovering at 10 percent, and everyone was glum. This is probably true.

FIGURE 3-3   Comparison of Price–Earnings Ratios and Interest Rates, 1959–1999

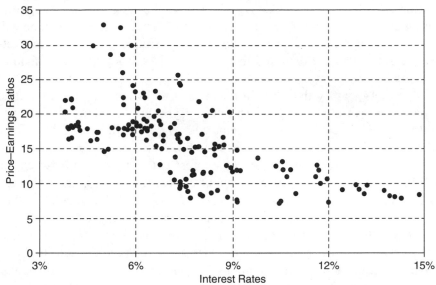

One can also argue that at the end of 1999 stocks were overvalued and everyone was crazy and optimistic and much too upbeat. The truth of this remains to be seen. However, both of these arguments have strong elements of excuses in them without some idea of why there should be a shift as large as 27 percent. Before turning to what else is going on, one more caveat is in order. The analysis is good, but it is not razor sharp. One should not give a lot of credence to relatively small amounts or leap to invest in a market that is 5 percent undervalued. These kinds of measures are just not that precise.

TABLE 3-1   Effects of Inflation, Interest Rates, and Earnings on Stock Prices

Factors	1982	1999	Impact of Change
Inflation rate	6.5%	2.0%	1.61x
Real interest rate	6.8%	3.4%	1.51x
Increased earnings per share	$12.64	$50.00	3.96x
Total impact on stock prices	—	—	9.63x
Actual rise in stock prices	120	1465	12.21x

Earlier we talked about how attitudes shift in bull markets. While investors ordinarily buy stocks because they believe the price is undervalued compared to the future dividends and earnings the stock offers, in euphoric bull markets investors buy stocks because they firmly believe someone will appear to buy it from them at a higher price. Simply put, in bull markets people are more confident and they see less risk in buying stocks than in bear markets.

We can quantify this shift in riskiness. Stocks tend to bounce around a lot more than bonds or Treasury bills. If you buy a six-month Treasury bill with an interest rate of 5 percent, you pay approximately $9750 for a $10,000 T-bill. Six months later when the bill matures, the government will pay you the $10,000. Your return or interest is the difference between the $9750 you paid and the $10,000—about 2.5 percent of $10,000 in this example. However, the key item here is that if you watch Treasury bills, they don't bounce around much in price. Your $9750 T-bill is likely to trade between $9500 and $10,000 or maybe $10,250 during the six months. Stocks are different—much more volatile. Over six months a stock is likely to move much more than plus or minus 2.5 percent. Investors—and the rest of us—don't like uncertainty. Other things equal, we would prefer to own stocks where the prices are predictable and don't bounce all over the place. Yes, we do want to own stocks that go up, but we also want the price rise to be believable, reliable, and predictable.

Of course, given the choice between two stocks—one where the price never changes and another where it bounces around like crazy but has a seven-in-ten chance of being up by 50 percent in a year—a lot of us would choose the volatile stock that offers the 50 percent return. How much extra return you expect or want to make up for the agony of the bouncing around is a measure of your willingness to trade between accepting risks and getting returns. Your own opinions about some randomly chosen stock may not seem important, but in the aggregate these concerns can be important. Over the 75 years since 1926, when reliable data on returns on stocks and T-bills began, the average annual return on stocks has been about 6 percent greater than the return on Treasury bills. In other words, people got 6 percent more each year—on average—for agreeing to hold volatile risky stocks instead of docile, plain T-bills. Even if 6 percent sounds puny, it isn't. At 6 percent per year, your money doubles in 12 years.

Economists are somewhat puzzled by why the amount should be so large. They have given the 6 percent a name: the "equity-risk premium (ERP)"—the premium in returns paid for accepting the risks of equities. The size of the premium suggests a hatred for risks (risk aversion in the jargon) that makes little sense. However, the puzzle has some benefits for investors. Economists have spent a lot of time studying the ERP. We know that it can vary a lot over time, depending on market conditions. We also know that seemingly small changes in the ERP can result in large changes in the market's reasonable value.

All this suggests an explanation for the 27 percent missing in the market value discussed above. As the bull market of the 1990s gathered steam, investors became optimistic and fell in love with the market. They came to believe that it is closer to a sure thing. In the process, the ERP slipped and the market's reasonable values climbed. Arguing that the market is overvalued now or was undervalued in 1982 needs some kind of a benchmark. Given the concerns about inflation, recession, unemployment, and economic disaster that many people had in 1981–1982, the market's low values then may have been reasonable or even a little high. For the low-risk premium—and modest concerns about risk, volatility, and falling stock prices—that investors have today, the market may be reasonably valued. In fact, some people have argued recently that the market is dramatically undervalued even though it has surged in the last five years.[10]

There is one aspect of the ERP that we should recognize—when people think things are getting better and better, they are setting the stage for stocks to do worse, not better. Suppose that the normal or average equity-risk premium is the historic average of 6 percent. This means that when the risks of stocks and T-bills are close to their historic averages, stocks earn returns that are 6 percentage points higher than T-bills. But, if everyone believes we are in some golden era where stocks are so trustworthy they are no riskier than T-bills, then stocks would only earn as much as T-bills and that 6-percentage-point bonus would vanish. In the best of times—no extra risk in stocks, stocks earn no extra return, and they are no fun.

Wait! Don't give up yet. Getting to the best of times is a lot of fun. Suppose back in 1994, before the great bull market took off, the risks of stocks and T-bills were close to the historic averages. Then as inflation and unemployment fell to 30-year lows and the Fed showed it could handle one financial crisis after another with great aplomb, the (apparent) risks in stocks collapsed. As the risks got to be less and less while the companies the stocks represented made profits and benefited from the strong economy, the stocks would get to be worth a lot more. Why? Much less risk combined with the same or better underlying profits and dividends. If the stocks got to be worth a lot more, then their prices would surge upward, as they did in 1995–1999. But, the bull market is sowing the seeds of its own demise—once all the risks are squeezed out of stocks, they can only rise as fast as their earnings grow. And that growth, while impressive, accounts for only 20 percent of the gains seen in the 1982–1999 period.

So where did the bull market come from? First, earnings grew almost four times from 1982 to 1999. Second, inflation came down and boosted the p–e ratios. Third, real interest rates came down as well and further boosted p–e's. Finally, the lower inflation rates and lower interest rates helped set the stage for an economic boom that encouraged people to think stocks were getting less risky. In this road to low risk, getting there is all the fun—as the late 1990s have proven.

Where is the Internet in this story? It is certainly part of the tale of the strong economy, but it may not be a big part of the stock market's overall gains. It is a big part of the technology stocks, but that is another story.

4

JUDGING THE MARKET

Bull markets end. It is difficult or impossible to predict when, but they all end. While there will be others, we would all like to know how to invest while we await their arrival. Since the speed of the market far exceeds the speed of publishing books, there is a chance that between the time this manuscript is written and the time it reaches the reader, the bull market may perish. There is a better chance it won't end, but preparation is usually a good idea in investing. This chapter takes a brief look at what could be around the corner and what to do about it. First the good news: how to invest if the bull market is roaring. Second, the mixed news: what warning signals to watch for. Third, the not-so-good news: what to do if the bull market is faltering. In the process, we preview Part IV of the book, which shows you how to build your portfolio given your feelings about risk and how much time you have until you plan to start spending your money.

IF THE BULL MARKET CONTINUES—WHERE TO INVEST
In a word—stocks. Through thick and thin, stocks do better than just about anything else. Yes, stocks do fall at times, even for long periods of time. But, so far they have always come back and have always been the best bet if you could hang on long enough. In the dark days after 1929, stocks fell for another three years. And the road back was long—it took until 1954 for

the Dow Jones to reach its 1929 high. But, if you had bought the S&P 500 at the peak in 1929, held on and kept reinvesting the dividends, you would have broken even in June 1945, about 16 years later. To be fair, there would have been some very nervous moments since the original stake fell to less than 17 percent of the initial investment in June 1932. If you had been smart enough to wait from August 1929 to June 1932 before investing, your June 1945 nest egg would have been almost seven times larger.

What stocks? A broad-based, diversified, low-cost portfolio. The choice is probably an S&P 500 index fund or an exchange traded fund (ETF). Some people argue that stocks in smaller companies, "small-cap" stocks, do better in the long run than the blue chips. When small caps are hot, they are very hot indeed. If you like playing long shots, then some of your money should be in small caps. If you think stocks have some risks without adding anything extra, stay with the large caps. Foreign stocks are another area gathering some interest in the current bull market. These should be split into two general groups: developed countries and emerging markets. Developed countries include Canada, most of western Europe, Japan, Australia, and New Zealand. There is a place for these in a portfolio, but they are not likely to boost your results by huge amounts. Like the United States, these are all modern economies. There is little reason to expect companies to be fundamentally more, or less, profitable in Germany or England or Japan than they are in the United States. So, we wouldn't expect a huge increase in investment returns either.

Emerging markets are different, very different from the developed countries. They are like small caps, but more so. When they go up, they can go way up. But, when they fall, they can collapse completely. For the long-shot players who find small-cap stocks boring, this is the ticket. Choosing among these depends on two things: how much risk you want to take and how much you think you can time the market. We return to both of these in chapters to come.

COULD THE BULL MARKET END?

Not only could it end, but at some point it will end. First, let's look at how to spot the end; second, we'll look at what to do. The first sign that a bull market may be ending is falling stock prices. This sounds obvious, but sometimes people forget to look at the obvious. Stocks seldom go straight up for days and weeks on end. Instead, there are always ups and downs. The 1990s bull market has been more consistently straight up than most, but even it has had some interruptions. In 1998 the S&P 500 fell almost 20 percent in August and September after Russia defaulted on its bonds.

In 1999 the market didn't fall much from July to October, but it certainly didn't advance either.

Market watchers usually assume that a drop of less than 10 percent from the last high is just normal shifting. A drop of 10 percent to 20 percent is a "correction" and a drop of more than 20 percent is a bear market. Equally important is how long the decline continues. A short steep drop of 20 percent over six weeks, followed by a rebound, is probably not enough time for many investors to rearrange their portfolios. A drop of 40 percent that goes on for a year is likely to seem much more than twice as bad.

Beyond the change in prices there are three other things that investors should watch in trying to decide if a bull market is being briefly interrupted or is about to be cast aside for a long time: interest rates, the economy, and stock values.

High or rising interest rates are the enemy of rising stock prices. The key interest rates to watch are the Fed funds rate, the yield on 10-year Treasury notes, and the yield on 30-year Treasury bonds. The Federal Reserve can pretty much set the Fed funds rate. If it is rising over the last six to nine months, the Fed is trying to slow the economy—not a good sign for stocks. If the yields on the 10-year Treasury notes and the 30-year Treasury bonds are higher than they were six months or a year ago, this is also not a good sign. It is hard to set an absolute level at which interest rates become a danger to the market, since there are many factors involved. However, if the yields on the Treasury notes and bonds top 8 percent, one should be wary. Finally, if the Fed funds rate is higher than the 10-year or 30-year Treasury yields, this is also not positive for the market. If all the interest rate signs are against you, there is at least a one-in-three chance that the stock market is entering a sustained retreat, not just a nervous pause.

Good economies and good stock markets tend to go together. Moreover, if the economy is good, people are finding jobs, inflation isn't rising, and profits are growing, it is hard to see why stocks should keep dropping and dropping. So, investors should watch the economy. Look at one or two general measures and check to see if they are getting worse. The ones worth considering are the unemployment rate (worse if it rises), consumer price inflation (also worse if it rises), and growth in real GDP. The last is sometimes called simply economic growth; a bigger number is better.

The last thing to look at is the most difficult to gauge—whether stocks are too cheap or too expensive. Stock prices bounce around a lot. Even if we could measure the exact "right" price we would probably find that prices vary from that level by a wide range. One thing that happens in a bull market is that stocks go from being undervalued to being overvalued. Of course the "right" value moves over time as well, so in a strong bull market the right value is rising as stock prices go up. There are many models for measuring the right value of stock prices, and no one can prove which one is the best at any particular moment. Therefore, they should all be used with a lot of caution. It is quite possible for the market to be over- or undervalued by 50 percent or more.

A simple rule of thumb is to take the expected earnings for the S&P 500 for this year or next year and divide it by the yield on the 10-year Treasury note, one of the interest rates mentioned above. This will give a figure for the "right" value of the S&P 500. If you are doing this in the first half of the year, use the current year's forecast earnings; if you are doing it in the second half of the year, use the following year's forecast earnings.[11] For example, if the earnings per share are $60 and the yield on the T-note is 6 percent, then the right value is $60 divided by 6 percent or $(60/0.06) = 1000$. Since the S&P 500 is around 1470 as of the end of 1999, it is also overvalued by about 47 percent.

If everything is pointing the wrong way—if interest rates are rising, the economy is slowing, and the market is overvalued—a good bet is that the market will continue to drop. If interest rates are rising, but the economy looks good and the market is not more overvalued than it was six months ago, the bull market could easily hang together, so don't panic now.

EVEN IF IT ENDS, WHAT NEXT?
Don't panic is probably the most important thing. Second, when stocks take a big dive, they tend to bounce part of the way back, no matter what may happen next. So if the market crashes, don't try and sell out on the day it all crumbles. Hold on for a moment and set up a program to gradually rearrange your holdings over a period of a few weeks or months.

Even more important, know where to put what's left of your portfolio. Chances are the choice is some kind of safe short-term investment like Treasury bills or a money market fund. Also, think before you jump out. From 1982 through the end of 1999 (when this is being written) those who abandoned the stock market made a mistake. The best thing to have done on October 19, 1987, when the market crashed, was . . . nothing. Those who stayed in did the best. If one reviews the history of the S&P 500 or other U.S. market indexes, you will see that there are no 20-year periods when bonds or T-bills did better than stocks. There are very few 10-year periods where bonds or bills did better than stocks. So, most likely you should stay invested. If you expect to spend this money within a year, you have no business putting it in the market anyway. The lesson for the long term is to hang in there.

5

HOW NOT TO JUDGE THE MARKET

Using some of the measures in the last chapter, you can make an educated guess about where the market is likely to go next and whether the bull market is still with us. You should not try to time the market, but you should consider controlling some of the risks in your investments. While these ideas often get confused, they are very different. In terms of the risks, there are two aspects worth mentioning: how much of your money to put in the stock market and what to buy in the stock market.

FALLACIES OF MARKET TIMING
Market timing is the idea that you can guess *in advance* when the market will go up and when it will go down. If you own stocks when they are rising and T-bills when stocks are falling, you will do much better than owning stocks all the time. Of course, the big word is "if." In almost two decades on Wall Street, I have yet to see any real evidence of successful market timing. Once you consider how hard it is to time the market, the absence of any success should not be a surprise. First, you need to be right not once, but several times in succession. There are numerous stories about people who got out of the stock market in the spring and summer of 1987, before the October crash. All these tales end with investors holding bonds for a long time—no one seems to have been able to get back in even close to

the bottom. The bottom was the crash—the market never looked back, it just kept climbing after the break.

Second, lots of people try to time the market, and some of them are really smart. If none of them have gotten it right, what makes you (or me) think we can do it now. There are probably more numbers and statistics available for study about the stock market than anything else, including baseball. Those hunting for regular and repeating patterns in market behavior face two kinds of problems. First, if you look hard enough, you can find patterns and regularities, even though they are only random events. Suppose you take a deck of cards, shuffle it, and deal out the top ten cards. You get seven red cards. You do it again, and get six red cards; again, and get five red cards. Does this mean you will get four red cards the next time? No. If you really shuffled, each deal is not affected by the last deal. Until you started the game, you never even thought of a pattern of fewer red cards on each deal. But, the apparent patterns are easy to see. This is the second big problem with looking for consistent patterns. Instead of deciding what they are looking for first, most would-be market timers tend to let the data tell them what to look for. Amazingly enough, the data always seem to have something to say if you look at it long enough. If that's not enough, the market is probably a lot more random and volatile than most of us imagine.

There is another reason why market timing isn't likely to work for any length of time, even if you seem to find some system that appears to work once. Not only is everyone involved in investing watching the market, they are also watching each other. Now, suppose someone discovers that the way to time the market is to buy stocks if they rise at least 10 percent in the week before a full moon. (Yes, this is silly, but so are some of the more serious theories that float around.) If this idea appears to work, it will develop a following and the next time stocks are climbing in the week before a full moon, adherents of this idea will rush into the market and start buying. By the time the full moon arrives, stocks will have been bid up. Once the full moon fades, someone will wonder why prices rose and someone will start to sell. In short, any gains will have been arbitraged away and the theory will have self-destructed.

There is another aspect of this that is worth thinking about. Suppose the S&P 500 is selling at 1450 today and someone tells you he is quite sure the index will be at 1700 in a year's time, a rise a bit over 17 percent. This prediction may well come true, but it is far from a sure thing. If it were a sure thing, everyone would borrow money today—easily done at less than 17 percent—and buy the index now, confidently expecting to make 17 percent. Of course, given the rush to the market, prices would rise and most investors would pay a lot more than 1450 for the stocks. Some might even pay more than 1700 and the prophecy would be anything but self-fulfilling. The biggest problem with timing the market is that the market reacts to every move everyone makes, including the market timers and the people watching the market timers. The next time someone promises you a surefire way to time the market, maybe you should ask "If you're so smart, why ain't you rich?"

CONTROLLING RISKS: HOW MUCH TO PUT IN THE MARKET

Is there ever anything wrong with stocks? Yes, sometimes the prices fall and they lose value. Moreover, in the tradition of Murphy's Law, one can depend on stocks to go down at precisely the wrong time. But there are some easy ways to reduce some of the risk of falling stock prices—easy as long as you remember that there is a cost to reducing risk, just like there is a cost to almost anything you do. If you are concerned about the risk that stocks might fall, you can put part of your portfolio into the market and the rest into Treasury bills or a money market account. The T-bills won't pay enough interest to make you rich (about 5.5 percent as of the start of 2000), but they will dampen the swings in your portfolio.

How much risk can T-bills take out of your portfolio and what will it cost? If the market goes down 5 percent and you have half your money in stocks and half in T-bills, you will lose 2.5 percent of your money in the market, but make 2.75 percent on the other half invested in T-bills. Likewise, if the market goes up 15 percent, but you put half in T-bills and half in the market, you would make 7.5 percent on the market half and another 2.75 percent on the T-bill portion for a return of 10.45 percent (7.5 percent plus 2.75 percent) on your portfolio. What did reducing your risks cost you? If the market went up 15 percent, it cost you 4.55 percent compared to being 100 percent in stocks. It probably would have also saved a lot of sleepless nights. There is always a temptation to be a Monday morning quarterback when you look at your investments. Maybe you can learn something, but if keeping the risks reasonable is important, that 4.55 percent cost may be money well spent.

Figure 5-1 shows how much a portfolio of stocks and T-bills would earn for varying proportions of stocks and different market moves. The calculations used to build the chart assume that T-bills earned 5.5 percent. Each line represents a different market return from -10 percent to $+20$ percent in 5 percent increments. The horizontal axis shows the proportion invested in stocks. Look at the line marked -5 percent, which corresponds to a market drop of 5 percent. On the horizontal axis at 50 percent you can read off a re-

FIGURE 5-1   Portfolio Returns for Different Proportions of Stocks and Cash in Different Markets

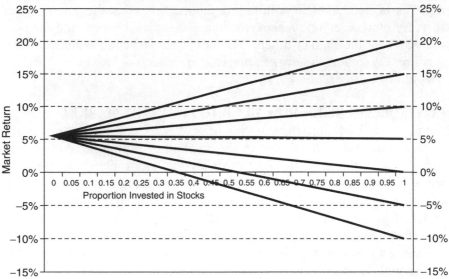

turn of about 2.75 percent, what the portfolio split 50/50 between stocks and T-bills would make if stocks fell 5 percent and T-bills returned 5.5 percent. As a first cut, this kind of chart can give you an idea of how much you can cut the risk by putting only some of your money in the market.

Most people worry about losing money. Figure 5-1 gives you an idea of how much you might want to have in Treasury bills to avoid losing money. Since 1970, the S&P 500 was down in only six years. Moreover, in one of those years the loss was small enough to be made up for by the dividends on the stocks in the index. In two of the down years, 1973 and 1974, when the economy was falling apart and interest rates were high, the market fell about 17 percent and 30 percent. Let's assume this seems sufficiently rare and that it is a risk you can take. But, you want to be protected against a 10 percent drop in the market. From Figure 5-1 you can see that if you have 35 percent to 40 percent in the market, you will be protected from a 10 percent market drop. In a similar fashion, you can use Figure 5-1 to look at other stock T-bill proportions or construct your own table or chart to consider other possible returns on T-bills.

THE KEY TOOL: STOCK INDEXES

Being caught in a falling market is not the only risk. Even when it goes up, not all stocks go up. In fact, this market has become infamous for being "top heavy." Relatively few large stocks are climbing and pulling the market indexes up, even though the average stock (whatever that is) may be dropping. If you could own only the ones that go up, things would be fine. But that is even harder than market timing. So, the answer is to own a lot of stocks on the bet that the ones that go up will outweigh the ones that don't. In other words, own a diversified stock portfolio.

Owning a lot of stocks is not any more expensive than owning a few. In fact, it is often cheaper. Choose a broad-based index like the S&P 500 and find a mutual fund or an exchange traded fund based on the index. This is the most efficient way to own a lot of stocks. Exchange traded funds or ETFs are similar to mutual funds, but they can be traded during the day the way stocks are. ETFs don't have an automatic reinvestment of dividends and capital gains feature, but do let you check prices during the trading day. Either way, the answer is to own a lot of stocks through one of these.

Even if you want to focus on only certain stocks, or avoid some others, indexes and index funds are very effective, because of diversification and low cost. Cost is easy. Depending on whether you use funds or ETFs, the costs of trading—commissions—are comparable or less than those on stocks. There are operating expenses in funds. These are the costs of running the fund and paying the fund manager. These costs are paid out of your money, so you should watch them. However, in index funds the managers are simply following the indexes rather than researching and choosing stocks. As a result, the operating expenses tend to be lower.

If you don't use index funds, someone is investing some time and effort in picking stocks. We know that professional managers don't do it all that well. After all, two-thirds of the actively managed mutual funds underperform the S&P 500 in most years, so two-thirds of the managers are spending more than their gains from good selections on doing the selecting. Maybe you can do better by yourself—but remember that the pros usually miss and they have more experience and probably more information than you do. In the next chapter, we will see just how successful stock indexes have been in recent years.

CHAPTER 6

SOME REAL MARKETS

The bull market in the second half of the 1990s was truly remarkable; some of the numbers are worth repeating to remind ourselves how strong the equity markets can be and just how rewarding investing in stock indexes sometimes is. There is another lesson hidden in these numbers. Almost anytime since 1995, someone could have looked at the results seen so far and said, "It can't continue like this; if I'm not in, it's too late and I missed it." More mistaken words may have been rarely said. Given how strong the gains can be, it is hard to see why a serious long-term investor should ever be 100 percent *out* of the market. There are many times when many of us should not be 100 percent in the market, but unless we claim incredible clairvoyance, it is hard to tell why we should ever be all out of it. Certainly, the last five years were rewarding, even for those only 20 percent invested.

How well did the market do? A $10 investment at the beginning of 1995 became $35 by the end of 1999, only five years later. That's three and a half times in five years for the S&P 500. The compound annual total return for the S&P 500 was 28.6 percent for 1995 through 1999, inclusive. There have been better five-year runs, but not too many of them. Note that a "year" in this discussion is 12 consecutive months, not a calendar year. Among calendar years, the five from 1995 to 1999 are even more impressive standouts. For the numerological historians, most of the outstanding periods begin with June 1932—the market's bottom during the Great Depression in the aftermath of the 1929 crash.

Table 6-1 shows the returns for the S&P 500 over the last 1, 2, 3, 5, 10, and 20 years as well as the best and average total returns for all 1-, 2-, 3-, 5-, 10-, and 20-year periods since 1926 and since 1950.

The bull market is not absolutely the best, but it is very good. Moreover, the two decades of the 1980s and 1990s (January 1980 through December 1999) are the best 20-year period ever. For those who really worry about being in the market at the wrong time, remember that the last 20 years include the 1987 market crash, the sky-high interest rates and severe depression of 1981–1982, the Asian Financial Crisis, and a host of other disasters.

The first lesson of the 1990s is never be completely out of the market. The second is that one doesn't need to invest in obscure, exotic, strange, or incomprehensible securities to do well. The S&P 500, the most widely used benchmark, was one of the best performers. In any market, the best performer is likely to be a single stock—often and unfortunately one you haven't heard of before. Moreover, the best stock will surge way beyond any broad-based index—just as the worst stock will collapse far worse than any index. However, in the 1990s the best corners of the market were some of the traditional, almost blue-chip, neighborhoods.

TABLE 6-1   Multiyear Market Performances

	1 Year	2 Years	3 Years	5 Years	10 Years	20 Years
			1926–1999			
Best	160.1%	56.5%	48.3%	37.6%	21.2%	17.9%
Worst	−67.1%	−53.2%	−39.8%	−16.5%	−3.9%	2.2%
Average	13.6%	12.3%	12.0%	10.9%	11.1%	11.1%
End date of best period	Jun-33	Jun-34	Mar-36	May-37	May-59	Dec-99
			1950–1999			
Best	61.2%	43.2%	34.9%	29.6%	21.2%	17.9%
Worst	−38.9%	−21.5%	−10.7%	−4.2%	0.5%	4.1%
Average	14.8%	13.9%	13.9%	12.9%	12.6%	11.6%
End date of best period	Jun-83	Sep-55	Aug-87	Jul-87	May-59	Dec-99
Most recent	21.0%	24.7%	26.7%	28.6%	18.2%	17.9%

The S&P 100, an index of some of the larger and more established stocks in the S&P 500 did even better than the S&P 500. The S&P 100 returned 404 percent over the five years through 1999 for an average annual return of 32.3 percent. It is also notable because it is the basis of the OEX index options. Another demonstration of the power of blue chips is the S&P 500/BARRA Growth index, which includes the half of the S&P 500 market capitalization that is growth stocks. This index returned 426 percent in the 1995–1999 period. Of course, if you could have picked economic sectors and chosen Communications Equipment, you would have enjoyed a gain of over 880 percent. However, that is more stock picking than index investing. Moreover, getting to the sector would have meant a lot of work to choose the right one and some risk that you might have gotten the wrong one. Perhaps the surest sign that one of the ways to prosper in the bull market was index funds is that investors have begun to buy them in greater and greater numbers.

IF THE END IS NEAR . . .

No one really wants to talk about what might happen if the bull market were to end. However, it will end someday, and we will all still need to find someplace to put our money. Further, if it ends in a crash, we may have a lot of our money (or our former money) in the market. What should we do? First, don't panic. Second, even though you are sure that the bull market won't end tomorrow, read this section anyhow. When it does end you will have spent a few minutes thinking about the unthinkable.

Some bull markets do end in a crash. The most infamous was the 1920s bull market (really 1928–1929) and the crash of October 1929. Other bull markets end in a long, slow, painful fizzle. This is the story of the 1974 bear market. In many ways the long, slow, and painful is worse because many are tempted to keep believing it will turn around any moment, as it keeps going down and down. One way to deal with the 1974 variety is to set yourself a series of benchmarks in advance—what you will do if the market falls 10 percent, 15 percent, 20 percent, or 25 percent from its most recent peak. At each benchmark you can sell some stocks or hedge your position with index puts.

If you don't sell stocks and the market drops further, you lose money on what you didn't sell. If you do sell and the market rebounds, you end up buying in at a higher price. Hedging can be done by buying index puts or even futures. Suffice it to say that none of these offer a free ride. Hedging means you can be assured of getting today's price, although you will pay something for the privilege. Hedging is not a free ride, but it can sometimes be less expensive than just holding your stocks or simply selling them when you're worried. The key goal is not to panic.

If the market crashes you will definitely know it. Still, don't panic. Markets often seem to bounce around and rebound shortly after a crash, no matter what the future holds. In 1929, the market rebounded and had some good months before sinking to its ultimate bottom in 1932. In 1987, the market bounced, settled back slightly, and then took off in 1988. In either case, there were better moments than the day after the crash to get out. (Obviously getting out before the crash would have been better, but since few did, let's be a bit realistic.)

THE LONG HISTORY OF STOCKS BEATING BONDS

After the initial shock of the end of the bull market, what should we do? One of the few clear messages of financial history—and one that few people are willing to argue should be ignored—is that given enough time, stocks always beat bonds. Table 6-2 shows how long an investment was

TABLE 6-2   Stocks Outperforming Bonds

Holding Periods		Bonds Beat Stocks
Months	Years	(% of the time)
12	1	34%
15	1.25	32%
18	1.5	31%
24	2	28%
36	3	26%
48	4	23%
60	5	19%
72	6	17%
84	7	18%
96	8	14%
108	9	10%
120	10	8%
144	12	8%
180	15	7%
240	20	0%
300	25	0%

held (in months) and the percentage of times that stocks outperformed bonds. The data cover 1929 through 1998.[12] The stock data are for the S&P 500, the bond returns are for long-term U.S. government securities.

A glance at Table 6-2 tells the story—the longer you hold stocks, the better chance you have of doing better than bonds. Of course, bonds can also go down. One can do the same kind of thing for stocks and find that the longer one holds stocks, the better chance there is that they will go up.

Any period beyond 180 months seen since January 1926 has never seen stocks decline. Is it possible for stocks to drop over a 15- or 20-year period? Yes. But if history has any meaning at all, it is rather unlikely. A careful review of Table 6-3 might make someone wonder why the chances of losing money for a 120-month holding period are slightly greater than the chances of losing it in only 108 months. Suppose you take two periods beginning at the same time, one ends just before a bear market and the other, longer, holding period, ends in the middle of a bear market. That is what happened—the particularly damaging moment seems to have a severe mar-

TABLE 6-3   Stock Loses Over Various Holding Periods

Holding Periods		
Months	Years	Stocks Lose (%)
12	1	24%
15	1.25	20%
18	1.5	18%
24	2	16%
36	3	14%
48	4	10%
60	5	10%
72	6	9%
84	7	6%
96	8	2%
108	9	2%
120	10	3%
144	12	3%
180	15	0%
240	20	0%
300	25	0%

ket pullback in 1937 when the economy slipped into a recession after a five-year expansion from the depths of the Great Depression in 1932.

All these data cover time periods beginning in bull markets, in bear markets, and in any other kind of market seen in the last 75 years. In short, if you plan to stay invested for a long time, getting out is likely to be a mistake. We would all like to think that we will see the end of the bull market before it happens and that we can sell at the top. That is nonsense—no one ever sees it before it happens. And, if we all did see it, our selling would end the bull market anyway. So, while you're not panicking, think about keeping some of your money in the market, *in stocks.*

GETTING IN TOO EARLY IS BETTER THAN NOT GETTING IN AT ALL

In the last few years, as the bull market roared ahead, many would-be market pundits took to arguing that the bull market is the best time to buy stocks. Bull markets are the best time to *own* stocks, but the time to buy stocks is often in the darkest of moments. In 1982 the S&P 500 was selling at a mere 120 and the p–e was about eight times, inflation was still close to double digits, the economy was in the worst recession since the 1930s, and interest rates were as high as any time since the Civil War. In short, it seemed like the worst possible moment to buy stocks. It was also the beginning of the greatest bull market.

That bit of history certainly suggests that one should jump in when things look the worst. A more valuable lesson is that hesitating to invest is not always the best approach. Certainly there are reasons to spread investments over time so that if you don't get the timing exactly right, you don't get it exactly wrong either. Moreover, once your money is invested in the market, it will either rise or fall with the market. Since the market rises more often than it falls—in 62 percent of the months from 1926 through 1999, the market rose—you are better off in the market with your money growing than sitting on the sidelines waiting.

TELLTALE SIGNS OF THE ULTIMATE BEAR?

Skeptics among the readers will still argue that the recent multiyear run-up seems sure to end in one incredible collapse like 1929. There are no guarantees, including the inevitability of the mother of all bear markets. However, if one looks at the 1929 crash and the Depression, the 1974 bear market and subsequent recession, or other notable problems like the Panic of 1907, one thing usually rings true: it takes more than just a stock market crash to create total disaster. In 1929, the economy was in a slump from August 1929, three months before the market dived. Moreover, the Crash was followed by some of the worst monetary policy on record. In 1974 the bear market struck in the midst of the first OPEC oil crisis. Moreover, in early 1974 the Fed misread the economy and raised interest rates at precisely the wrong moment, sending the economy into a tailspin.

If the market collapses *and* the economy looks horrid and policy makers aren't doing anything about it, all bets are off and selling out may be sane though painful. If the market collapses but the economy looks okay and the policy makers are moving quickly to limit damage from the market crash, it probably pays to hold on or keep some of your money in the market. The low point in 1987, and the time to buy, was midday on October 20, 1987—Crash Day plus one.

7

INDEXES

TO TRACK THE MARKET

The last few chapters have told the story of bull and bear markets and of fortunes made and lost in the stock market. Through much of this we have relied on one or another stock index to tell the story of the market. Usually we have used the S&P 500, though other indexes may have crept in from time to time. Stock indexes are useful tools to track the market, to gauge today's market against the lessons, or follies, of history, and even to build investments out of.

The idea of a stock index is a single measure that can be used to describe how well the market is doing and what is happening to it. Indexes were not scientifically developed measurement devices. They were developed by newspapers and commentators looking for a way to sell more papers. The first regularly reported index or average in the United States was the Dow Jones Industrials, which began in 1896 with 12 stocks. It was simply an average of the 12 stock prices—take all 12 prices, add them up, and divide by 12.

In the 1920s, the Standard Statistics Company, a forerunner of Standard & Poor's, introduced a composite stock index which was an average of the *market value* of the companies rather than their prices. Market value is stock price multiplied by the number of shares outstanding. Done this way, the index represents a portfolio of stocks where one holds all the shares of each stock, or the same percentage of the outstanding shares of each stock. Currently, Standard & Poor's estimates that index funds own around 8 percent of the total market value of the 500 stocks in the S&P 500. Those portfolios total a bit over $1 trillion.

The idea is to use changes in the index as a gauge of the overall market. One could try to total the value of all the stocks in the market and use that as a measure of what the market is doing. This approach has been tried and has some practical difficulties. There are about 8000 stocks traded in the United States. Some trade hundreds, thousands, or even millions of shares daily with prices quoted on widely available computer feeds. Others trade a few times a day or even a few times a week with prices rarely quoted. You have to draw a line between available and unavailable stocks some place, but where. Moreover, some stocks will see their prices surge or collapse because an investor tries to buy or sell a modest amount. Again, someone needs to draw a line between stocks that should count and those that shouldn't count. If the only thing that mattered was a daily or weekly calculation, a list that claimed to be "complete" might be okay. But when the goal is quotes every 15 seconds, a set list of manageable size is useful.

In stock indexes, as in many things, tradition and familiarity count for something. The Dow Industrials has been an average of the prices of 30 stocks since 1928. The S&P 500 has been 500 stocks since 1957 and has been an average of the overall market values since 1923. In strict terms, neither of these are the total market. However, the S&P 500 is close enough to the total market, and because it is based on the companies' market values, it reflects the total market. If one wants to try to measure the total market, there is the Wilshire 5000. Despite the name, it is about 7700 stocks. However, anyone who tries to base investments on it tends to buy about 3000 stocks, less than half. Some academic studies use data from the Center for Research in Securities Prices (CRSP) at the University of Chicago, which publishes value-weighted indexes of all stocks in the market. The CRSP data are useful, but are not real time.

From a practical point of view, if you want to know what the market did today, you look at the Dow or the S&P 500. The Dow, reflecting its heritage in *The Wall Street Journal*, is more widely quoted. However, Dow Jones itself now calculates a value-weighted index of over 500 stocks that looks like the S&P 500, although it is not very widely used by anyone. The S&P 500 is the measure that most professional investors use.

The S&P 500 and the related data not only tell us whether the market is up or down now, today, this week, or this month. Given the related information on earnings, dividends, returns, and so forth, the index lets an investor compare the market today with the market at any other time. Do stocks pay higher or lower dividends today than 10 years ago? The answer is in the S&P 500 data. What about earnings? Does an investor pay more for a dollar's worth of earnings now than she did last year? Again, the S&P 500 data hold the answer. Have technology stocks done better than consumer stocks? Again, through a system of industry classification, the S&P 500 data hold the answers. Moreover, many of these statistics extend way back in history, making it possible to make comparisons between stocks today and stocks over the last 100 or more years.

Stock indexes provide the crucial measuring system that an investor needs to decide if he is making real progress or just treading water and paying commissions.

INDEXES AS BENCHMARKS

Keeping score matters. For investing it is a key aspect of knowing how things are going. Making 15 percent in 1999 was good, but not all that good—the S&P 500 returned a bit over 20 percent. Making 15 percent in 1994, when the market was flat, was very good. So, indexes provide a key benchmark to tell investors what is a good and bad performance. With any benchmark, it is only good if it is fair. If a police officer gives a speeding ticket for going faster than 20 miles an hour on a superhighway, no one would think this is fair play. But, get a ticket for doing 75 in a 65 mph zone and you may be mad, but you can't say the whole thing is unfair. The S&P 500 is a fair benchmark in that it is really possible to own all 500 stocks and get the same results that the index gets. A number of index funds do it every year.

Even if keeping score weren't important for investing success, it would still be important for many investors. There is a competitive element to investing, and at times the bragging rights are almost as important as the financial rewards. Moreover, there are other times when our feelings may color the results—as in not selling a stock we like—but the scorecard helps make the response more rational.

The score keeping can cover both returns and risks. Returns appear simple—the amount of money one makes. Investment theory usually deals with "total returns" that include both the change in the price of the stock and any dividends that the stock pays. Total returns are calculated for the S&P 500, and other indexes, by treating the index as if it were a portfolio where any dividends received are reinvested in the overall portfolio, not just in the stock paying the dividend. After all, the idea of getting cash from a company you own stock in instead of just more stock is that you can invest the cash in anything you want. These returns are usually stated as a percentage as in the total return for the S&P 500 was 15 percent per year or 2 percent per month, or whatever the number happened to be.

The actual calculation is done on a daily basis—any dividends paid by any stocks in the index are totaled for each day and reinvested (on paper) in the index to calculate the return for that day. The daily results are then converted to weekly, monthly, or annual numbers, as need be. Since the companies in the S&P 500 represent something like $12 to $15 trillion in market value, the numbers can be rather unwieldy. Moreover, it would be a mouthful to report every 15 seconds. Instead, the index uses a scale factor called a divisor to give us numbers that are easier to handle. One takes the total value of the stocks in the index and divides it by the divisor to find the index level, about 1450 as of January 2000. In a similar manner, one can take the total value of dividends paid by all the stocks in the index in the last year and divide it by the same divisor to get the dividends per share for the index. (Earnings per share (EPS) are calculated in the same way using the total income earned by all companies. The EPS on the S&P 500 may be the most widely quoted, and least understood, number on Wall Street.)

One can get a good guess of the total return by adding the percentage change in the index price to the dividend yield. The dividend yield is the current dividend per share divided by the price of the index. Lately dividend yields have been a bit over 1 percent. But, with the power of compound interest, an extra 1 percent or so each year adds up. Even in the bull market of 1995–1999, the cumulative total return was 351 percent versus the cumulative return without dividends of 320 percent—a bigger difference than one might expect for only 1 or 2 percent a year over five years.

Risks are often more important than returns, and risks can also be calculated with the index. Risk is a measure of the volatility of the returns. If an investment has steady, stable, and predictable returns, it is low risk because an investor can be confident that she knows what the investment is worth. If the returns and the value of the investment bounce around a lot, there is little confidence about the value and the risks are high. Usually volatility is measured with a statistical calculation called the standard deviation. A high number suggests a lot of volatility, a low number very little. Over the last five years the monthly figure for standard deviation is about 4 percentage points. Since the average monthly return is a bit over 2 percent, this means that two-thirds of the time the monthly return is between −2 percent and +6 percent. By comparison, the standard deviation for a 10-year Treasury bond, which had an average monthly yield of 0.7

percent over the last five years, is 0.5 percentage points. This means that the Treasury bond yield ranged from 0.2 percent to 1.2 percent per month in two-thirds of the months.

The calculation of the standard deviation (easily done in a computer spreadsheet program and described in most elementary statistics textbooks) counts unusually high returns the same way it counts unusually low returns. This upsets some people who argue that risk should reflect only the chance of losing money and not the chance of seeing unusually high returns. Of course, an investor who is short (who borrowed stock and sold it and is hoping the price will fall so he can buy it back more cheaply) will see things reversed—for him chances of high returns are bad. However, for most stock indexes measured over months or years, there is little difference between calculating standard deviation the normal (two-sided) way and using specialized one-sided calculations.

The market's volatility—that is volatility measured as the standard deviation of the S&P 500—varies over time. Figure 7-1 shows the volatility since 1930 on a trailing five-year basis. One can see a huge run-up in the collapse in 1929–1932, a jump associated with the 1974 bear market, and another bump associated with the 1987 crash. In the last few years volatil-

FIGURE 7-1   Stock Market Volatility Since 1930 (Based on 60-month standard deviation)

ity fell as the market racked up a series of consistent gains and then rebounded after the plunge in 1998, when Russia defaulted on its debts and scared a lot of investors around the globe. Today's level of market risk is pretty close to "normal."

There is another very important aspect to volatility. Time will do wonderful things for it. If one measures returns over the same time period, say as annual rates (how much the investment would in one year), the volatility of the annual returns declines as the time frame extends.

With the last few pages, there is enough background about risk, stocks, and stock indexes to make a very important point. Technically this is called time diversification. Practically it might be called stocks reward patience. In Table 7-1 we show the average annual returns and risks (standard deviations) for the S&P 500 and for 10-year Treasuries. The data cover holding periods ending anytime after December 1989 using data that start in January 1970.

The standard deviation of annual returns for either stocks or bonds falls the longer the holding period. As a rule of thumb, 95 percent of the time returns will be two standard deviations from the average. Someone with a two-year time horizon might see stocks as low as 3 percent—19 percent less two times the standard deviation of 8 percent. Moreover, this wide range means stocks could easily be beaten by bonds in a two-year period. But, in a 20-year period, a bad 20 years in stocks is likely to mean a re-

TABLE 7-1   Average Annual Returns and Risks

Holding Period	Stocks		Bonds	
	Average	Standard Deviation	Average	Standard Deviation
1 yr	19%	12%	9%	8%
2 yrs	19%	8%	10%	4%
3 yrs	17%	8%	9%	3%
4 yrs	17%	6%	9%	3%
5 yrs	16%	5%	10%	2%
6 yrs	16%	4%	10%	2%
7 yrs	16%	3%	10%	2%
10 yrs	16%	2%	11%	2%
15 yrs	16%	2%	11%	1%
20 yrs	14%	2%	10%	1%

turn of 10 percent (14 percent less two times 2 percent standard deviation) and this equals the average bond performance. In other words, unless you are very worried about risks, stocks will come out ahead if given enough time.

Presumably you wouldn't have read this far if you hate the idea of owning stocks. But, in case you have, this is one idea you should consider with some care. Of course, now that you will consider stocks, which ones? There is an easy choice—a stock index. For many people choosing to invest in stocks is easy compared to choosing which stocks to buy. Choosing stocks takes either a lot of work and research or a willingness to gamble with your money. Moreover, just as more time reduces risks, more stocks can reduce risks as well. If you buy one stock and the management is unusually inept or the industry is unusually unfortunate, you lose. But, if you buy the entire market, all these company-specific and industry-specific risks average out. That is the secret behind buying the entire market. It is true you won't do as well as the best stock or as poorly as the worst stock. But, history suggests you will do better than average—in most years two-thirds of the professional money managers don't beat the S&P 500. So, buy the S&P 500 (or some other broad-based stock index).

Later chapters will go into details about how to own the S&P 500 and other indexes. However, having come this far, a couple of words are in order here. One way to buy the index or the market is through a mutual fund. Most of the major fund companies offer index funds which are designed to track the S&P 500 or some other major stock index. Since there are a number of index funds available, it makes little sense to pay a large sales fee (load) to buy an index fund. Moreover, it may pay to check on the expenses charged to the fund or for features like minimum investments, check writing for withdrawals, and so forth.

If you don't care about automatically reinvesting your dividends and do care about being able to easily trade in and out, you might also consider an exchange traded fund. These are similar to mutual funds, except that they trade on a stock exchange, usually the American Stock Exchange. The oldest and largest exchange traded fund is the S&P 500 SPDRs (pronounced spiders like the insect from Standard & Poor's Depository Receipts).

No matter what, buying stocks by buying the market through an index is a good idea.

WHO'S WHO OF INDEXES

As we have seen, stock market indexes are important tools for measuring market performance, judging how well your portfolio is doing, or designing portfolios and picking stocks. To really use these tools in a wide range of investments, we need some background information about what they are, how they work, and where they come from. This section gives that background and a Who's Who list of some major indexes. Just as markets change and evolve, so do indexes. Moreover, it is important to have current information about indexes. That means that while we can give you a lot of background, you may also want to visit various Web sites that contain more up-to-date information, including current market performance and measures.

A stock index is a model portfolio of stocks. Ideally it should be a fair index in the sense that an investor can really buy the stocks in the index in the right amounts and can get the same investment performance that is calculated with the model portfolio. In any investment puzzle there are a lot of details, hidden expenses, and transaction costs that may mean it is very hard to match the model performance. However, with a growing number of widely followed stock indexes there are mutual funds or exchange traded funds that track the index and provide actual performance results. Sometimes the actual results may even be slightly better than the model results.

To completely define an index, one needs at least a list of the stocks to be included and some way to determine how much of each stock will be included in the calculation. The oldest and simplest approach is the one used by the Dow Jones Industrials. The prices for the 30 stocks are added together and then divided by a scale factor. One could use the number of stocks as the scale factor so the index would be simply the average price for all 30. When the Dow began there were 12 stocks and the divisor was 12. From time to time, the list of stocks changes because companies may be acquired or even go out of business. Investors want an index that only moves when the market does, not for other reasons. So, if the index ends one day at a value of 1000 and a stock is added or removed, investors still want it to open the next morning at the same level of 1000. To make this work the divisor is adjusted when the change is made.

An example may be helpful. Suppose one has a very simple index consisting of three stocks and the approach, like the Dow, is simply to average the prices. We begin with stocks A, B, and C as shown:

Stock	Price
Company A	10
Company B	13
Company C	22
Sum	45
Index (A + B + C)/3	15
Divisor = 3	

Now, suppose that Company C is acquired by another company and the resulting corporation is named Super C. The index decides to replace Company C, which is no longer trading, with Super C. Under the terms of the deal, each share of Company C became 1.25 shares of Super C, and Super C sells for 18.75. Now, the last time the market closed before the deal, the index was at 15. When the market opens the next morning, and if the stock prices are the same as the night before, the index should still be 15:

Stock	Price
Company A	10
Company B	13
Super C	18.75
Sum	41.75
Index (A + B + C)/2.7833	15
Divisor = 2.7833	

All we did was change the divisor to keep the index smooth. Indexes or averages set up this way sometimes have some strange aspects that make them less than ideal for tracking the stock market. When an investor talks about a big move in a stock, she is referring to the percentage change in the price, not the dollar increase or decrease. If a stock selling for 200 rises by two points or 1 percent that is a lot smaller than when a $10 stock rises one point or 10 percent. Yet, the two point rise in the $200 stock will make a bigger difference to the index value than the one point rise in the $10 stock. Seems almost the reverse of what one might expect.

A similar problem occurs when companies appear to be very different in size, but really aren't. Suppose Company A in our example has 100 million shares outstanding priced at $10 and is worth $1 billion while Company C, priced at $15 has 66.67 million shares and is also worth $1 billion (up to a small round-off error). Since the two companies are the same size, they should have the same impact on the stock market or on an index designed to track the stock market. If Company A's value climbs by 10 percent, its price goes up $1 to $11 and the index rises by $1 divided by the divisor of 3, or 33 cents. Suppose Company C's value also climbs by 10 percent. Its stock climbs by $1.50 from $15 to $16.50 and the index climbs by $1.50/3 or 50 cents. Yet, both companies added 10 percent to their value. The difficulty is not with the companies, but with an index based on an average of prices.

A better way to build an index that reflects the stock market is to use the total market value of the companies instead of the prices. The total value of a company is called its market capitalization and this kind of index is called capitalization-weighted or "cap-weighted." The first index example discussed above is "price-weighted." In cap-weighted indexes there are also divisors for the same reasons of consistency. We can show the example all over again as a cap-weighted index:

Company	Share Price	Shares (Millions)	Market Capitalization (Billions)
Company A	10	100	1
Company B	13	500	6.5
Company C	22	45.45	1
Sum			8.5

Index = 15, Divisor = Market Cap/Index = 0.566 Billion

The divisor looks a lot bigger, but by using the divisor we can make the index the same size as in the price-weighted case. If we change a stock, we can recalculate the divisor just as we did in the other case to assure a smooth index. Note one side benefit: If a stock splits in the cap-weighted index, there is no divisor change required since the changes in shares outstanding and the share price offset one another.

Although there are other ways to calculate indexes, capitalization-weighted indexes are the standard throughout the investment world. Price-weighting is only used in a handful of older indexes that were started long before computers and that have never been revised or changed.

The list of stocks and the calculation method are the two keys to a stock index. Life would be simple if the list of stocks never changed and if no adjustments were necessary. Unfortunately, that is far from reality. In the last few years the S&P 500 has seen about 30 to 50 stocks added and an equal number removed from the index each year. The Dow has undergone two revisions in the last few years, changing four stocks each time. These changes are required to keep up with things like mergers and acquisitions, companies that change, shrink, or grow, and changes in the market that the index needs to reflect. So, part of defining an index is what the index does when the market changes or companies appear and disappear—in short, a set of procedures for managing the index and keeping it current and up to date. For investors these kinds of things can make a big difference. If you use an index as an investment vehicle, it pays to know how the index is run and what that means for your investments.

The major stock indexes are compiled, managed, and published by a variety of organizations. The most widely quoted are the Dow Jones Industrials and the S&P 500. The Dow is published by Dow Jones & Co, which also publishes *The Wall Street Journal* newspaper. The S&P 500 is published by Standard & Poor's, a division of The McGraw-Hill Companies.[13] A number of stock exchanges also publish indexes based on the stocks listed on the exchange. Currently the NASDAQ, published by the National Association of Securities Dealers which runs the NASDAQ stock trading system, is another popular index. The New York Stock Exchange also publishes indexes, led by the NYSE Composite, based on stocks traded on the exchange. Other indexes are published by financial advisory firms such as the Wilshire 5000 by Wilshire Associates and the Russell 2000 offered by Frank Russell & Company.

So far we have mentioned indexes on U.S. stocks. However, the international field is as wide and varied as the domestic offerings. Increasingly companies offering indexes are taking a global approach. Among the longer

THE INDEX EFFECT

Almost anyone who follows indexes becomes familiar with the "index effect" even if they don't know the term. When a stock is added to a popular, widely followed index, the stock tends to rise in price. Over the last two years the average increase in a stock added to the S&P 500 from the time the addition was announced to when it was actually added was 5 percent or more. Moreover, stocks don't give that back in the next few weeks or months—or maybe ever. Typically, Standard & Poor's announces a change in an index about five business days before the change is actually made. For example, if everyone knows a particular merger will close at the end of the month and open up a position in the S&P 500, about a week before the expected closing date Standard & Poor's will announce what stock is being added to the index. The index effect takes place in the period from announcement to implementation when the stock joins the index.

The first studies of the index effect focused on the S&P 500 because so much money is managed by matching the index stock for stock. The explanation is straightforward: When a stock is added to the index, index funds must purchase substantial positions. In total, the funds' purchases probably represent about 5 percent to 8 percent of the outstanding shares of the stock. This demand for shares drives the price up. Moreover, unless the index funds dump these shares, the price is likely to stay up. The effect is often magnified by arbitrageurs who try and profit by buying stock at the announcement in hopes of selling it to index funds before the stock is actually added to the index. In some cases, with popular or widely followed stocks, the effect can be greater. The record is probably the addition of Yahoo to the S&P 500 in December 1999, when the price climbed over 25 percent in about two weeks.

Similar effects are seen with other indexes as well. While changes in the Dow Jones Industrials are less frequent, they also generate a lot of trading and substantial index effects. Removing a stock from the Dow—and usually from the S&P 500—generates a reverse effect as the price falls. Another example is the annual reconstitution of the Russell indexes, especially the small-cap stock Russell 2000. Russell announces the changes in its index a month in advance. However, since the Russell 2000 has grown in popularity and since the stocks tend to be smaller and often less liquid than the stocks in the S&P 500 or the Dow, there can be some large dislocations around this annual revision.

standing and better known global indexes are the MSCI, EAFE, and the FTSE-Actuaries World Indexes. MSCI stands for Morgan Stanley Capital International, a company owned jointly by Morgan Stanley Dean Witter, a leading investment bank, and Capital International, a Swiss company. EAFE stands for Europe, Australia-Asia, and Far East—in other words, developed industrial nations other than the United States. The FTSE-Actuaries World Indexes are a set of world indexes maintained by the *Financial Times* and the London Stock Exchange; FTSE represents the initials of these two organizations. There are also indexes run by stock exchanges around the world. Some of the more famous ones include the DAX in Germany, the FTSE-100 in London, and the CAC in Paris.

With a list this diverse, it would take several volumes to catalog all these. Further, by the time one were even halfway through, they would have changed. Instead of a complete catalog, the following pages give a summary of some key points for a handful of leading indexes, mostly in the United States. This list does not pretend to be complete. Rather, it reflects some of the author's opinions and beliefs. However, it does cover a wide range and also includes Web site addresses for most of the index providers. Investors should consult these Web sites for recent information.

THE MAJOR PLAYERS

The major domestic index players are Standard & Poor's, Dow Jones, Russell, and Wilshire. We will look at each of these briefly and then mention four players in the international arena: Standard & Poor's (again), Dow Jones (again), MSCI, and FTSE. Indexes are a rapidly growing and ever-changing part of the financial world. As a result, any complete list of index offerings is likely to be out of date quickly. Therefore, you should look at the Web sites maintained by these index providers for an up-to-date listing of all their indexes. Despite the fast pace of change, once an index becomes established, it is not likely to see any revolutionary change, so the objectives and general guidelines are likely to remain the same. Indeed, the S&P 500 had its last major overhaul in 1957 and the Dow Industrials have been 30 stocks since the late 1920s. Moreover, both use the same calculation methodology as they did before their last major reviews. On the other hand, indexes do have to keep up with the markets—in 1998 and 1999 there were over 40 changes in the S&P 500 as companies merged out of existence and underwent other changes.

Standard & Poor's

Standard & Poor's is the leading indexer based on money managed to its indexes. Standard & Poor's estimates that over $1 trillion is managed against the S&P 500. The largest is one of the nation's largest mutual funds, the Vanguard 500 Index Trust, with more than $100 billion in assets.

Standard & Poor's flagship index is the S&P 500 consisting of 500 stocks covering the U.S. market. The index includes a few non-U.S. com-

WHO ARE THOSE GUYS AT THE
STANDARD & POOR'S INDEX COMMITTEE?

Standard & Poor's indexes are managed by a committee of nine people, all of whom are full-time employees of Standard & Poor's. Although indexes and the index committee have been around for a long time, it is only in the last 10 to 15 years that the index committee has gained its current notoriety. Any readers who skipped over the introduction may want to glance at it—your author is the Chairman of the Standard & Poor's Index Committee.

Standard & Poor's Index Committee is responsible for the management of the indexes—choosing which stocks to add or delete, deciding on changes in policies that might exclude one or another kind of stock, and setting rules for when changes are announced or how different results are calculated. While the committee publishes general guidelines (see Standard & Poor's index Web site, www.spglobal.com), in the end it is the committee that makes these decisions. Although some index providers use computers and "objective" rules, Standard & Poor's believes that a committee of experienced analysts and investors is better than some computer. After all, the computer merely runs a program that was written by a committee, so one might as well skip the electronic middleman.

The Index Committee manages all of Standard & Poor's domestic U.S. indexes together. In addition, there are regional index committees covering other portions of the world. It meets in a closed session approximately once a month. At these meetings the committee reviews pending corporate actions,

(continued)

panies. However, these are considered to be grandfathered and would not be added to the index today. The stocks are predominately large-cap stocks and are selected to reflect the overall U.S. stock market. The index is managed by a committee; there are always 500 stocks and changes are made as necessary or when the committee wishes.

In addition, Standard & Poor's offers a range of other indexes covering the United States and other markets. Among the U.S. indexes are the S&P 100, S&P MidCap 400, S&P SmallCap 600, the S&P Super Composite 1500, and a full series of growth and value indexes done jointly with a financial analysis firm, BARRA. The S&P 100 consists of 100 stocks drawn from the S&P 500. It is the basis of the OEX options trading. The index was originally developed for options trading by the Chicago Board such as mergers or reorganizations, involving companies in one or another Standard & Poor's index. In addition, the committee also reviews companies being proposed as candidates for addition to the index. While a candidates list is maintained, it is closely guarded and not made available to anyone not directly involved with the management of the Standard & Poor's indexes.

From time to time, the committee will also meet with companies that are in the index or which are interested in becoming members of the index. These meetings are held when the Index Committee feels it is mutually beneficial to meet. If a company simply wants to be in the S&P 500 and Standard & Poor's is familiar with the company, its size, financial condition, and recent financial history, it is unlikely that the committee will agree to a meeting. On the other hand, if a company in the index is involved in a complex merger, the committee will agree to a meeting and will use the occasion to make sure that it understands the details of the pending merger. While Standard & Poor's does not announce such meetings, companies may tell the press they have met with Standard & Poor's as long as they do not suggest what the Standard & Poor's decision will be on their index status. Since the Index Committee hasn't made any decisions at the time it meets with a company, there is no way the company would know what that decision would be.

Companies do, from time to time, lobby the Index Committee. Experience suggests that a company that will send one member of the committee a series of letters asking for consideration is likely to send the same series to all the members. Therefore, Standard & Poor's prefers not to publish the names of all the committee members.

of Options Exchange (CBOE), one of the nation's leading exchanges. Standard & Poor's took over the management of the index from the CBOE.

Standard & Poor's indexes are subdivided by economic sectors, industry groups, industries, and subindustries. There are 10 sectors; at the most detailed level there are about 125 subindustries. While many index providers have systems of sector and industry classification, Standard & Poor's and Morgan Stanley Capital International (MSCI, another leading index provider) have joined together to sponsor a single shared system of industry classification.

Dow Jones & Company
Dow Jones & Company, the publisher of *The Wall Street Journal,* is also the publisher of the Dow Jones Industrial Average, probably the most widely quoted stock market measure. The "Dow" is a simple price-weighted av-

erage of 30 leading companies chosen by a committee of editors from the
Journal. The Dow is also the oldest average in the United States to be con-
temporaneously calculated. Other indexes, including the S&P 500, were extended backward after their development to "create" history. The Dow has
been around since 1896. There are two less known companions to the Dow,
the Transports and the Utilities. Together with the Industrials these make
up the Dow Composite, a somewhat broader index.

The Dow is widely followed, partly because it has been around for a
long, long time, partly because of the publicity from *The Wall Street Journal,* and partly because most of the stocks are well known household names.
In recent years Dow Jones has begun to dramatically expand its range of
index offerings, including a capitalization-weighted index of U.S. stocks
that looks like the S&P 500, a range of national and global indexes, and a
series of Dow Industrial look-alikes for the European Market. None of these
new indexes have caught on in the United States.

Frank Russell Company and Wilshire Associates

Frank Russell Company and Wilshire Associates are two other U.S. index
providers. Both companies offer a range of investment-related services for
professional money managers. Wilshire Associates also offers mutual funds
based on its indexes. Unlike the Standard & Poor's and Dow Jones indexes,
these are based on formulas and are generated by computer. Also, while
the Standard & Poor's and Dow indexes are changed from time to time, as
necessary, the Wilshire and Russell indexes are reconstituted once a year
by rerunning the computer programs and data. Some investors argue that
the computers do a better job of running "passive" investments, which are
supposed to track markets not follow human commands. Others doubt that
a computer formula can be any more long lasting than a well thought out
committee decision. Moreover, the programs were written by people so
there are committees behind these indexes as well.

Table 8-1 summarizes many of the leading indexes from these four
providers. While this gives an idea of what is available, this is far from an
exhaustive list. Interested—or curious—investors should invest some time
on the World Wide Web hunting down indexes. Some suggested sites are
listed in the appendix.

As long as the table is, it only scratches the surface. There are many
other U.S. indexes. For one thing, most of the major index series, such as
Standard & Poor's or Dow Jones, divide their indexes by economic sector,
industry groups, and industries. This provides a wide range of specialized
indexes. It also provides very useful tools for investors since one can

TABLE 8-1 Leading Indexes

Index	Number of Stocks	Management and Method	Security Criteria	Comments
		Standard & Poor's	www.spglobal.com	
S&P 500	500	Committee, Capitalization-weighted	U.S. Companies	
S&P 100	100	Committee, Capitalization-weighted	Drawn from S&P 500	Basis for OEX options
S&P MidCap 400	400	Committee, Capitalization-weighted	Midcaps—$1–4 Bln in market cap	
S&P SmallCap 600	600	Committee, Capitalization-weighted	Small caps— less than $1 Bln	
S&P Super Composite 1500	1500	Committee, Capitalization-weighted		Combination of S&P 500, S&P MidCap 400, and S&P SmallCap 600
Standard & Poor's 500/BARRA Growth and Value indexes	500 stocks in S&P 500	Split of S&P 500 based on price–book ratios to split market capitalization	S&P 500 stocks only	Joint effort of Standard & Poor's and BARRA
S&P MidCap 400/BARRA Growth and Value indexes	400 stocks in S&P MidCap 400	Split of S&P MidCap 400 based on price–book ratios to split market capitalization	S&P MidCap 400 stocks only	Joint effort of Standard & Poor's and BARRA

TABLE 8-1 Leading Indexes (*Continued*)

Index	Number of Stocks	Management and Method	Security Criteria	Comments
S&P SmallCap 600/BARRA Growth and Value indexes	600 stocks in S&P Small-Cap 600	Split of S&P SmallCap 600 based on price–book ratios to split market capitalization	Standard & Poor's SmallCap 600 stocks only	Joint effort of Standard & Poor's and BARRA
Dow Jones & Company			http://averages.dowjones.com	
Industrials	30	Committee, price-weighted	Most widely followed average	
Transports	15	Committee, price-weighted		
Utilities	20	Committee, price-weighted		
Composite	65	Committee, price-weighted	Combination of the previous three averages	
Dow U.S. Equities	550	Capitalization-weighted	Has sector and industry sub-indexes	Overshadowed by the "Dow"

		Frank Russell Company	www.Russell.com	
Russell 3000	3000	Reconstituted annually on Data as of May 31, cap-weighted index of 3000 largest stocks.	Top 3000 NYSE, Amex, or NASDAQ stocks	Computer-driven without any adjustments
Russell 1000	1000	Top 1000 of Russell 3000 index		
Russell 2000	2000	Stocks 1001 to 3000 in Russell 3000		Popular small-cap index
Growth/Value indexes	varies	Split based on price–book ratios and forecasts of earnings per share	Computer-based formula	Stocks can be both growth and value.
Russell Top 200	200	200 largest stocks in Russell 1000		
Russell Midcap	800	800 smallest stocks in Russell 1000		
Russell 2500	2500	2500 smallest stocks in Russell 3000		
		Wilshire Associates	www.wilshire.com	
Wilshire 5000	>7000	Capitalization-weighted index of all stocks with readily available prices	Must be headquartered in the United States	
Wilshire 4500	6500	Wilshire 5000 excluding the S&P 500		A "completion" index

TABLE 8-1 Leading Indexes (*Continued*)

Index	Number of Stocks	Management and Method	Security Criteria	Comments
Wilshire Large Cap 750	750	750 largest stocks in Wilshire 5000	Reconstituted annually as of June 30	Overlaps with Large Cap 750
Wilshire MidCap 500	500	Stocks 501 to 1000 in Wilshire 5000 by market capitalization	Reconstituted annually as of June 30	
Wilshire SmallCap 1750	1750	Stocks from 751 to 2500 in Wilshire 5000	Reconstituted annually as of June 30	
Wilshire Microcap Index	About 6000	All stocks from 2501 to end of Wilshire 5000	Reconstituted annually as of June 30	
Growth/Value	various	Growth/value splits of Wilshire indexes	Reconstituted annually as of June 30	Methodology not defined

TABLE 8-2   Indexes Returns, 1995–1999

Index	Compound Annual Returns 1995–1999 (%)
S&P 500	28.56
S&P MidCap 400	23.05
S&P SmallCap 600	17.04
S&P 100	32.24
S&P Super Composite 1500	27.55
Russell 1000	28.05
Russell 2000	16.69
Russell 3000	26.94
Wilshire 5000	27.06
Wilshire 4500	23.68

SOURCE: Standard & Poor's Fund Services Micropal Data.

compare the performance of a single stock with the performance of its industry, its broad economic sector, and the overall market. That way, if you look at a popular computer stock like Dell or IBM, you can tell if it is the company, the industry (computer hardware), the sector (technology), or the whole market that is responsible for your fortune (or misfortune).

There are also indexes covering countries other than the United States. The four major index players in the global game are Standard & Poor's, Dow Jones, MSCI, and FTSE. Two we met above. MSCI is Morgan Stanley Capital International. MSCI maintains a series of indexes covering 51 countries around the world. FTSE is owned by the *Financial Times* and the London Stock Exchange, from which it took its initials. It is best known for an index of 100 stocks traded in London, the FTSE-100. However, it also offers a global series of indexes, the FTSE World Indexes. These cover 29 countries.

While there is more to choosing an index than just looking at the best performance in the last year, the question inevitably arises. One should recognize that any comparison using the 1990s should be suspect because the U.S. market did so unusually well during the decade. Nevertheless, Table 8-2 shows the returns over the five years from 1995 through 1999 for a number of the indexes discussed above.

II

INVESTING WITH INDEXES

Part I provided some background on the stock market and on stock indexes. Simply put, the stock market is not without risk—but if you have the time to wait, it will be rewarding. Sometimes, as in the late 1990s, the market rewards very quickly. Other times, such as in the 1970s, it can take a while. Stock indexes are a way to gauge and understand the market and what it is doing. However, stock indexes can be much more—a way to invest and a way to judge individual stocks or groups of stocks in the market. Part II of *Outpacing the Pros* is about investing with stock indexes; Part III will look at how to use indexes to choose stocks.

Investing through indexes is becoming more popular these days. Over $1 trillion is indexed to the S&P 500, the most widely used index. Another half trillion or so is indexed to other indexes including the S&P MidCap 400 and S&P SmallCap 600, the Dow, various indexes offered by Frank Russell Company, Wilshire Associates, Morgan Stanley Capital International, and others. Indexing as an investment approach has been around since the mid-1970s but has only become mainstream in the last five or so years. For many years investment managers argued that index funds were condemned to have only "average" performance because they would do not better than the market indexes or averages.

While index funds seldom do much better than the indexes, they often do a lot better than many investment managers. In a typical year only about one in three mutual funds outperform the S&P 500. This is not a theoretical result—it is the lesson of real numbers in real markets. If you truly believe you can pick out the funds that will beat the indexes, good luck. But, remember that someone put money into those two-thirds of the funds that don't beat the index. The rationale for the good results from index funds is not that difficult to see. As a group, all the index funds plus all the investment managers should average out to results equal to the indexes, *before expenses*. Simple arithmetic says that if everyone averages 12 percent, the index funds average 12 percent, then the nonindex investors also average 12 percent. However, while index funds have expenses of one-fifth of a percent to about 1 percent, the managed funds have expenses that range from about three-quarters of 1 percent to 2 percent or more. The toll charges represented by the expenses mean that the return index investors get, after the expenses are taken out, tend to be much better than what's left for the other investors.[14]

We begin this section with a rapid review of U.S. stock market history since the end of the Second World War. While we use the S&P 500 as the benchmark, remember this is a real investment today. In fact, it has been a real investment since 1976 when the Vanguard 500 Fund was introduced.

CHAPTER 9

A CRASH COURSE IN MODERN FINANCIAL HISTORY

Many have written books about financial history and the history of the stock market. Our goals here are far more modest. We are going to take a quick look at recent financial history to get three simple ideas across. First, stock prices go up. Not all the time, but with reasonable consistency. There are certainly some notable bumps on the way, but if history can teach us anything, it is that investors who hang around long enough get paid for waiting. Moreover, "long enough" is usually not that long. We will look at the history of the market, as described by the S&P 500, since 1945. We could have started earlier, but 1945 is getting to be quite a long time ago. Second, the way to play the game is to buy and hold—get into the market and stay in the market. We will look at what would have happened if an investor missed the 5 or 10 best or worst days in the market and at what happened to someone who bought just before the crash of 1929. These examples will also remind us of the importance of dividends, even in today's market. Third, to round out the arguments, we will compare the results in three difference stock indexes—the S&P 500, the Dow Jones Industrials, and the New York Stock Exchange composite—just to confirm that the results are not peculiar to one index. We can also make a quick comparison with some foreign stock markets for more recent periods. There the details are different but the general idea is the same.

MARKET HISTORY SINCE 1945

Figure 9-1 shows the S&P 500 since 1945. The index is based on an average value of 10 for the 1941–1943 period. At the beginning of 1945 it was about 13.5, not much beyond the base level. The year turned out better than its start with the market up by about a third by the beginning of 1946. The chart barely reveals that, because of the long time period shown. A better way to look at the market's history is with Figure 9-2. This chart uses an old statistician's trick and plots the logarithm of the index instead of the index. You don't need to know anything about logarithms except that this flattens out the vertical scale so the chart is more readable and that the steepness of the line shows how fast the market is rising or falling. (Old-time stock market charts call these ratio charts instead of logarithmic or semilog charts.) Enough of the mathematics; just realize that this chart is easier to read and that you can see the jump in 1945. You can also see that much of this was given back in a drop in 1947 and a slide until 1949. The market can be fickle in the short term of a few years.

However, look at the overall expanse of the chart. The market can be rewarding in the long term. From that 13.5 level in 1945 the S&P 500 climbed, with a lot of interruptions, to over 1400 at the end of 1999. Moreover, these levels do not take into account dividends or the results of in-

FIGURE 9-1   The S&P 500 from 1945 to 1999

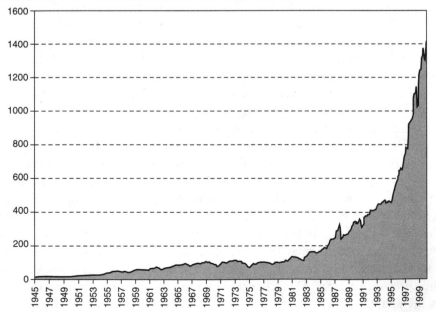

FIGURE 9-2   Logarithm of the S&P 500 from 1945 to 1999

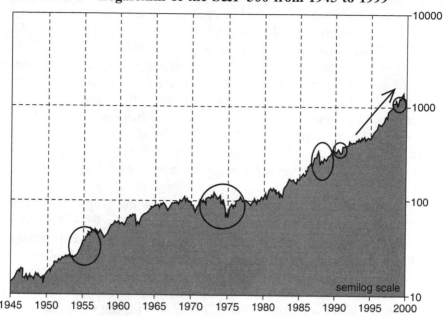

vesting those dividends back into the stock market. A brief review of the chart shows some aspects of the market. First, it has a lot of bumps and tumbles. Moreover, the last few years (at the arrow) have been a lot smoother than most periods. Second, the results aren't always exactly what we remember. The 1950s were an unusually good time for the market despite the volatility. In the summer of 1955 the market was up more than 40 percent from its level of only a year before. In contrast, the 1960s—a decade usually recalled as the best of times for the economy—was not as good for the market as the 1950s had been.

Some of the downside can be seen in the 1970s. First the market took a big tumble in 1973 and 1974, as shown by the circle around those years on the chart. In January 1973 the market was around 118. By the end of 1974 it was down more than 40 percent; it didn't reach a new high (and surpass the January 1973 level) until 1980. That tumble, the 1973–1974 bear market, was the worst collapse since the 1929 crash and was far larger than anything seen since. Oddly though, investors don't seem to either remember or research the 1973–1974 bear market; almost anyone who studies history seems to focus on 1929.

The late 1970s saw a generally flat stock market as economic policy makers turned to fighting about inflation. Finally, in 1979 Paul Volcker, the

newly appointed chairman of the Federal Reserve, set out to bring inflation down from levels of about 15 percent. Volcker raised interest rates,
sending the economy into a deep recession and the stock market into a deep
funk beginning in the fall of 1979 and extending into the summer of 1982.
Initially inflation tumbled and stock prices followed. Then, in the summer
of 1982 the markets reached a point where prices were so low there was
no way the economy could be that bad. Moreover, the Fed began to relent
and interest rates began to move down from their heights. First bonds, and
then stocks, began to rally. By June of 1983, stock prices were up by 50
percent from their level of a year earlier, a bit before the markets took off.
That rally extended into the bull market that continues to this day, 18 years
later.

The rise from the summer of 1982 was not uninterrupted, but all the
pauses proved to be pleasantly brief and temporary. In 1984 the Fed got
nervous about inflation and tightened policy, and stocks skidded before re-
suming their gains. In the spring and summer of 1987 stocks surged, reached
a peak in August and then began to slide from August through a devastating crash in October 1987. On one day, Monday, October 19, stocks lost
about one-fifth of their value. That collapse remains the most memorable
recent event in stock market history, even 13 years and a number of nasty
bumps later.

Various people claim to have foreseen or predicted the 1987 market
crash. We won't make any such claims here, although we will remind investors that predicting the crash is *not* enough for success. The real skill
would have been to predict the crash and then to have gotten back into the
market on October 20, 1987. There are a few facts about the crash and the
market of 1987 that are worth remembering. First, the stock market actually was up in 1987. The total return on the S&P 500 from December 31,
1986, to December 31, 1987, was 5.2 percent. Second, the crash may have
been a one-day event, but the market slide was not. Stock prices fell 8.1
percent from their August 25 high to October 12, 1987, a week before the
crash. They fell another 8 percent in the week of October 12 to 16 and also
broke all kinds of volume records. Then came Monday, October 19, when
they took their big tumble, losing 20.4 percent in one day. The loss as measured by the Dow Jones Industrials was slightly greater, 22.6 percent.

There are some lessons to be learned from the 1987 collapse. First, an
economic collapse is not inevitable when the stock market takes a tumble.
In 1929, the economy was already in a recession when stocks crashed in
October 1929. Second, investors who think they can time the market and
profit must be right twice in a row—when to get out and when to get back

in. There are many who claim they knew to get out sometime between August 25 at the high and October 19 or 20 at the low. Very few of these will tell you when they got back in.

Market history has been less exciting, though more profitable, since the 1987 crash. The recession of 1990–1991 and the Gulf War sparked a correction in the stock market and a substantial pullback in stock prices. This kind of activity is typical—the economy slowed, specific risks associated with the Gulf War were prominent and stocks tumbled. However, stocks began to recover well before either the recession or the Gulf War was passed and resumed the climb that began in 1982. For investors the reminder is that both recessions and wars matter to the stock market, but again the key to any short-term tactics is both when to get out and when to get back in. In October 1990, when the stock market bottomed, things looked rather grim. First, the economy was clearly slipping and the recession's start two months earlier had just been officially declared. Second, a large-scale military buildup was getting under way. For investors, this darkest of moments turned out to be the time to *buy* stocks.

When one looks at an account of stock market history or at the chart, the period from early 1994 to early 1995 doesn't seem very interesting at all. Stock prices moved sideways and 1994 overall saw little change with a total return on the S&P 500 of only 1.3 percent. Yet, this was one of the more interesting and encouraging years for the market in the 1990s, if not much longer. In early 1994 the Fed became quite concerned with the possibility that inflation would begin to climb and responded with aggressive monetary policy. The Fed funds rate, the Fed's primary interest rate tool, was pushed from 3 percent at the start of the year up to 5.5 percent at the end of the year. In the process, the Fed devastated the bond market where prices collapsed and losses were widespread. Equities largely avoided the bloodshed as stocks went essentially nowhere. At the same time, earnings per share for the S&P 500 climbed by 40 percent and the p–e ratio fell from 21 times at the beginning of 1994 to 15 times at the end of the year. For those who believe that the Fed *always* raises havoc with stocks, 1994 is a pleasant exception.

From the beginning of 1995 until the end of 1999, the market has enjoyed a spectacular run putting together the best five calendar years in modern history. Even in this roaring market, there have been some reversals. These should be a reminder that stocks are often subject to gyrations. In July 1997, Thailand's currency collapsed and the Asian financial crisis was upon us. Stocks took some notable one-day tumbles, especially a loss of 6.9 percent on October 27, 1997. A little less than a year later when many thought the international financial crisis was largely behind us, Russia defaulted on some bonds and sparked a 20 percent drop in stock prices over a periods of six weeks. The market's troubles weren't helped by the widely reported collapse of Long Term Capital Management, a now-infamous hedge fund that made some spectacularly bad bets in the bond markets. Investors should come to expect these kinds of tumbles.

THE BEST AND THE WORST

Suppose that an investor could have avoided the five worst days of the 1928 to 1999 time period or had somehow missed the five best days. Would things have turned out a lot differently? Looking only at stock prices and ignoring dividend reinvestment (because there is no daily dividend data available that far back), an initial investment of $1000 on January 2, 1928, would have become $78,520 on January 31, 2000. That is an annualized return of about 6.26 percent. (Again, no dividends which is why it looks a lot lower than the 9 percent to 11 percent number you may have been expecting to see.)

If you really manage to miss the five worst days of the last 70 years— days like October 19, 1987, or October 28 and 29, 1929—you would be both an incredible investor and magnificently lucky. You would also be richer, with $154,000 rather than $78,500 for your efforts. Of course, if you missed the five best days, things would have been a bit different. That $78,500 would be only $42,500 and the 6.26 percent return would have been more like 5.38 percent. See Table 9-1.

Realistically, no one is going to time things so well that he or she avoids the five worst and hits the five best days in over 70 years of market activity. Rather, the point is that getting in and staying in means you will be there for those good days, although you may suffer on those worst days. On average and over the long haul the market goes up and being in is what counts.

There is a second aspect to this that also merits some thought. Suppose stocks take a nasty bounce and you, getting worried, bail out of the mar-

TABLE 9-1   The Best and Worst Returns on $1000 Invested from January 2, 1928 to January 31, 2000 (no dividend reinvestment)

Return over entire period	$ 78,517	6.26%
Missed five worst days	154,183	7.25%
Missed five best days	42,579	5.38%
Missed both five best and five worst	83,613	6.35%

ket. Have you lowered your risks? Well, by getting out you have certainly cut to zero the chances of being caught in the market on a terrible day. But, you have also cut to zero the chances of being there for one of the great days as well. Now, let's look briefly at when a few of the really good days were—more often than not, just when things looked as bad as could be. The best day was March 15, 1933. Franklin Roosevelt declared a bank holiday when he was inaugurated and closed the markets as well as the banks. When the markets reopened, stocks surged at one of the grimmest moments in U.S. financial history. The second best day was a bit of a false start. On October 30, 1929, the markets staged a rebound from the crash of October 28 and 29 and rose 12.5 percent. If there was any moment when the nervous would have bailed out, it would have been October 28 and 29 in 1929.

Other strong days, though not among the top 10, were the two days following October 19, 1987, when stocks began to rebound—and unlike 1929, the rebound stuck. Other strong moments were the ends of corrections in 1998 and 1999, two other times when everything certainly looked pretty rotten. The moral of all these numbers is that over time the market rises and the only way to benefit is to be in the market. Getting out of the market may seem to cut the risk of losing money, but it also cuts the risk of making money. A little bit later we'll look at more versatile ways of cutting risks.

FIGURE 9-3   Comparison of the S&P 500, the Dow Jones Industrials, and the NYSE Composite Indexes, January 1973 to January 2000 (1973 = 100)

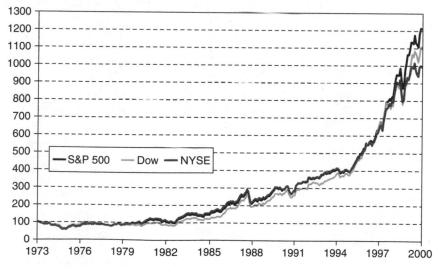

THE S&P 500 AND OTHER MEASURES

Figure 9-3 shows three major indexes for the United States: the S&P 500, the Dow Jones Industrials, and the New York Stock Exchange (NYSE) Composite Index, for the period from January 1973 through January 2000. All three have been restated, so that the January 1973 level is 100. A glance at the chart shows that they all move closely together for most of the time. Even in the last few years, when they seem to spread out a bit, the month-to-month bounces follow the same pattern. From this, it is clear that while much of the foregoing discussion used the S&P 500 as the benchmark, the comments about market history would have been essentially the same with one of the other indexes.

The widening spread in recent years is due to two things. In the last few years technology stocks have been a large and growing factor in the market. Some of the biggest of these are not listed on the New York Stock Exchange and are not included in the NYSE composite. Further, until recently they weren't part of the Dow 30 either. They have been in the S&P 500 for a number of years. This has given the S&P 500 an extra boost. Further, as the numbers have climbed, small movements have been magnified.

10

C H A P T E R

RISK

DECREASING RISK USING CASH

As attractive, or frightening, as the history of the stock market over the last 50 years may seem, there is certainly a good deal of risk. Pick the wrong month or the wrong moment and you can lose a lot of money. If getting rid of risk means never making a mistake, then there is no way to get rid of risk. But, if controlling risk means reducing the chances of losing some money at some price, then risk can be controlled. This section discusses some aspects of risk in the stock market and suggests one way to mitigate the risk.

For investors risk may mean that the value of their investments bounces around a lot more than they would like or that when you go to cash in the investments and spend your money, there is less than you thought. (Almost certainly, there is less than you would like—but that is less a risk than a certainty.) Suppose you have invested in the S&P 500 index through an index fund. In the 661 months from the beginning of 1945 to January 2000 you would have lost money in 186 months, or a bit more than one in five times. Although you would have been ahead on balance with an average gain of 1.12 percent per month, there would have been some nasty moments when you were losing. In October 1987—a particularly nasty month—you would have lost about 21.5 percent of your money. Suppose that there were some easy way to trim that loss to "only" 11 percent for October 1987.

There is: if the portfolio were half in Treasury bills (or money market funds) and half in stocks, the worst drop would have been only 11 percent. Of course, the upside wouldn't have looked as nice either. For the market the best month, October 1974, was up 16.8 percent, while for the half cash and half stocks investor, the best gain was only about 9 percent. Likewise, the investor splitting his money between cash and stocks would have only enjoyed a monthly average return of 0.76 percent compared to the more daring soul who was 100 percent in stocks.

Which investor you are better off being is not something this book can answer, because the question of how much risk is not too uncomfortable is a question each investor must address for himself or herself. Table 10-1 gives some idea of the likely results of mixing stocks with cash. The data cover the last 55 years and show what results would have been seen from portfolios that mixed Treasury bills and the S&P 500. One thing that is clear is that lowering risk is not a free ride. As one reduces the size or chance of a big monthly loss, he or she is also reducing the chance or size of a big monthly gain.

The sample portfolios in Table 10-1 are based on the actual returns of the S&P 500 and Treasury bills from the beginning of 1945 through January 2000. In developing these figures it was assumed dividends from stocks are reinvested in stocks and interest from T-bills is reinvested in T-bills and that every January the investor rebalances his or her portfolio by buying or selling stocks or T-bills to get back to target proportions. If this isn't done, the proportion of stocks will gradually rise since stocks return more than T-bills over the long term. For comparison, the last column shows the 50/50 portfolio where rebalancing is done every three years instead of every year.

The first three rows in Table 10-1 give some general summary data: the monthly average return, the standard deviation, the number of months the portfolio lost money between 1945 and 2000 (a total of 661 months), and the percentage of months that it lost money. Look across the first five columns and you get an idea of the trade-offs between higher returns and lower risks. As you move across the table the returns rise from 4.8 percent to 14.3 percent per year and the number of months that the portfolios lost money climbs from never to 241 months out of 661 or 36 percent of the time. The second row shows the standard deviation. This is a measure of volatility or risk that shows how close the monthly results are to the average of all the monthly results. For the first portfolio, the standard deviation is quite small at 0.8. You can interpret this to mean that the vast majority of the time, the monthly returns will be close to their average and if you

TABLE 10-1   Results for Various Cash/Stock Portfolios, 1945–2000

	Cash/Stock Proportions					
	100/0	25/75	50/50	75/25	0/100	50/50*
Return (%/yr)	4.8%	7.2%	9.5%	11.9%	14.3%	9.6%
Standard deviation	0.8	3.6	7.2	10.7	14.2	7.4
Number of losing months	0	177	221	236	241	221
Percent of losing months	0%	27%	33%	36%	36%	33%
	Monthly Percent Changes					
Maximum	1.27	3.70	6.95	11.23	16.81	7.32
Minimum	0.03	−6.17	−11.97	−17.05	−21.54	−12.58
	Based on Counting Months from 1945 to January 2000					
Count <−1%	0	37	121	159	186	124
Count <−2%	0	6	53	103	132	61
Count <−3%	0	2	24	61	100	24
Count <−4%	0	1	11	34	63	12
Count <−5%	0	1	3	22	42	5
Percent <−1%	0%	6%	18%	24%	28%	19%
Percent <−2%	0%	1%	8%	16%	20%	9%
Percent <−3%	0%	0%	4%	9%	15%	4%
Percent <−4%	0%	0.1%	2%	5%	10%	2%
Percent <−5%	0%	0.1%	0.5%	3%	6%	1%
Percent of months down after two years	0%	1%	4%	6%	8%	4%

*Rebalanced every three years versus yearly rebalancing in columns 1–5.

look at the average you have a very good idea of what you'll get each month. For T-bills it is no surprise that there are no losing months.

However, when we start putting some money into stocks, the chance of losing money and the spread among the returns rises and the standard deviation is a much larger number.

As you work your way down the table you can get more of an understanding of how mixing cash and stocks will affect a portfolio. One thing having some cash does is reduce the likelihood of some extreme results. Look at the rows marked maximum and minimum. These numbers refer to *monthly* results, not the annual averages shown above. These figures are still another way to compare the portfolios. The all-cash is rather mundane—the best of months is up only 1.27 percent and the worst is still positive at a scant 0.03 percent. The 100 percent stocks is far more exciting—or scary—with the best month up 16.8 percent, which is more than the average *annual* return, while the worst of months is a shocking loss of 21.3 percent in October 1987. Of course, there is more to over 50 years of investing than just the best and worst months.

If, like most investors, you worry more about losses than about gains, look at the last two groups of rows on the table. These show you how many months, and what percentage of the months, each portfolio lost as much as 1, 2, 3, 4, or 5 percent of its value. Once again you can see the shift from few if any losses to a measurable number of big losses.

It is important to remember that since stocks always go up and down, there should be a time dimension to any considerations about risk. If you plan to hold an investment for 20 years, whether it goes up or down a bit this month makes little difference to what you'll have in 20 years. Of course, it isn't easy to forget about a big loss last month by repeating, "It's the next 20 years that matter" over and over again. Moreover, who wants to lose money for 5 years straight on the outside hope that the following 15 years will be fantastic successes. To give a little flavor of this time dimension, the last line of the table shows how often (in terms of the percentage of months since 1945) each portfolio was worth less than its value two years earlier. Two years is far less than 20 years, but if you're a worrier, two years may seem like forever.

For the all-stock portfolio, 0/100 in the next-to-last column, 8 percent of the time one would be looking back at a loss over the previous two years. The last time this happened was in 1983, and most of the times this was a problem were in the mid-1970s following the 1973–1974 bear market. Almost at the other extreme, look at the portfolio that is 25 percent stocks and 75 percent cash. Even here there are some moments—though many less than with all stocks—when you would have been down over a two-year time horizon.

These examples suggest that if you are worried about the ups and downs of the market—market risk—you can reduce market risk by mixing some cash in with your stocks. The mix is not a free ride; you are likely to make less money over time in a portfolio of stocks and cash than a portfolio of only stocks.

Some readers may wonder if bonds would work even better than a money market fund, Treasury bills or some other cashlike investment. Bonds might work better, but they are more volatile and more complicated than cash. Further, there is a risk that some event that sends stocks down would also send bonds down just as much. For instance, if interest rates rise as the Federal Reserve (for whatever reason) tightens monetary policy, both stocks and bonds would see their prices tumble and both stock index funds and bond funds would fall. The risk protection we are seeking would most likely also collapse along with stocks and bonds. Further, not all bonds are the same, so we can't build one series of simple examples. As a result, if it is controlling risks that you want, mix cash, not bonds, with your stocks.

DECREASING RISK USING TIME

As we hinted in the last section, another way to handle risk is with time. At first this may seem useless; it is like saying, you can worry in the short run, but don't bother worrying in the long run. But using time to mitigate risk does make a lot of sense. It even has a name, *time diversification.*

The stock market does go up and down and good years do tend to follow bad years. To be sure, the ups and downs are not predictable and any suggestion that they are is fraught with danger to your wealth. But, since the best periods tend to offset the worst periods, an investor who expects to be in the market for the long haul and who feels confident enough to wait out some of the bad moments can use time to mitigate some of the risks. But this is not easy because an investor who was planning to hang in for the long haul and then panics on a bad day is likely to be worse off than even those who never play the game. Investors who sold stocks in the aftermath of the 1987 crash discovered that they sold at the worst moment. Investors who held on broke even for the year (the S&P 500 was actually up 2 percent in 1987 before dividends).

Table 10-2 is similar to the one used above in the discussion of using cash to cut risks; however, this time we vary the holding period—how long the investment is held. The table uses the portfolio that is 75 percent stocks and 25 percent cash, one of the portfolios looked at in Table 10-1. For this portfolio, we have calculated statistics assuming it is held for 1 year, 2 years, 3, 5, 10, and 20 years.

The data cover the period from January 1945 through January 2000. The first group of calculations are based on all possible holding periods of a given length. For example, for the 10-year column, we look at periods from January 1945 to January 1955; February 1945 to February 1955; and so forth. Over the period from 1945 to 2000 there are 541 such holding

TABLE 10-2   Holding Period Returns Based on Portfolio of 75 Percent Stocks and 25 Percent Cash

Years Held	1	2	3	5	10	20
Count (months)	650	637	625	601	541	421
Average annual return	11.8%	11.9%	11.3%	11.1%	10.8%	10.0%
Standard deviation	11.8	8.0	6.1	4.7	3.6	2.3
Count <0	114	39	25	1	0	0
% <0	17.5%	6.1%	4.0%	0.2%	0.0%	0.0%
Maximum	46.2%	32.8%	26.6%	24.0%	16.6%	15.3%
Minimum	−27.9%	−14.0%	−5.8%	−1.2%	2.0%	6.3%

Years Held	Same Time Period (1965–1/2000) for All					
Count	421	421	421	421	421	421
Average annual return	11.6%	11.8%	11.1%	10.6%	10.1%	10.0%
Standard deviation	11.7	8.0	6.2	5.0	3.7	2.3
Count <0	72	28	17	1	0	0
% <0	17.1%	6.7%	4.0%	0.2%	0.0%	0.0%
Maximum	46.2%	28.8%	26.6%	24.0%	16.3%	15.3%
Minimum	−27.9%	−14.0%	−5.8%	−1.2%	2.0%	6.3%

periods. These periods overlap so that much of the information in the 10 years ending with February 1955 is used again for the 10 years ended February 1956. Statisticians will argue that these data are being used again and again. This is true. Rather than argue that the sample size is a very large group of 541 observations, remember that we have only one history of the stock market. If the twenty-first century turns out to be completely different from the twentieth century, a lot of these historical examples may be misleading. However, if we didn't look at history we would have no idea of what might happen.

There is a second statistical quirk worth noting. There are far more 1-year periods than there are 10-year periods because we don't have any 10-year periods ending before 1955. (Remember, the data start in 1945.)

The second group of results at the bottom of the table cover only those years where there are 20-year holding periods (1965 and later) so that all the numbers are based on the same overall time period and the same number of sample size.

Now, lets see what waiting does to investments. We will look at the lower part of the table for this discussion. All the returns are stated as annual returns, no matter what the holding period. This makes it easier to compare results across different holding periods. The average one-year holding period gives a return of 11.6 percent; the largest ever was 46.2 percent and the worst was −27.9 percent. Further, 72 of the 421 in the sample, or 17.1 percent, were negative. Now, look across the last two rows of the table. As the holding period increases, the best result declines and the worst result improves. At 10 years, the *worst* result is a *gain* of 2 percent. Now, 2 percent isn't very much, but it sure beats the −27.9 percent seen for the one-year holding periods. At a 20-year holding period, the worst result is a positive 6.3 percent return.

The more statistically or analytically inclined readers can look at the row labeled "standard deviation" and see the same thing. If you take the standard deviation and add it to the average return, then take it and subtract it from the average return, about two-thirds of the holding periods will be in between these two numbers. For example, for the one-year holding period, two-thirds of the returns fall between 11.6 plus 11.7, or 23.3 percent, and 11.6 minus 11.7, or −0.1 percent; for the 20-year holding period the range is 12.3 percent to 7.7 percent; a much smaller range.

Sharp-eyed readers will note that the average annual return has slipped as one goes across the page. The returns for each holding period are calculated as compound annual returns using the beginning and ending points. We all know that compound interest can be wonderful; that is, 5 percent compounded daily is worth more than 5 percent as a simple annual percentage rate. The result is that the if one goes from $100 to $200 over 12 years, the compound interest is going to be a smaller number than the simple annual interest rate. At the same time, the longer holding periods trim off the extreme values and tend to push the average returns around a bit. Notice the return rises from the one-year holding period to the two-year period, but then falls from the two-year period to the three-year period.

One final caveat about all this time stuff: These examples assume that one locks up the portfolio for the holding period. Faith is required and panic must be avoided. Those who panicked in the 1987 crash regretted it; those who never heard of the crash went on to riches in later years.

WHAT ABOUT LEVERAGE AS A WAY TO INCREASE RISK?

So far this chapter has tried to lower risk; how about increasing it. That may sound strange but in the spirit of nothing ventured, nothing gained, it is worth looking at. Moreover, this is merely the reverse of mixing stocks and cash. The idea is simple—borrow money and buy more stocks. If the market goes up, the winnings are bigger. However, if it goes down, so are the losses. We will leave aside the question of why you might want to do this, but note that many people do. In fact, borrowing money to buy stock—buying on margin—is a common practice for both individual and institutional investors.

Table 10-3 shows both the benefits, and the risks, of leverage. The column "No Leverage" shows the results of investing $1000 if the market rises or falls 20 percent. As one would expect, in the good times the rise generates a 20 percent return while in the bad times the 20 percent decline in the market means a 20 percent loss. Now, suppose one borrowed $500 and put up $500 of his or her own money. What would happen. In good times the return would be 40 percent, not 20 percent, but in bad times the loss

TABLE 10-3   Leverage Example

	No Leverage	Leverage
Own money	$1000	$ 500
Borrowed money	0	$ 500
Total invested	$1000	$1000
Results If Market Rises 20 Percent		
Gross returns	$1200	$1200
Pay back loan	0	$ 500
Own money	$1000	$ 500
Net returns	$ 200	$ 200
Return on own money	20%	40%
Results If Market Falls 20 Percent		
Gross returns	$ 800	$ 800
Pay back loan	0	$ 500
Own money	$1000	$ 500
Net returns	−$ 200	−$ 200
Return on own money	−20%	−40%

would be −40 percent, not −20 percent. Simply put, half your own money and half someone else's can double the risks. Moreover, this simple example assumes there is no charge for interest on the loan.

If this seems a bit like magic (or black magic on the downside) walk through Table 10-3 for a moment. In the case of no leverage, the $1000 in a rising market has a gross return of $1200, or a 20 percent gain. (Subtract the $1000 investment from the gross return to get the net return on the investor's own money of $200, and $200 divided by $1000 is 20 percent.) Still in the No Leverage column, if the market goes down, the $1000 investment becomes $800 (a loss of 20 percent), and the net after deducting the investment is a loss of $200, or a return of −20 percent.

Now, move to the Leverage column in Table 10-3. The investor puts up $500 and borrows $500 to invest $1000. If the market goes up, he or she now has $1200. Subtract the $500 for the loan and the $500 originally invested to show a net gain of $200. Now, the return is this $200 divided by the $500 the investor put up on his or her own. This means the return is 40 percent. On the downside, the investment falls to $800; after deducting the $500 loan and the $500 investment, the investor is $200 in the hole and has lost $200 of the original $500—a 40 percent loss. Things could be even worse. If the market went down by more than the original investment, our luckless investor would have to shell out more money to pay off the loan. (Imagine the table with a 60 percent market drop that leaves $400 to repay the $500 loan.) In a rising market, leverage is a thing of wonder; in a falling market, a source of terror.

There are other ways to both add, and subtract, risk. However, they need to wait until we look at some real investment tools for index investing: mutual funds, exchange traded funds, and others.

C H A P T E R 11

INSTRUMENTS FOR INVESTORS

Now we begin the process of moving from ideas and discussions to some real investments. We have seen what stock indexes are and some of the things that we can do to control risks. We have also seen what one stock index, the S&P 500, did over past market cycles. Now its time to put some of this to work to make some money. To start, we will look at different kinds of investments—mutual funds and exchange traded funds.

MUTUAL FUNDS

In theory one could buy all 500 stocks in the S&P 500 in the same proportions as in the index and hold the stocks. If you had enough money to cover the trading commissions—and enough money so that your portfolio wouldn't be mostly fractional shares—it would work fine. There are, however, some much easier ways to invest in stock indexes. In this section we look at the two most common ways to invest with stock indexes: mutual funds and exchange traded funds. We start with the S&P 500. In Chapter 12 we will move beyond the S&P 500 to other indexes and other ways to divide the market.

Mutual funds have been around since the 1920s and have been increasingly popular over the past 50 or so years. The initial arguments for mutual funds were that it gave individual investors an opportunity to benefit from professional money management. In a mutual fund, an individual investor purchases shares in a stock portfolio; the portfolio is managed by a team of professionals. Moreover, the team has access to information about the market, can employ skilled security analysts, and should be large enough to be able to trade at the lowest available commission rates. In practice, for funds that invest in stocks, this translates into operating expenses of 1 to 2 percent annually. In other words, each year 1 to 2 percent of the money you have in the fund is used to pay for the money managers and related expenses. If a fund has a banner year and gains 40 percent, paying 2 percentage points of the 40 percent for money management doesn't seem too painful. Suppose the market slides and the fund *loses* 10 percent; you still pay 2 percentage points in management fees. Funds with professional managers are called *actively managed funds* (index fund adherents might suggest that this term is an attempt to suggest that the managers actually do something).

Sometimes the professional fund managers do well, but some times they don't. As we noted in Part I, most years about two-thirds of the money managers don't do as well as the S&P 500. In the mid-1970s, The Vanguard Group introduced a new idea—an index fund. Indexing was a relatively new concept, although it had been used by pension funds for a few years. The Vanguard 500 Index Trust, which is designed to track the S&P 500, was the first index mutual fund offered to individuals.

In an index mutual fund, there are no money managers selecting stocks to buy or sell. Rather, there is a manager but with a different goal. His or her job is to match the index. The simplest way to do this is to buy all 500 stocks in the S&P 500 in the same proportions, and with the same timing, as the index. Because the fund manager doesn't pick stocks, index funds are often called *passively managed funds*. Other than the costs of buying and holding the stocks, the fund's results should match the index. Expenses for index funds are often much lower than for actively managed funds. Index fund expenses typically vary from 0.2 percentage points up to about 1 percentage point. In addition to simpler money management issues, there are some things the index fund managers can do to offset the inevitable costs of trading, custody (expenses related to holding the stocks), and other fund expenses (such as bookkeeping, accounting and sending reports to shareholders). One of the more lucrative options is lending securities.[15]

The S&P 500 is the most widely used index for index mutual funds; it accounts for well over half the assets in index mutual funds.[16] Not all index funds choose to hold all 500 stocks in the index, and other funds are "closet indexers" that stick close to the index even though they may not claim to be index funds. While many large index funds do hold all the stocks in the "right" proportions, there are some index funds that take other approaches. Some funds believe that they can do better by holding 200 or 300 stocks and using mathematical models to determine exactly which stocks to hold and in what proportions so that their results will mimic the overall index. This is not as difficult as it seems since the index is weighted by the market capitalization of the individual companies and a relatively modest number of companies can represent a large portion of the total index. At the beginning of 2000 the index was unusually concentrated and the 35 largest stocks accounted for 50 percent of the index's market value. (This is a bit extreme; normally it takes about the 50 largest stocks to account for 50 percent of the index.) Table 11-1 shows how much of the index market capitalization was accounted for by the 25, 35, 50, 75, 100, 200, and 300 largest stocks in the index.

Some index funds that do not hold all the stocks use more elaborate systems that just hold the 100 or 200 largest stocks. They develop quantitative models to minimize the risk that the *tracking error*—the difference between the return they earn and the return an equal amount invested in a true S&P 500 fund would earn—gets too large. For most investors it may not make much difference if a fund holds all the stocks or if it tries to get by with only some of the stocks.

Mutual funds have some special benefits and also some unusual problems that investors should be aware of. Some funds are sold directly by mutual fund companies which deal with the public through toll-free phone numbers, Web sites, and through the mail. Other funds are sold by stockbrokers, financial planners, or other investment professionals. In reviewing funds, investors should recognize that sometimes the investor pays a sales commission, or *load*. This is a fee that goes to the broker or the fund com-

TABLE 11-1   Proportion of S&P 500 Market Capitalization in Largest Companies (February 29, 2000)

First 5 companies	17.3%
25	43.5%
35	52.1%
50	60.5%
75	70.2%
100	76.4%
200	89.4%
300	95.5%

pany. If you buy an actively managed fund to get the benefits of a particular fund manager, the load may be warranted. However, if you are buying an index fund, such a fee is probably not warranted, and it is highly likely that another fund based on the same index is available without any sales load.

Another fee that is charged by some funds is called a 12b1 fee. This can be used to cover certain marketing expenses and is part of the fund's operating expenses. These fees are increasingly common both in active funds and in some index funds.

Taxes are one of those nasty inevitabilities of investing life. Investments in mutual funds are taxable unless the fund is in a tax-protected account like a 401(k) retirement plan or an individual retirement account (IRA). In a mutual fund, investors pay taxes on the increased value of their shares when they sell the shares. They also pay taxes each year on any capital gains or dividends. Supposing you have a choice between two mutual funds and you are confident that both can offer total returns of 20 percent before taxes this year. One fund is a typical actively managed fund where the manager is doing a lot of buying and selling of stocks. In this fund, the manager sells about half his holdings and buys other stocks each year. If the stocks he sells have gone up, you will be paying capital gains taxes on all these sales. (If the stocks went down, you chose the wrong fund!) Now, consider an index fund where there is likely to be a lot less turnover in the stocks held because the only time that the fund sells a stock is when it is dropped from the index. The index fund has fewer sales and less capital gains to be taxed on.

Another aspect of mutual funds is convenience. Whereas convenience may not be the obvious road to better investment returns, it certainly is important in choosing mutual funds. If getting information on a supposedly great fund is very difficult, you might never invest—in which case you might have been better off in an easier-to-deal-with fund. Market research by fund companies often "discovers" that service is as important as investment performance for a lot of investors. In any event, it is worth taking a little time to check on how easy it is to make additional investments, get tax information, or get your money out when you do choose a mutual fund company. Most, though not all, of the big mutual fund companies and fund supermarkets offered by discount brokerage firms, offer index funds. With most of the large, well-known fund companies you can choose from a range of index funds as well as actively managed funds.

When you buy, or sell, mutual funds all your trades are done as of the close of the day. Most of the time this doesn't make much difference, but every so often it does. You can't sell your mutual funds at 10:30 a.m. if you think the market is about to collapse. All you can do is put in a sell order that will be executed at the closing price for that day. In fact, you can't even get a quote on a fund as of 10:30 a.m. on a trading day; all you'll get is the value as of the previous trading day's close. In days gone by, when sending things by U.S. mail was as fast as needed and when electronic communications and live stock quotes were not generally available, no one cared that all they had was end-of-day pricing. In today's electronic world, many investors want to know what their funds are worth *right now.* Hence, the emergence of a new category of funds, discussed next.

EXCHANGE TRADED FUNDS

Exchange traded funds, or ETFs, are one of the most successful new investment products of the 1990s—and the next century as well. ETFs are essentially mutual funds that are traded on regular stock exchanges. Prices are quoted continuously, and you can trade in and out any time of the day. You could even day-trade ETFs, though this author is certainly not going to recommend the idea. ETFs originated in 1993 with the introduction of Standard & Poor's Depository Receipts, or SPDRs (pronounced "spiders"), which are traded on the American Stock Exchange.

ETFs are traded in the same way as stocks. They have ticker symbols and use a broker to do the trades. There are a lot of ETFs to choose from, covering a range of different indexes. Moreover, the number of alternatives is beginning to expand rapidly with increasing competition from both index providers and money managers. Among the money managers, two of the largest are Barclay's Global Investors (BGI) and State Street Global Advisors. Both of these organizations are expected to introduce numerous ETFs in the near future. On the index provider side, most of the large index providers are becoming active in ETFs. This includes Standard & Poor's, which helped pioneer the idea with SPDRs, and MSCI, which has a series of index-based country funds. Both of these firms and other index providers are increasingly active both in the United States and in other major markets.

In addition, some of the larger investment banks are now offering ETFs based on narrowly defined specialized indexes created only for the ETFs. Recent examples include offerings from Merrill Lynch named HOLDRs (for **Hol**ding Company **D**epository **R**eceipts). These are not true indexes—the indexes haven't been around for any length of time and investors have no way to gather other information on the past performance of these securities.

Behind an ETF is a system that assures that the ETF will always trade very, very close to the value of the index it is designed to track. There is a custodian who holds the stock that backs up each share of the ETF. At the exchange where the ETF is traded, there is a specialist who is authorized by the exchange to facilitate trading in the ETF. If there is heavy buying of the ETF, the specialist will purchase the shares in the underlying stocks and deliver the shares to the custodian. The custodian then creates new shares in the ETF. In the other direction, if there is net selling in the ETF, the specialist redeems shares in the underlying company from the custodian and sells the shares to raise the funds to cover the ETF shares that have been sold to him. This complicated-sounding process goes on continuously in the background, assuring that the ETF price is always in line with the index price. Note that sometimes there is a constant adjustment between the ETF and the index. The SPDRs trade at one-tenth the value of the index so if the index is 1400, the SPDR is trading at 140.

ETFs are similar to mutual funds, but certainly not the same. The biggest difference is that ETFs trade on an exchange all day long at varying prices, instead of just at the end of the day at the closing price. ETFs pay dividends—although it is hard to get excited about this since dividend yields are currently rather low for most indexes. Normally, capital gains distributions and capital gains tax liability are small because in the creation and redemption process the ETF can redeem shares with large tax liabilities and thereby limit the overall tax exposure. This means that the tax treatment is closer to what would happen if one owned a normal share of stock and cashed the dividend checks: the capital gains taxes are paid when the position is sold and tax is paid on the dividend income each year.

Like mutual funds, ETFs have operating expenses. In most cases the expenses incurred by ETFs are comparable to index mutual funds and are lower than actively managed mutual funds. However, investors who are concerned about expenses should read the fine print in ETFs the same way they would with any other mutual fund. ETFs that hold foreign stocks or stocks in one narrowly defined industry or sector may have higher expenses than broad-based ETFs tied to the S&P 500 or some other popular stock index. As to convenience, since ETFs are traded like stocks, the service offered depends on your broker. In general, most of the services you can find from a mutual fund company you can probably find from a broker.

As of the early part of 2000, ETFs are being used only for index funds. So far there are no ETFs that are designed to be actively managed funds. Initially it was thought that ETFs would only be of interest to index fund investors. However, the rapid growth and rising popularity of these new investment products strongly suggests that before long there will be ETFs that are actively managed. Already there are a wide range of index and indexlike vehicles being used to support ETFs. The first notable expansion was to funds designed to track indexes for foreign countries based on the Morgan Stanley Capital International (MSCI) indexes. These also set in motion the idea that any ETF needed a cute name. Since MSCI was following the SPDRs, they chose the name WEB, as in **W**orld **E**quity **B**askets. Recently, names were in play again as Barclay's Global Investors expanded the offerings and renamed them iShares MSCI Series. Other early ETFs stayed closer to the SPDR name. There are MidCap SPDRs based on the S&P MidCap 400, another index from Standard & Poor's. There is also a series focused on different sectors of the economy called the Select Sector SPDRs.

Dow Jones has licensed its Dow Industrials index for an ETF called Diamonds, giving a new twist to the names. Creativity in naming does not seem to be able to keep pace with creativity in financial products. During 2000 BGI will introduce a large series of ETFs. These will collectively be known as iShares. The rapid expansion in the menu of ETFs suggests that index fund investors and traders have far more to choose from than just the S&P 500. Before exploring the wide variety of offerings in later chapters, two other investment vehicles are discussed next.

VARIABLE ANNUITIES AND UITs

Variable annuities and unit investment trusts (UITs) are occasionally used for index investing. Variable annuities are investment programs structured around insurance policies. Because of the tax treatment of insurance policies, individuals investing in variable annuities enjoy certain tax benefits that permit their investments to be sheltered from federal income taxes. It is not quite a free lunch. Variable annuities require a long-term commitment and normally are subject to penalties for early withdrawals from the program. Moreover, some variable annuities have substantial fees because the fees must cover both the insurance features and the usual investment management fees. The combination of the need to make a long-term investment and the fees means that index funds—low fees and favorable long-term performances—are very attractive vehicles for variable annuity programs.

UITs, or unit investment trusts, are similar to mutual funds except that the securities are all chosen at the beginning of the program and there is no active management except in extraordinary circumstances. Traditionally UITs were used to package municipal bonds to allow small- and medium-sized investors to buy a diversified portfolio of bonds. In the last decade or so, the focus has shifted to equities with portfolios of stocks chosen by a particular investment approach or strategy. Index-based UITs are rare. While indexes do not change as much as actively managed portfolios, there is some turnover. Moreover, for indexes, UITs are probably less effective than normal mutual funds or ETFs.

12

C H A P T E R

BEYOND THE S&P 500
Investment Styles and Segments of the Market

So far we have discussed investing in the entire market using the S&P 500 or another broad-based stock index. There are two powerful arguments why this is the way to go: more often than not this marketwide strategy beats most other approaches, and it accomplishes this with less risk and less expense. Nevertheless, there are many times when investors want to focus on specific bits and pieces of the market. One way to focus is by choosing stocks. But, choosing individual stocks means giving up any of the risk-reduction benefits of diversification, even when your bet is really about an industry or a sector of the economy rather than a single company. If you are a big believer in the future of technology (a popular idea in recent years) or if you think a particular industry is a future hot spot, one way to invest could be with indexes. There are probably stock indexes and associated investment vehicles ready and waiting. One recent Wall Street development is the creation of specialized ETFs for industry- and sector-focused investments. Another is to choose strategies like small-cap stocks or growth stocks or international stocks. In this chapter we will look at some indexes keyed to these different parts of the market and some of the investments that are based on these indexes. We start with broad strategies, then turn to sectors and finally to a few industries.

100

CAP SIZE

One popular idea that makes periodic reappearances in Wall Street lore is small-cap stocks. *Cap* means market capitalization, a company's size as measured by the value of its outstanding shares. You can calculate market cap by multiplying the number of shares by the stock's price. The idea is that small-cap stocks give better investment results than large-cap stocks.

There seems to be a mixture of romance and investment appeal to the thought of investing in young growing companies that are a bit past their two-guys-in-a-garage startup stage but have not yet become behemoths of American Industry. Certainly everyone would like to have bought Microsoft at its public offering and then rode with it to its present position as one of the largest companies in the U.S. stock market. There are two lively debates about small-cap stocks. The first is whether there really is any "small-cap effect" or if we are just seeing a few quirks in the data. On one side there is an argument that most of the unusual gains to small-cap stocks occurred in the late 1970s and that excluding that one moment there really isn't anything there.[17] Counter to this are numerous studies, many using long-term data compiled by Ibbotson and Sinquefeld[18] and the experience of Dimensional Fund Advisors,[19] a firm specializing in index investing. There is a second argument against small caps that concedes that there really are gains to be had from small-cap stocks, but argues that their higher risks offset the value of these gains.[20]

The place to look for an answer is in the risks. From studies at Standard & Poor's it appears that the small-cap effect is real, but relatively rare. If someone is an aggressive investor who is willing to take some extra risks for a chance of extra gains, then holding some small-cap stocks is a good idea. But, if you are a more staid investor—or if you think there are better places to place your bets—small caps may not be for you. One thing is clear—when small caps outperform, they often do so by wide margins.

Indexes and index funds are ideal ways to play small-cap stocks. For one thing, the benefit of diversifying your portfolio is even larger here than across the entire stock market. Small-cap stocks are often more volatile and more risky than their large-cap brethren.

The most widely quoted small-cap index is the Russell 2000 index developed by Frank Russell & Co. Russell is a pension consulting firm. The index was developed as a benchmark for money management and is part of a series of indexes. The main index is the Russell 3000, consisting of the 3000 largest stocks in the U.S. markets. Stocks number 1 to 1000 make up a large-cap index, the Russell 1000, and stocks number 1001 to 3000

make up a small-cap index, the Russell 2000. Essentially all U.S. companies are included in the index with only minor considerations to liquidity,
trading, or any other measures. The index is rebuilt once a year with a massive series of changes on June 30 of each year, based on market conditions
as of May 31, a month earlier. This rebalancing results in a lot of shifting
and churning in the index.

The Russell 2000 is certainly not the only small-cap index around. Another widely followed index is the S&P SmallCap 600, maintained by Standard & Poor's. This index differs from the Russell 2000. First, it is small
with 600 stocks rather than 2000. Second, it is managed differently. Unlike
the mechanical once-a-year revamping used by Russell, the S&P SmallCap
600 is managed by a committee at Standard & Poor's.[21] The Committee
oversees the index and chooses which stocks to add or remove. The stocks
are screened for trading liquidity, financial viability, and related concerns
and chosen to assure that the index reflects the overall market. In a typical
year the S&P SmallCap 600 may have a little less turnover than the Russell 2000. Moreover, the changes in the S&P SmallCap 600 are spread out
across the year instead of all taking place at one moment. Investors choosing between the two indexes should compare specific funds rather than just
the indexes. The comparison should look at risks and returns in recent years
and also recognize any major changes at the funds, as well as other benefits a particular fund company might offer.

Another interesting small-cap option is offered by Dimensional Fund
Advisors. This is one of the purist approaches to small-cap stocks. A bit of
investing history would be helpful. In 1976 a landmark study of investment
performance was published by Roger Ibbotson and Rex Sinquefeld.[22] The
study compiled data on monthly total returns for large-cap stocks (measured by the S&P 500), small-cap stocks, corporate and government bonds,
and Treasury bills. It has become the basis of much of the performance
analysis done in the last two decades, including most of the work analyzing performance by cap size. Dimensional Fund Advisors (DFA) was
formed by Sinquefeld to put the results of the original study to work. Following their research, DFA defines small-cap stocks as the smallest 20 percent of stocks ranked by capitalization. Because many analyses are based
on dividing the entire market into tenths, or deciles, and numbering the
deciles from 1 (for the largest stocks) to 10 (for the smallest stocks), the
fund with the bottom 20 percent is the Dimensional Fund Advisors U.S.
9–10 Small Company Fund.

The DFA fund is aimed at stocks that are often smaller than those in
the Russell 2000 index of the S&P SmallCap 600. Moreover, these are

stocks that may be thinly traded and where taking a significant position can push the stock's price higher. It is a portion of the market where the skills of the traders buying the stocks are very important. DFA has returned good results—some of the credit goes to the strategy, but some also goes to their trading room.

In addition to small-cap indexes and funds, there are also indexes and funds that focus on midcap stocks—stocks between the small caps and the large blue chips. The first midcap index was introduced by Standard & Poor's in 1991. That action, which was designed to expand the range beyond the S&P 500, had the effect of establishing a new asset class. Over the last 10 years this segment of the market has gotten more attention and other indexes have been introduced. Today both Russell and Wilshire, two companies that began as pension consultants and have subsequently expanded into money management, have introduced midcap indexes. In one sense it is clear that Standard & Poor's midcap index has gained a following. When stocks are added to the midcap they tend to rise in price shortly after the announcement, just as stocks added to the S&P 500 do. In the last few years, the midcap index effect has been as large, or larger, than the S&P 500 index effect.

The big question is how to know when to focus on small caps, or midcaps or large caps. There is no easy answer, although there is often no shortage of forecasts either. However, there do seem to be sustained periods of several months to a few years when one or another capitalization size range predominates in terms of investment returns. Seeing one or two months of apparently consistent performance in a row is not enough to "know" that one or another style is assured to take the lead. However, if one sees a period of six to nine months where one style predominates, chances are that it will continue to hold sway for a while longer. Experienced investors and money managers will consider capitalization size ranges in selecting stocks or betting on one or another sector of the market. However, they seldom make all-or-nothing bets. If small caps have recently done well and if conditions in the economy and the stock market haven't changed, an experienced investor is likely to bet on small caps continuing to outperform midcap or large-cap stocks. However, he or she won't abandon all midcap or large-cap stocks. Rather, if small caps represent 7 percent of equities, the investor may arrange his or her portfolio to include approximately 10 to 15 percent small-cap stocks.

GROWTH VERSUS VALUE

Two of the most misnamed styles or strategies on Wall Street are growth and value. No one wants to buy an investment that won't grow and no one wants to buy an investment that has no value—so why would anyone avoid either growth or value? A glance at some stocks and how they behave will do more to illuminate these terms.

Popular, or hot, stocks tend to rise in price as more and more investors buy them. As their prices rise, the ratio of the stock's price to its earnings or its book value will rise as well. (Book value is what company's accounts—and it's auditors—say it is worth based on its history and how much it paid for whatever it happens to own.) These kinds of popular hot stocks are usually called *growth stocks*. The idea is that investors buy them because they expect their earnings to grow rapidly and to justify their high price–earnings ratios. One popular way to gauge which high p–e stocks are reasonable choices and which other high p–e stocks are simply overpriced is to compare the p–e ratio to the growth of the stock's earnings per share. This is done by dividing the p–e by the earnings growth rate to find the *peg ratio*. A low peg ratio (that is, earnings growth that is large compared to the p–e ratio) is good. Sometimes growth stocks are the hot stocks of the market.

At other times, people like "value" stocks. *Value stocks* have low price-to-earnings ratios and low price-to-book value ratios. If a growth stock is one where the price has been bid up, a value stock is one where the price has been pushed down by bad news and disappointments. Investors buy these because they think the stocks are cheap and that eventually the stocks will be recognized for their hidden values and their prices will rise. As plausible as these tales may be, both growth and value strategies can work, though not always at the same time. Those who buy growth stocks are buying into currently popular ideas that they expect to continue to command attention. Those who buy value are betting they are smarter than the rest and can recognize a diamond in the rough.

Index fund investors can place bets on either growth or value. Moreover, they can mix these bets with their bets on market capitalization. But first, let's look at growth versus value. A number of index providers offer growth and value indexes. These are sometimes described as splitting an index into its growth and value halves. For the Standard & Poor's indexes, this is exactly what's done. For other indexes, including the Russell indexes, the split is a bit more complicated and some stocks can appear in *both* the growth and the value categories.

The Standard & Poor's division is done with the inverse of the price-to-book ratio, the ratio of a stock's book value to its price. (In some of the academic literature, price is called *market value* and book-to-price ratio is called *book-to-market*.) The ratio is done as book to price because every so often one finds a stock with a zero book value—and a ratio of price to zero book would confuse the computer. (Try dividing a number by zero on a calculator or a computer.) The stocks in the S&P 500 are sorted from lowest book-to-price ratio to highest book-to-price ratio. Starting at one end, the market capitalizations of the stocks are added up until one covers half of the total market capitalization of the index. The half with low book to price—or high price to book—is the growth-stock index; the other half is the value-stock index. This idea was developed by BARRA, an investment consulting firm. The approach is based on a good deal of financial and economic research done by two economists, Eugene Fama and Kenneth French, to identify statistically what drives stock prices. Fama and French found that two key factors were market capitalization and price-to-book ratios.[23]

The data on the growth and value halves of the S&P 500, properly on the S&P 500/BARRA Growth Index and the S&P 500/BARRA Value Index, extend back to 1975. Until recently, value always had higher returns than growth over any extended period of time, including the whole period since 1975. Further, the value index is less volatile and less risky than the growth index. A lot of people saw this as getting something for nothing— higher returns at lower risk. When the late 1990s are included in the data, growth comes closer, but value still leads over the entire history since 1975.

One thing that does seem clear is that either growth or value tends to lead for several months at a time. So, one strategy is to look at the recent past and then identify which style has done better in the last 6 to 12 months and then bet that the trend will continue. Nothing is without risk, but if one keeps an eye on the market, this approach is likely to be helpful. There are a range of index funds, including funds based on the growth and value divisions of the S&P 500.

Investors can also mix the large-cap/small-cap and growth/value strategies together. A familiar diagram to anyone who has studied mutual fund reports from Standard & Poor's or Morningstar is a little three-by-three grid comparing market capitalization and growth/value, as shown here.

	Growth	Blend	Value
Large cap			
Midcap			
Small cap			

Mutual funds are sometimes classified into these nine different categories. While actively managed mutual funds may wander from one box to another depending on how the market moves or what the fund manager wants to do. (For example, if most of the stocks in a fund fall, it could shift from large cap to midcap despite "active management"!) However, index fund investors can choose their own strategy and their own positions in the grid.

Don't just write this strategy off as some investor's approach to tic-tac-toe. Most professionally managed pension funds spend a good deal of time and effort deciding how to spread their money across this kind of box. Moreover, pension funds have learned that money managers who do well in one corner of the box are often terrible if they venture into another corner. Therefore, it is often important to decide which part of the grid each manager is assigned to. Since indexes are likely to do better than most professional managers, using index funds to fill the boxes is a good idea.

How should investors play this kind of tic-tac-toe? First, gather some information on recent shifts and trends. One can find data on recent index results on Web sites from Standard & Poor's, BARRA, Russell, Wilshire and others.[24] Each of these, using the index provider's own indexes, will show recent results for the last month, few months, quarters, or even years. You can see different trends and patterns and then choose a pattern that has been established over a few months and which is likely to hold unless there is a major change in the markets or the economy. Some investors do try to link growth or value with different conditions in the economy or the markets. The patterns are certainly not simple and are always easier to find after the fact than in advance.

SECTORS OF THE ECONOMY

There is another game that can be played with index funds that divide the market into pieces, or sectors. This strategy is gaining in popularity, both in the United States and in Europe. *Sectors* are groups of similar industries. For example, we can talk about technology companies, financial companies, consumer products, and so forth. The key is to group the companies in the market into a useful number of sectors in which the companies have much more in common with their sectormates than they do with companies in other sectors. From time to time, there have been attempts to do this automatically with a computer and some advanced statistics. While the results are often interesting, the sector classifications that stand the test of time seem to be the ones developed by people using some common sense.

Since stocks are valued for their future profits, it seems that it would make sense to sort companies into sectors based on where they make their profits. The idea has value but often proves impractical. Profits tend to have big swings from year to year, so a company that is classified by profits might be switched back and forth between sectors each year, or even each quarter. Moreover, a lot of companies don't even report their profits broken out by their lines of business. As a result, practical approaches use revenues, not profits.

Each of the major index providers has its own approach to defining sectors and assigning companies to them, with the exception of Standard & Poor's and MSCI, which joined together in 1999 to use the same system for both sets of indexes. The two systems are really one and the same— any company should be in the same sector in both sets of indexes. Moreover, the system is defined in terms of 10 economic sectors, about 25 industry groups, around 60 industries and about 125 subindustries. For index users following sectors this has some advantages since they can compare one of Standard & Poor's indexes to one of MSCI's indexes more easily. Russell, Dow Jones, and FTSE-International each have sector and industry classification systems. While one may argue with the details in one or another, for most individual investors what matters is a general understanding of the broad sectors and how the stocks are divided among them.

Sector investing has developed a lot of appeal lately. It is not difficult to see why. Technology is all in the news and at times everyone seems to believe that technology stocks only go up while others often go down. Of course this isn't the case, but the idea of focusing on one sector or industry has its appeal. For an investor, indexes aimed at sectors have the benefit of zeroing in on the sector and offering a group of stocks that are spread across a defined sector or industry. The key investment decision is to bet on technology or financial services or health care, not to choose 5 or 10 stocks from a list of 100 technology companies. Rather than being weighed down in research, the investment is put into action.

One of the easier ways to make some technology bets is through sector SPDRs. These ETFs based on the S&P 500 are sponsored by Merrill Lynch in a joint effort with Standard & Poor's and the American Stock Exchange. (The ETF is the Standard & Poor's Select Technology Sector SPDR, ticker XLK.) Each of the sector SPDRs is an exchange traded fund based on companies from the S&P 500; all the sector SPDRs together add up to the S&P 500. Of course, it is easier to buy an index fund, or the S&P 500 SPDR itself, than to use the sector SPDRs to assemble the index. However, if you think that you want to have more of your portfolio in technology than the index offers, you could buy the S&P 500 SPDRs and the Technology index SPDR to overweight technology.

No matter what you do with sectors, you will need to form an opinion about which sectors arc likely to do well or do poorly. Some of this may seem easy, because there are plenty of discussions of technology, technology stocks, and the new economy. However, you should carefully compare the stocks in the different sectors and assure yourself that your idea of utilities, financials, or technology stocks is close to the ideas used when the indexes were put together. If not, you might end up buying some things you didn't intend to own.

Choosing a good or bad sector is not as simple as deciding to invest in an overall index like the S&P 500, the S&P Super Composite 1500 or the Wilshire 5000. Choosing a sector means you are making a bet on a part of the market. In effect, we have just taken a step away from index funds and index investing and toward active management. You are assuming some risk—the risk that you made the wrong bet and the sector you ignored goes up while the sector you embraced takes a tumble. There is no easy way around making these bets, so if you think betting on one part of the market over another is not for you, skip to the next section on International Investing.

If you like the idea of betting on hot sectors, there are a number of different approaches worth considering. Probably the best idea is to use some combination of different ways to choose which sectors you like or dislike, placing your strongest bets when different kinds of analyses tend to agree. No matter how you look at sectors, doing the analyses is fairly data intensive and is likely to require a bit more work than deciding how much financial risk is comfortable and then putting some, or all, of your money in an S&P 500 index fund. The next few pages quickly cover ideas for choosing among sectors.

Over- and Underweighting and the Market
When money managers decide to make a "sector bet" in favor of technology or against utilities, they rarely put all the money in technology stocks or none of the money in utility stocks. Rather, they will look at the S&P 500 (or some other broad market measure) and put a slightly higher proportion of their portfolio in technology stocks than in the rest of the S&P 500, making up the difference by putting a smaller proportion in some less-favored sector in the index. The weights are measured by the amounts invested in the portfolio and are compared to the market capitalization weighting of the index. In effect, the manager is hedging his bets a bit so that if—surprise—utility stocks do very well, the manager isn't caught without any position in utilities. This may seem a bit chickenhearted, but many professional money managers are judged against indexes and index funds

and don't want to risk being so different from the benchmark measuring rod that they might look completely misguided. Of course, if you are absolutely sure that health care is the only place to invest, you can put all your money in health care stocks.

Technical Analysis

Technical analysis consists of using past trends in stock prices and trading volumes to try to predict future developments. It goes in and out of style, but at times it is very popular. Technical analysis is usually done by drawing charts of stock prices, and hence it is occasionally called *charting*. Without going into much detail, there are a couple of simple approaches that can be used to compare sectors to one another or to the market as a whole. One basic tool that is used to show whether the index for a sector is gaining or losing compared to the overall market is to measure its *relative strength*. To do this, one divides the sector index by the overall market index and plots the ratio. If this ratio is rising, the index is rising faster (or falling more slowly) than the market. If the ratio falls over time, the sector is doing worse than the market. If you are overweighted in an index, you would like it to gain in relative strength. Determining this ratio is particularly useful because many analysts believe that trends in relative strength tend to persist. In simple terms, if a sector is outrunning the market, it is likely to keep outrunning the market for a while longer. Certainly this can't go on forever, but these trends seem stable. Further, the trends in relative strength don't usually turn on a dime and collapse. So, while only fools believe they can get out of an investment at the precise market top, many technical analysts believe that you can escape well before all your money is given back and the sector is at a bottom by using technical analysis.

A second idea in technical analysis is *momentum*. Once things get moving they will keep moving in that general direction. Some academic studies suggest that there is statistical evidence for momentum over a period of up to several months. While most of the formal studies focus on individual stocks, analysts often argue for momentum in following sectors, or even mutual funds. The idea is straightforward: If the sector has been gaining, it is likely to keep gaining. Of course, if things can't go on forever, this idea won't work forever.

The last simple idea from technical analysis is a *moving average*. A 200-day moving average is simply the average price of the last 200 days. Each day this is calculated by dropping the earliest observation, adding in the latest, and recalculating the average. It is usually charted as of the most recent date. If the sector (or the market) has been rising, the current price will be above the average of the last 200 days; if the market is falling, the current price will be below the moving average. A simple way to judge the trend is whether the sector is above its moving average—trending higher— or below the moving average and trending lower.

Dedicated technicians will go far beyond these tools, but they will be looking at the same basic questions of price movements in one sector relative to the market or to other sectors.

Fundamental Analyses

Fundamental analysis looks at different gauges of investment values and compares sectors to their past norms and to the overall index or the market. Almost any financial ratio that can be calculated for a single company can be calculated for an index of companies. However, these calculations are sometimes rather complicated and require a lot of data and some investment in computerized number crunching. Rather than pursue complete income statements, one can look at a few widely used fundamental ratios. In all these, the comparisons are being made between current levels and normal or typical levels. If a sector is far from its normal ratio values, fundamental analysts may argue it will return to its normal levels by its prices either rising or falling more than other sectors.

Probably the most widely used financial ratio is the price–earnings ratio or p–e. This is simply the price of the index divided by the earnings per share. Sometimes earnings per share are calculated using analysts' forecast of next year's earnings and sometimes it is done using earnings from the recent past. Either method is reasonable, but it is important to be consistent. The basic idea is that there is a normal level of the p–e ratio and if it gets far from normal, it is likely to move back toward normal. For instance, for the S&P 500 the average p–e ratio over the last two or three decades is about 15. (That is, prices are 15 times earnings.) So, if the p–e is 35, it is likely to fall. It can fall either because earnings rise or because prices fall, or some combination.

What makes fundamental analysis challenging—and as much art as science—is that things are seldom this simple. For the S&P 500 overall, the "normal" p–e may vary with economic conditions. The lower the rate of inflation, the higher the p–e ratio is likely to be. So, an investor who ignored the decline in inflation in the mid-1990s would have seen the p–e ratios on the S&P 500 as much higher than they really were.

In much the same way technicians calculate relative strength, fundamental analysis will calculate relative p–e ratios between sectors and the overall index. However, here it is important to look at past trends and averages. Sectors that tend to be volatile such as capital goods or consumer durables usually have low p–e ratios. So, a low relative p–e for consumer durables compared to the S&P 500 may simply be the typical condition rather than a sign that consumer durables are cheap compared to other sectors in the market.

Trends in p–e ratios often follow trends in price-to-book ratios discussed earlier in the growth and value comments. Similar approaches can be taken using price-to-book ratios instead of p–e ratios. While other ratios are increasingly common in gauging the attractiveness of individual stocks, most have not yet spread to sector analyses.

Economic Angles

Another way to look at sectors is to look at conditions in the general economy. If capital investment in technology is strong and everyone is talking about computers, the technology sector may be hot. If housing starts are strong, consumer spending on durable goods—including furniture for new homes and cars for new garages—is likely to be gaining, so consumer-related sectors should look attractive. However, there are some sectors that are hard to link closely to the general economy. Prospects for the health care sector may have as much to do with politics and revised Medicare legislation as with the economy. Utilities seem to be rather staid except when energy and oil prices get out of hand. The economic angles require a detailed review of the economy but only yield some general ideas.

Overall, sector investing should be based on choosing sectors that appear attractive for a variety of reasons. It also depends on paying a lot more attention and investing more time than simply buying an index mutual fund or ETF and being patient.

INTERNATIONAL INVESTING

Investing internationally, putting some of your money to work in a foreign country, can be a very worthwhile and profitable use of indexes. Most investors and analysts divide countries outside the United States into two broad groups: developed nations and emerging markets. The developed nations generally include Western European countries, Canada, Australia, New Zealand, and Japan, while the emerging markets include most of the rest of the world. There are a number of different index systems that cover some or most of these countries in differing levels of detail. The two most complete index systems are maintained by Morgan Stanley Capital International (MSCI) and FTSE International. MSCI's indexes cover 51 countries including both developed and emerging markets. MSCI also provides some combinations of indexes covering regions of the world. The best known is the EAFE index, standing for Europe, Australasia, Far East and pronounced "efa."[25]

FTSE International is owned by the *Financial Times* and the London Stock Exchange. It publishes a series of indexes called the FTSE World Actuaries. While in the United States actuary seems like an archaic term for an insurance analyst, in London the Society of Actuaries is a leading professional society in the financial community and is widely respected. The FTSE World Actuary Indexes have been around for a number of years under various ownerships, which included Standard & Poor's for a brief period in the mid-1990s as well as Goldman Sachs & Co. and others. Like MSCI, the FTSE World Actuaries covers a wide range of 29 countries and includes some combinations and composites.[26]

Standard & Poor's maintains international indexes as well as the widely followed U.S. indexes. Standard & Poor's international flagship is the Global 1200 index covering the United States along with the S&P 500; Europe with the Euro 350; Canada with the S&P/TSE 60; Japan with the S&P/ TOPIX 150; the rest of the Asia-Pacific region with the S&P Asia Pacific 100; and Latin America with the S&P Latin America 40. In addition, the S&P Global 100 provides a single narrowly defined multinational index of global companies. Standard & Poor's also runs additional indexes in Canada in cooperation with the Toronto Stock Exchange and in Australia in cooperation with the Sydney Stock Exchange.

Standard & Poor's international index activities also include a complete set of indexes covering the emerging markets, the S&P/IFC Indexes. These cover 54 emerging market countries throughout the world. The S&P/IFC Indexes were developed by the International Finance Corporation, a division of the World Bank. The World Bank is an international agency that provides assistance and financial aid for economic development. The IFC started the indexes to provide investors with benchmarks to judge foreign markets and to help attract equity investments to emerging markets.

In addition to these, Dow Jones maintains some international indexes and participates in a group that runs the STOXX indexes in Europe. Both Frank Russell & Co. and Wilshire Associates have some international index activity. However, for investors, it is the index funds and the ETFs that matter, not just the indexes. While new ETFs are appearing, the longest-established international ETFs are the iShares MSCI, formerly called WEBS or World Equity Baskets. These are based on the MSCI indexes and are traded on the American Stock Exchange.[27] Whether one uses exchange traded funds or index-based country mutual funds, our comments below should apply to developing an international portfolio.

Putting some of your money to work outside the United States is not a magic formula to higher returns or sudden riches; however, it is likely to reduce your risk a bit. If one looks across the major industrial nations of the globe—the United States, Japan, Canada, Great Britain, Germany, France, Switzerland, Italy, Spain, the Netherlands, plus some other smaller European countries—it is hard to make a strong case that the companies and investments are fundamentally more profitable in one place than another. With communications and transportation, it is difficult for any country to have a monopoly on a better or more efficient means of production or business. Increasingly, workers, especially skilled and professional workers, are willing to move across borders to find better jobs. Even taxes and regulations are being driven by competition to become more alike in one country or another. Over long periods of time the return to equity investments in one industrialized nation are likely to be close to those in another. You can pick countries, but it is a bet you can time the markets.

While choosing one nation over another is not an easy bet to make and win, most investors who venture overseas would do well to at least look around a bit. Industrial countries, including the United States, go through business cycles of recession and expansion. These are not regular or easily predicted, and they vary in length but they do occur in all countries. While it is usually easy to determine if a country is in an expansion or a recession, this may not be the answer to the international investor. For better or worse, stock prices tend to be *leading* indicators of business cycles. In other words, at the bottom of a recession, when everything looks hopeless, stocks will begin to move up *before* the general economy improves. Moreover, at the end of an expansion, when everyone optimistically thinks the good times will go on forever, stocks may take an unexpected and unexplainable dive—and herald the end of the good times.

Despite these difficulties, a brief review of economic conditions should be helpful. Japan may be a case in point. It enjoyed a long, long boom from the early 1970s until the late 1980s. During this time Japanese stocks consistently outperformed the U.S. market. Japan fell into a recession in 1989 which has proved rather deep and very long; a clear recovery is not yet visible more than 10 years later. Once the recession had settled in and the Japanese stock market had plunged—a drop that eventually erased almost half its peak value—most observers took a properly extremely cautious view of Japan. During the 1990s Japan's stock market has been one of the more volatile ones around. The lesson of Japan is to look at a foreign

VOLATILITY AND INTERNATIONAL DIVERSIFICATION

Analysts usually measure risk or volatility with a statistical measure called *standard deviation*. If one is looking at a long series of data, such as monthly returns for different indexes, the standard deviation gives you a measure of how much these bounce around. If the index represents a staid quiet market, the standard deviation will be a small number, probably under 10. If the index represents a volatile market, such as technology stocks of the Nasdaq index, the standard deviation is likely to be a lot higher. For Nasdaq, over the five years to June 2000, the standard deviation is 27.1.

The idea of diversification is to mix different investments so that when one is down the other is up and the sum is a lot less rocky than any of the parts. To see how this might work, we took a small group of the MSCI country indexes for the period from January 1970 through February 2000 (about 30 years). We constructed a portfolio of 60 percent U.S. stocks and 8 percent each in France, Germany, Japan, Switzerland, and the United Kingdom. All figures are in U.S. dollars. The weights were chosen arbitrarily, but most U.S. investors would keep a majority of their money at home. The portfolio was rebalanced (brought back to the original weights) once a year. Then we calculated the standard deviation and the annualized returns for each country and for the portfolio. The following table shows the results.

The first column of figures gives the annual return for each portfolio. The two best performers were the composite portfolio and Japan alone; both returned 14.2 percent annual over the period. However, the composite portfolio had a standard deviation of 14 and the Japanese portfolio had a standard deviation of 22.9. In practical terms, one can say that the chance of losing money in any year in the composite portfolio was about 15 percent; in Japan it was close to 30 percent.

This table is a simple example of diversification across different markets (or different stocks) that are not perfectly correlated. If all the markets in the table were synchronized with one another, there would be nothing to gain. But since some are up when others are down, spreading one's money across the markets can be a big help.

	Return	Standard Deviation
Composite	14.2	14.0
United States	13.1	15.3
France	13.8	23.0
Germany	13.4	20.5
Japan	14.2	22.9
United Kingdom	13.4	24.0
Switzerland	13.5	19.1

market before you jump in and to remember that you are now betting that your sense of timing is better than anyone else's. Given the number of people trying to time markets, that is a rather aggressive bet.

The fact that different nation's stock markets bounce around makes choosing which one to invest in very difficult. It also means that spreading your money among a number of markets will reduce your risks. The idea of diversification is to have your money in many places at once, so it doesn't all get caught in the wrong place at the wrong time. This is why domestic indexes are attractive—you have eliminated the risks associated with any single stock or small group of stocks by spreading your wealth around. International investing does the same thing. The accompanying box on volatility and international diversification offers some numbers to show you how international diversification can lower your risks.

EMERGING MARKETS

Emerging markets are stock markets in developing or emerging nations. These cover a wide range—the Eastern European nations that were part of the Soviet Union or the Eastern bloc, massive countries such as India and China, rapidly developing Asian nations like Taiwan and Korea, and most of the Latin American countries. The first thing to recognize is that this group may include more differences and disparities than similarities. Issues facing these nations can range from government instability to currency crises to the level of education in the labor force.

For the investor interested in these emerging markets there is little one can say except that the rewards and the risks are both very large. For such investors there are some country funds—mutual funds that specialize in a single country—and there are a few index funds. However, most of the investing is still done through money managers located outside the markets and is not done with indexes.

PART III

USING INDEXES TO CHOOSE STOCKS

This part of the book begins with a discussion of why indexes often do well and then turns to how to use the lessons of indexes for picking stocks and managing a portfolio of stocks. After arguing that index funds outperform a majority of active managers, it may seem odd to talk about picking stocks. However, a lot of investors want to choose their own stocks and run their own portfolios. Other investors prefer to combine a portfolio of their own with one or more mutual funds—either index funds or actively managed funds. Most longtime mutual fund investors have found themselves at some point thinking they can do better than their portfolio manager—and save money besides. In any event, indexes have proven to represent some of the most successful portfolios, so why not use them as models.

13

WHY INDEXES DO SO WELL
What We Might Learn for Picking Stocks

The success of index funds stems from various factors. One of the key reasons is probably fees and expenses. The typical index fund charges expenses of 15 to 50 basis points (0.15 percent to 0.5 percent). In contrast, a typical actively managed equity fund charges fees of around 100 basis points (1 percent) to 200 basis points (2 percent) or more. The difference in fees represents one of the biggest factors in the differences in performance and results. Both Bill Sharpe, Stanford finance professor and Nobel Laureate, and John Bogle, founder of Vanguard funds and the Vanguard 500 Trust (the largest S&P 500 index fund and now the largest mutual fund in the United States), have presented this argument.[28] As Sharpe argues, the combination of all the money and mutual fund managers and all the index funds add up to the market. So, their total performance is simply the market. Since the indexes are the market, the active managers as a group also average out close to the market. But then they deduct their fees, and the returns they give to investors is the market's return less the fees. Bogle presents numbers to make the same argument.

Can an individual investor operate a portfolio as inexpensively as an index fund? Probably not. Even with discount brokerage commissions and free quotes, it may be difficult to match the efficiencies and low costs of some large institutional investors. However, before giving up on picking stocks, the investor should realize that there are some other lessons to be learned from indexes, and that, since the active managers *average out* to the market, some may do better than the market.

There are some aspects of indexes that are difficult for an investor owning a more modest number of stocks to emulate successfully. One of the reasons the S&P 500 has done well is that a lot of acquisition targets—companies taken over after their stock prices are bid up—were in the S&P 500. Identifying takeover targets in advance of any public announcement is very difficult without insider knowledge (but profitable). Because the index owns so many widely followed stocks, it tends to own a lot of target companies.

LETTING THE WINNERS RUN

Deciding when to sell a stock is usually more difficult than deciding when to buy. Index funds don't sell very often because indexes don't remove stocks very often. In the S&P 500, the most widely used index, the majority of removals occur because a company is being taken over by another company. As most investors have profitably learned in the last two decades, owning a stock when it is taken over by another company can be quite rewarding. Typically, a takeover involves a price that is 10 percent or 20 percent or more above the target's price before the takeover is announced. True, a few stocks are dropped from the S&P 500 each year because they really don't fit at all. These stocks usually have performed very poorly and, had they been in an investor's portfolio, they would have been labeled dogs. However, the takeovers tend to outnumber the dogs by a wide margin.

What's the lesson here? Occasionally prune the deadwood, but in general let the winners run. An example is Microsoft, which was added to the S&P 500 in 1994. At the time Microsoft was added to the index, it represented about 1 percent of the index's market capitalization. Over the next six to seven years it rose four times faster than the market or the index. By 1999 Microsoft was 4 percent of the market. Most active portfolio managers, watching a stock surge to four times its original portion, would have gradually sold into the rising market to keep the weight of the stock from rising "too high." In so doing, the managers would have given up some profits. Indexes don't sell rising stocks—they let the profits run. The lesson is that it is often ironically easier to sell winners than losers. For most investors, selling stocks that have lost money is akin to admitting failure, while selling stocks that have risen is like declaring a great victory, even if the stocks keep rising after they are sold. Remember, when a stock falls, the money is lost—whether the stock is sold or held.

Some indexes are restructured and rebalanced from time to time. Among those commonly used by investors, the best-known annual restructuring is probably that of the Russell 2000 Small Cap index. Each year, at the end of June, the index is completely rebuilt. The annual rebuilding does remove stocks that have done very well and are no longer small-cap stocks at all. The trading and tax costs that this would impose on an individual investor makes this a bad strategy for many investors. However, the idea of periodically reviewing the entire portfolio may not be a bad idea. Other midcap and small-cap indexes, such as the S&P MidCap 400 and S&P SmallCap 600, also face the question of what to do when small-cap or midcap stocks grow enough to become large-cap stocks. This kind of selling doesn't give the investor as clear a message, but it can be a reminder to review the good ones as well as the bad ones. If nothing else, reviewing the good ones is more fun.

LOW TURNOVER
One direct result of the index fund patterns, especially if one really does hold the winners, is low turnover in a portfolio. Low turnover has some benefits of its own for taxes and expenses. On the tax side, it is clearly better to sell stocks that have been held long enough to qualify for capital gains tax treatment. There is a related reason to hold stocks: until they are sold, no taxes are due. If one is subject to a 20 percent capital gains tax, then selling a stock with a gain of $10,000 means $8000 in profits to reinvest and $2000 for the tax man. If one holds the stock, all $10,000 stays invested and can keep growing.

Trading doesn't make an investor rich; it makes the brokers rich. Owning and holding on to good stocks makes investors rich. One reason index funds do well is that they keep costs very low. Any individual investor, even in the new era of electronic trading, is going to spend more on a trade than a professional money manager. Unfortunately, most of us start far behind when it comes to controlling trading costs, so lets make sure we know what we're doing. Some recent academic research strongly suggests that trading costs money and doesn't usually generate a lot of higher returns.[29]

DIVERSIFICATION
Diversification means not putting all your eggs in one basket. It is one of the oldest and most important rules of investing. Once you realize that there are no guarantees in investing and that sometimes even the most skillful of stock pickers end up buying stocks that go down, you understand why you shouldn't put all your eggs in one basket. Some wags suggest that you can own too many different stocks and that you should have only a few, but

watch them like a hawk. Do watch them, but remember that diversification still pays off.

The idea of diversification is that each kind of stock, each investment strategy, or each sector has its day in the sun—and each has its day in the rain. If you can put two (or more) sectors or styles or strategies together, you can average out to stable and successful results. Figure 13-1 shows what might happen to the price of a single style of investing over time. There are some good times with high and rising prices and some bad times with weak and falling prices. Now, suppose we could find a second style which was not synchronized with the first. We would have a picture like Figure 13-2, where we put half our money in each style and get much more stable results. This picture is an ideal situation: the two investments are perfectly timed—when one is all the way down, the other is all the way up. Moreover, diversification is not a free lunch. In Figure 13-2, the returns on each investment are sometimes negative. However, diversification assures that their sum is usually positive.

It is very difficult to find two stock investments, or any two investments, that are perfectly timed like the curves in Figures 13-1 and 13-2. However, if you are looking for diversified investments in the stock market, an index is the place to look. Moreover, the index can give you some obvious guidelines about how to easily judge the diversification of your portfolio. A broad-based index, like the S&P Super Composite 1500 or the Wilshire 5000, represents the entire market. It has a mix of growth stocks and value stocks. If your portfolio is mostly growth or mostly value, you have lost some diversification. Similarly, a broad-based index has representation from different sectors in the economy such as technology, health care, consumer durables, and so forth. Again, if your portfolio is 50 percent technology and the index is only 30 percent technology you are overweighted in technology and less diversified than the market as a whole. By comparing your own portfolio to the representation of different sectors, of

FIGURE 13-1   The price of a single style of investing over time

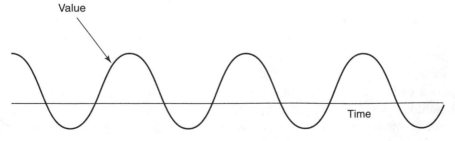

FIGURE 13-2   Two asynchronous investments over time

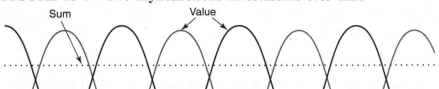

growth and value, and of stocks of different market capitalization in a broad-based index, you can see how diversified your holdings are.

An index like the S&P 500 or the S&P Super Composite 1500 is well diversified. However, you don't need to hold 500 or 1500 stocks to achieve reasonable diversification. You can probably get close with 10, 15, or 20 stocks. Moreover, there may be some areas that you don't really want to worry about representing in your portfolio, and you can omit those.

When you use indexes to gauge diversification, be careful which index you select as a benchmark. The Nasdaq composite is one of the most widely discussed indexes these days. It may have a lot of appealing properties, but reflecting the total market isn't one of them. The weight of technology stocks in the Nasdaq composite is roughly twice as large (70 percent versus 33 percent) as in the overall market or in the S&P 500 or the S&P Super Composite 1500.

RISKS

Diversification also helps control some subtle risks related to the way portfolios are constructed. Sometimes stock markets reverse very suddenly and a corner of the market that was out of favor becomes the hot spot. As it becomes recognized, money managers rush to get in and their rush pushes stocks higher and higher. This kind of sudden shift should bring smiles to index fund investors or others who use indexes as a guide to staying diversified. For instance, small-cap stocks were notoriously poor performers in the late 1990s. A thousand dollars invested in the S&P 500 in the first quarter of 1995 grew to $3270 by the end of 1999; the same sum in the S&P SmallCap 600 would have grown to only $2220 in the same time. Certainly small caps were not the best place to be. Yet, in the first quarter of 2000, small caps returned 5.8 percent and large caps (the S&P 500) returned only 2.3 percent. A diversified portfolio would have had some small caps and would have participated in the sudden shift. Moreover, if the shift turned into a steady pattern, the new hot sector would become a bigger and bigger part of the portfolios—an example of letting the winners run.

LIQUIDITY, TRADING, AND ANALYSTS' COVERAGE

Costs of trading commissions were discussed previously. There are other costs related to trading, including liquidity and bid-ask spreads. Some indexes, including Standard & Poor's, only include stocks that pass tests for liquidity so that that the stocks don't surge anytime someone buys more than 100 or 200 shares. This isn't a problem if you're considering buying Microsoft or General Motors. But, if you come upon some unrecognized gem that has languished for a year, be a bit wary whether buying a position of a few hundred shares will suddenly push the price way up. Certainly be careful about trading almost any stock after-hours when you don't know how deep or liquid the market it.

Probably all investors dream of finding some obscure unknown stock and buying it just before it is discovered. Even with the recent popularity of growth stocks and momentum plays—stocks that go up because they recently went up—investors still dream of that ugly duckling that turns out to be a swan. You won't find stocks like that in most indexes, mostly because inclusion in a major index such as the S&P 500 (or the Dow Industrials) is likely to assure that at least a handful of analysts follow the stock. That is not necessarily all bad. First, for the ugly ducklings to be discovered, some analytical coverage is essential. Second, most stock analysts do have something to say and can present useful information about the stock, information that an investor can use to judge the stock. Third, and certainly important, if the stock is followed by some analysts there will be estimates of future earnings that can be used to help you evaluate the stock.

MARKET TIMING TALES

It would be wonderful if somehow your money were only invested in stocks on the days they go up, and it was safely tucked away in a money market fund on the days it goes down. Unfortunately, that's not possible. To some extent all investors try to time the market—anyone who ever wondered if he should wait a week or two before buying or selling a stock is trying to time the market. There are many who claim to have wonderful systems to tell them exactly when to get in or out of stocks. Probably the best question to ask one of these investors is, "If you're so smart, why ain't you rich?" If that seems impolite, ask him or her where the yacht is.

Index funds don't do any market timing. One often heard comment is that an actively managed mutual fund with one (or more) professional money managers is safer because the money managers will know when to get out of the market *before* it falls. Truth to tell, money managers are as human as the rest of us and no more likely to be clairvoyant than you are. In 1998, when the stock market went into a summer swoon brought on by Russia's decision to default on some of its bonds, the S&P 500 slid about 20 percent and actively managed funds fell by slightly more. Moreover, successful market timing requires not one right move, but two in a row. Not only do you need to know when to get out of the market, you also need to know when to get back in. There is a famous story of the endowment committee of a leading university that congratulated itself in 1991 for getting out of the market before the 1990 pullback and subsequent recession. Unfortunately, they spent the next few years congratulating themselves and missed several very good years when they could have done much better in stocks than bonds.

Getting back in the market after a slide is probably more difficult than getting out. In the aftermath of the October 19, 1987, crash, the time to get back in was October 20—one day later. Yet most investors were shell-shocked and could think only about selling. Those few who were crazy enough to buy were the ultimate winners.

Over the long haul the stock market has risen. Although there have been some sustained periods of a flat or falling market, the long-term direction is upward and the long-term rewards are there. (If you didn't believe this, you wouldn't be reading this book.) Simply put, unless you are convinced that the market is in a decline that will extend well past the time when you will be pulling your money out to spend it, you should remain invested and not try to time the market's seemingly random short-term moves. If you do plan to spend the fruits of your investments fairly soon, some significant portion should probably be out of the stock market *now* to limit your overall risk.

SUMMARY OF LESSONS FROM INDEX FUNDS' SUCCESS

The success of index funds provides some simple guidelines for investors who prefer to pick and choose their own portfolios rather than just buy shares in an ETF or an index mutual fund. In summary, the lessons are:

- Watch the expenses. Even if investing is part entertainment, spending too much on trading costs and brokerage expenses cuts into profits.
- Don't trade too much. Let the winners run and prune the losers, but keep turnover low.

- Diversify your holdings and don't put all your eggs in one basket. If you can only afford two or three stocks, you might be better off with a mutual fund or an index fund.

- You may love hunting for an undiscovered diamond in the rough, but stocks that are liquid, actively traded, and followed by some analysts are worth serious consideration.

- Don't try to time the market; it rarely works.

CHAPTER 14

MODELS OF THE MARKET

While the lessons of indexing are important guides to running a portfolio, they will not help you choose stocks or groups of stocks to buy. The stock market is huge—there are well over 5000 stocks to choose from and different ways to approach making this choice. We begin with one of the more widely accepted models of what stock will return to its owner, the three-factor model. This will let us cut the market into six basic sectors for further hunting. The next chapter looks at a different way to narrow down the choice of stocks; subsequent chapters discuss ways to screen out all the stocks that don't belong in a portfolio.

In the mid-1960s a series of academic articles introduced the capital asset pricing model or CAP-M. For most investors and market watchers there are probably only a couple of things worth noting about these ideas. First, the economics profession has come as close to agreement that CAP-M is important as it does on almost anything. William Sharpe won a Nobel Prize for his work on CAP-M.[30] Second, it is the genesis of *beta*. A stock's beta represents how much it rises, or falls, compared to the market. If a stock has a beta of 1, then the stock rises or falls the same percentage as the market; a beta of 1.25 means that the stock rises or falls 1.25 times the market's percentage change.

CAP-M is a nice simple model and a major step forward. However, it suggests that the only thing that matters is how much the stock moves, compared with market moves. This may seem too simple, and indeed later re-search suggests that it is. This simple model was expanded through work by others, especially Eugene Fama and Kenneth French, to include two ad-ditional aspects of a stock to become the three-factor model.

In CAP-M, the only thing driving a stock's return was the move in the market, usually measured by the S&P 500. In the Fama-French three-factor model two other measures are added. One is the stock's size mea-sured by market capitalization, the other is the ratio of the stock's book value to its market value. Both these measures reflect a combination of past academic research and Wall Street lore. Fama and French's research shows that both these factors are important in determining what a stock does. Both have become cornerstones of most pension plans and other long-term money management approaches. One abiding Wall Street story is that small-company stocks are the place to hunt for the next Microsoft or General Electric. Peter Lynch, the storied manager of the Fidelity Magellan fund nicknamed these discoveries "ten baggers" for stocks that rose 10-fold. The other long-running Wall Street piece is about growth stocks and value stocks—accepted high flyers or hidden gems waiting to be discovered. Small-company stocks are revealed through the addition of market capi-talization measures; growth and value is identified by the book-to-market ratio.

GROWTH AND VALUE

For better or worse, these two flavors have been named growth and value. The names are unfortunate: no one wants to buy a stock which he thinks has no value and no one wants to own a stock she thinks isn't going to grow. But, since some Wall Street pundit many years ago spoke louder and faster than others, it is growth and value that represent the yin and yang of the market.

Growth stocks are children of fad, fashion, momentum, and proven worth. A growth stock is not simply a stock where the earnings are ex-pected to increase. Rather, it is a stock where everyone expects the earn-ings to rise and has already bid up the price and the price–earnings ratio to reflect these expectations. Buyers of growth stocks expect (hope) that the earnings will continue to increase and will more than justify the price.

Growth stocks are in fashion because everyone expects their earnings to rise. A positive opinion about a growth stock is a safe opinion because it is widely shared in the market. Whether the numbers—the higher than average p–e or the sky-high prices—are safe numbers in the sense that they are consistent with other data is not a concern for most growth stock investors. Instead, it is the popularity and safety in the numbers of buyers that they seek. It is no wonder that growth investors often become believers in momentum. All that momentum says is that what has recently gone up is likely to continue rising. This is similar to the technician who argues that stocks trading above their moving averages are good buys. To stay above the moving average, a stock needs to be rising and to be gathering popularity.

If growth is safety in popularity, value is safety in logic—even if no one else seems to understand the logic. Value investors look at the numbers that describe the stock, not at the number of investors bidding the stock up. Value players prefer a low p–e, or a low price-to-book because the stock is cheap, as long as they are confident the earnings will come. By their nature, value investors are contrarians. They are not concerned with popularity and would prefer to be the first to buy a stock. Their investment faith rests with the numbers and the analysis, not with where investors are putting their money.

The research by Fama and French, and others, has found that the best way to divide stocks into growth and value is with the ratio of book value to market value. Book value is how much the company's accounting records say it is worth. It is value of all the company's assets—equipment, buildings, land, and financial assets—less its liabilities. The book value is based on the company's past history, what it has bought and sold and what it has done, as tracked on its accounting books and records. These records are based on rules, procedures, and customs. The company's market value is based on its stock price and what investors think it will be worth in the future. A comparison of these two shows whether it is a growth company or a value company. The comparison of book and market value uses a ratio. Wall Street tradition states the ratio as the price of the stock divided by the book value per share or price-to-book. Like it or not, the academics tend to use book to price and sometimes call it book equity to market equity or BE/ME. Occasionally one finds a company with zero book value, which makes the price-to-book ratio a bit difficult.

Low price-to-book, or high book-to-market, means a value company. The market's evaluation of this company is close to, or below, its accounting value. It is probably not a case of high hopes for the future and high expectations for future growth that have driven the stock price skyward. In contrast, a high price-to-book or low book-to-market company is a growth company. The stock has been boosted by earnings gains and is expected to continue to do well; these expectations push prices higher.

Which is better? Unfortunately, sometimes one, sometimes the other.

The S&P 500 is broken into growth and value stocks using the book-to-market ratio. If one takes the two halves and goes back to 1975, when the data begin, the cumulative results favor value over growth, as shown in Figure 14-1.[31] There are periods when growth beats value as well as when value beats growth. For some people, going back to 1975 seems a bit extreme; more recently growth has beaten value.

When you select stocks you should diversify by having some growth stocks and some value stocks. You should also look at the recent performance of some growth and value indexes, since one style is usually sustained for several months or even a few years before giving way to the other, and, therefore, it is worth knowing which is currently ahead. Look at the stocks in your portfolio and determine which proportion of your funds are in growth stocks and which are in value stocks. If one style is currently in favor, you probably want to overweight your holdings in that direction. Standard & Poor's indexes for the United States are split into growth and value halves. Other indexes, including the Russell indexes, such as the Russell 2000, are also split into growth and value.

FIGURE 14-1   Comparison of returns for growth and value stocks from 1975 to 2000

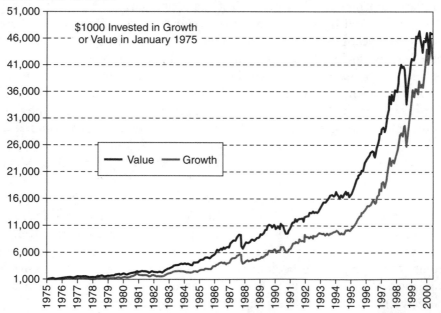

MARKET CAPITALIZATION

The other Fama-French factor is market capitalization. The idea that small companies are the place to invest is another enduring Wall Street rule that has been reconsidered in academic research. Research on this debate is far and wide, and often rather argumentative. Most researchers agree that there are periods when smaller stocks dramatically outperform their larger brethren and provide impressive returns. Most also agree that over the long haul, smaller stocks are riskier; they are more volatile and their returns are far more variable than large stocks, or all stocks together. But that is about where the agreement ends.

The arguments over small caps, or over whether investors picking stocks should focus on small-cap stocks, take two forms. The first, and more obvious, is whether one can really expect small-cap stocks to do better than large-cap stocks over any reasonable time period. The second is whether all the apparently better results merely reflect the greater risks in small-cap stocks. Some researchers, among them Jeremy Siegel in *Stocks for the Long Run,* suggest that if one were to drop one or two key periods of small-cap stock superior results, small-cap stocks would be far less attractive.[32] As Siegel notes, for most of the 1980s and 1990s, small-cap stocks were *not* the place to be at all.

Further, what many investors think about when they look for small-cap stocks is probably not what the academics study when they try to decide if there is a bonus to owning small-company stocks. Investors, with the benefit of the press, are looking for companies started in a garage (like the legends of Apple Computer or Hewlett-Packard) or sparked by some genius Ivy League college dropout. They are not considering a systematic investigation that ranks all companies available on the New York Stock Exchange (or the combination of the NYSE, the American Stock Exchange and Nasdaq) and then selects the bottom 20 percent by size ranking. Yet the academic studies typically use the latter because it is systematic and can be replicated in various databases.[33]

From all these debates a few conclusions are possible. First, small-cap stocks are riskier. If you are nervous about stocks, then loading up on small-cap stocks is likely to make you more nervous. More specifically, for investors who do not consider themselves "aggressive" investors willing to take significant risks in search of extra gains, small-cap stocks should best be kept to a small portion of your portfolio. And this probably means that no more than 10 percent of the money in stocks should be in small-cap stocks. Second, investors willing to take these risks should realize that the times when small-cap stocks do outperform are fairly rare. But, when they work, they work very nicely. Aggressive investors picking stocks should certainly not steer clear of small caps—and probably should look to put 10 percent to 20 percent of their money in small caps.

Professional money managers often put growth, value, and market capitalization together into a box diagram:

	Growth	Value
Large Cap		
Midcap		
Small Cap		

By design, growth and value are 50/50 splits of each index or size category. If one considers Standard & Poor's three indexes—the S&P 500, the S&P MidCap 400, and the S&P SmallCap 600—and defines large cap as over $4 billion, small cap as under $1 billion, and Midcap as between $1 billion and $4 billion, then large cap is about 83 percent of the market, midcap is about 10 percent, and small cap is about 7 percent.

Similar diagrams are often used in mutual fund reviews, including those published by both Standard & Poor's and Morningstar. The mutual fund reports add a middle column, often called blend. In dealing with stocks, most approaches divide stocks into growth or value—but not both. (Russell's indexes do leave some stocks in the middle and may count some stocks in both a growth index and a value index.)

Dividing into growth and value is a relative weighting game. Normally the division is done to leave half the market capitalization on each side of the divide. However, this usually means more stocks on the value side since growth stocks are typically larger than value stocks. Dividing by market capitalization is done either by looking at indexes designed to track different portions of the market or by adapting cutoff points for company size. All these measurements change over time.

Stock pickers can compare their portfolios to the box shown above and get an idea of where they are placing their growth, value, and capitalization bets in the market. While diversification is good, trends in performance of one part of the box compared to another seem to last for a while, so looking at the relative performance of the different sectors is also a good idea.

15

THEMES IN THE MARKET

This chapter expands the discussion of sectors to include different overall ideas or themes as regards choosing stocks. Some discussions about technology focuses on whether stocks of computer hardware and software companies will do well in the coming year. But other discussions are broader and talk about how technology will affect the economy and the future of the world and what stocks we should be buying. After all, if technology is to make us all as rich as Bill Gates, maybe we should buy stock in a company that builds luxury homes, even though homebuilding stocks are not technology stocks. While some of these themes do come from brokerage houses promoting the stocks they think we should all buy, these broad ideas do have a way of affecting the stock market.

During much of the 1990s, the market has focused on large well-established stocks. Blue chips have been in favor. One result was that the top 50 or so stocks (ranked by market capitalization) in the S&P 500 were strong performers. The S&P 100 also did very well, often outperforming the S&P 500. The S&P 100 is 100 large stocks selected from the S&P 500. It was originally created for the OEX index options. The S&P 100 has proved to be an unusually stable group of stocks with extremely low turnover. The dominance of a group of blue chips from a leading index suggests that there are times when the stocks to buy are the ones in a leading index. (This should not be confused with the "index effect" and trying to buy stocks shortly before they are added to a popular index.) Certainly when a theme or approach rises to dominance, one way to choose stocks that follow that theme is to look for an index and then buy the stocks in the index. If the theme or idea is likely to be supported by wide analytical coverage and a certain amount of notoriety, then the stocks in a popular index like the S&P 500 or S&P 100 should be a good choice.

Technology has certainly been one of the recently popular stories or themes in the market. Technology stocks—companies that really are in business related to computing, not builders of luxury homes in Silicon Valley—were one of the most popular areas of the market in the second half of the 1990s. The proportion of the S&P 500 represented by technology stocks climbed from 11 percent at the end of 1994 to 30 percent at the end of 1999. Another popular idea or theme seems to be that everyone is getting older. (If everyone were getting younger, that would definitely be news.) In this case, the average age of the American population is rising as the baby-boom generation, born between 1946 and 1964, ages. Some suggest that aging baby boomers mean that the successful stocks of the future will be health care and pharmaceutical companies, while the stocks of the past included companies selling camping gear, bicycles, and equipment for active sports. If you believe that golf will replace tennis as the fashionable participation sport, then you may be a believer in this idea.[34] Some themes make sense and lead to good stock picking, other themes make more nonsense than anything else. Telling which is which is very important.

An index fund ignores any theme in the market, but it provides a benchmark to tell how much your portfolio is tied to a particular story or idea. It also provides a powerful reminder that themes come and go and index funds keep on rolling. What should an investor do to pick stocks based on broad ideas or themes about the market?

Examine the idea and see if it seems to make any sense. Sending a man to Mars may be a popular topic in the press from time to time, but it will be hard to use this thought to choose stocks. First, the government would need to make a serious commitment to fund such a program. Second, additional research and planning is needed before there is even discussion of letting contracts to design or build the rockets and spacecraft. Third, we are years away from any substantial efforts. It is a bit early to use the idea of sending people to Mars to select investments among one or another aerospace company. In 1969, when the United States did land a man on the moon, one major airline put out a press release that it would accept reservations for travel to the moon, though no date was specified. The airline subsequently went bankrupt, so any stock investments based on that announcement would have proved a bit premature.

For a theme to be of any use, it should help an investor clearly identify the sectors of the economy, industries, and stocks that will benefit. The baby-boom aging of America story is very appealing since everyone can see himself or herself in the descriptions and the stories. But, it is less clear how this helps to identify the industries or stocks that will do well. The story is so broad and diverse, it is hard to pin down any specifics. Second, the details can fool us. One might think that the baby boom means a smaller proportion of the population is college age, so textbooks aren't a growth business. Yet, more and more people are returning to school of one kind or another when they retire, so education is no longer simply for young people.

Other themes and ideas do point to specific industries and can help identify stocks. Continued globalization and the spread of the Internet is raising the demand for communication services, especially for telephones and broadband services like cable television or high capacity Internet connections. At the same time, it is increasingly difficult to run new lines in crowded American cities or paved American suburbs. The same is true in other developed countries. In the developing world, running any kind of cable often means long distances and rough terrain. All these factors combine to make some kind of wireless technology popular. Unlike the aging of the baby boom, this theme, wireless technology to bring the Internet to anyone's door front, can be linked to specific industries in the technology sector and specific companies. However, before you rush into wireless stocks, recognize that there are a lot of other questions that need to be answered.

Is the idea viable and does it make sense? In the United States, wireless technology is not quite here yet. Cell phones are ubiquitous, but broadband wireless Internet access is still a thing of the future. For the moment this may be a "value" stock play in some undiscovered technology start-up, but it isn't a large established company getting most of its business from wireless Internet delivery. What are the sectors and industries that the theme points to? Technology is much too broad since it represents about 30 percent of the entire stock market.

Recognize that some themes may make common sense and still not prove to be good investments. One example may be a response to the Microsoft antitrust case. The case has attracted a lot of attention and has pushed Microsoft's stock price around quite a bit. The case is also likely to continue onward for quite a while unless some unexpected settlement is reached. One theme might be that the case opens up new opportunities in the software industry. If the Justice Department does force a breakup of Microsoft, one of the dominant firms in the industry will change into at least two new, smaller companies. Whether or not Microsoft is broken up, it will be distracted from doing business and will pay less attention to its business. This suggests that computer software could be a place to look for interesting investments.

The reader can judge if the general argument makes some sense. It certainly points to a specific industry (computer software) within a particular sector (technology) in the market. It also points to some details. One could look for large established software companies that either offer products that compete directly with Microsoft or could introduce competing products quickly. Names like IBM and Oracle are likely to pop up. One can also look at less-established existing competitors, such as those selling Linux and other versions of Unix, an operating system that competes with Microsoft's Windows products. Unlike the baby-boomer story, this one can generate specific stocks to look at. The stocks still need to be reviewed for their financials, but the theme has paid off with some ideas.

Once the sectors or industries are identified, one can use an index as a comparison for how much of the total investment should be in any particular spot. Suppose a contrarian investor buys the Microsoft breakup theme, but wants to hedge by buying Microsoft instead. Microsoft was over 4 percent of the S&P 500 at the start of 2000, though the announcement of the initial antitrust decision and other turmoil pushed it down to less than 3 percent of the index, as of. A portfolio of 20 stocks with around 5 percent in Microsoft is not a huge bet on its revival. After all, in good times that was no more than the average or market weighting one would have found in the index. If you believe in the theme, you should have a larger portion of your portfolio in the areas that your theme points to than the market would place there. A believer in technology who had 25 percent of his holdings in tech stocks at the end of 1999 was *underweighted* in technology by about 5 percentage points. The believer would have wondered why his portfolio didn't seem as tech-heavy as he thought it was.

At times, themes become simply selecting what sectors to avoid or focus on. The discussion in Part II on sectors and sector-based index funds covered some ideas for choosing sectors. Often the idea of a theme is a story or justification for choosing one or another sector. Certainly this has been the case in recent years with technology—the wonders of computers mean that everyone should buy computer stocks, the more the better. Not exactly. After all, if everyone has been buying computer stocks for quite a

TABLE 15-1   Market Capitalization Weights by Sector, May 31, 2000

	S&P 500	S&P MidCap 400	S&P SmallCap 600
Consumer discretionary	12%	13%	16%
Consumer staples	7%	3%	4%
Energy	5%	8%	5%
Financials	14%	11%	12%
Health care	11%	12%	13%
Industrials	10%	15%	20%
Information technology	30%	21%	24%
Materials	2%	5%	4%
Telecommunication services	7%	2%	0%
Utilities	3%	11%	3%

while, chances are that at least some of them have been bid up to prices far higher than anything remotely reasonable.

To establish market themes for stock pickers, first, take apart the ideas and see if they make some common sense. Second, identify the particular sectors and industries that the theme points to. If possible, use definitions for sectors or industries that come from a widely followed index so that you can check exactly what is in a sector. If you think there is something to the strategy suggested by the theme, compare your investment allocations with an index and really overweight your portfolio in the indicated direction. Table 15-1 shows the market capitalization weights by sector for the S&P 500, S&P MidCap 400, and S&P SmallCap 600 as of May 31, 2000. These weights do move around so you may want to find more up-to-date information.

Your portfolio is probably never going to be exactly the same as the indexes. Indeed, the indexes never match the total market, although they are usually within a few percentage points for of the proportions in the overall stock market.

16

QUANTITATIVE STOCK SELECTION AND INDEXES

Analysts and investors use various quantitative measures of stocks: price-to-book ratios discussed above, plus dividends, earnings, price–earnings and others. These measures are used to judge stocks as investments. Most of these measures can be moving targets; what was a high p–e ratio in 1990 may be a low one today. However, indexes are benchmarks that can be used to gauge one stock against another or a stock against the market. Indexes also provide measures that are specific to a sector or an industry. Since dividends are rare among technology stocks, it may not be useful to compare dividend yields when the benchmark includes electric utilities famous for paying dividends.

In this chapter we review many of these quantitative measures and offer comments for comparing stocks to indexes with these measures. Sometimes the measures can be used to sort out the good ideas from the bad suggestions, other times they only serve as a confirmation or a warning about a particular stock. For the discussion here we will use the S&P 500 as the key benchmark, since it is the most widely used broad index in the United States and one for which there is a wealth of available data on this kind around. The discussion focuses on some of the practical questions; formal definitions can best be found in accounting textbooks.

EARNINGS PER SHARE

Earnings per share, or EPS, is really part of the price–earnings ratio, or p–e, the most popular measure for judging a stock or the market overall. However, since most of the questions about the ratio relate to the earnings or EPS part, it is worth mentioning it first. As simple or basic as EPS may seem, it has undergone various changes in recent years, giving rise to some competing definitions. For a long time the earnings referred to the company's earnings or profits after tax, the bottom line.

Over the last two decades as corporations have rearranged, redefined, restructured, and reinvented themselves time and time again, it has become more and more common to see annual financial statements with write-offs, reserves, and other bits of accounting detail. All these tend to shift and change the financial results as one division is sold off or another is moved around or spun out. When the earnings have more to do with the way an old unit was dumped than with the ongoing businesses in the pieces that remain in a company, it is natural to question how meaningful the reported EPS number really is. On top of that, stock analysts find it difficult to project EPS when the biggest swing factor is the accounting advice being given to the chief financial officer. As a result, a new concept was borne: *operating earnings*.

The idea of operating earnings is to exclude one-time charges related to corporate rearrangements and focus on continuing operations. After all, if the EPS is going to be used to evaluate the stock's future prospects, then the operations that will still be around are the ones to watch. Further, a stock analyst has a good shot at forecasting the operating earnings accurately; he or she has only a long shot at guessing the right projection for the write-offs and other stuff. The concept is fine, the practice is a bit muddy at present. There is no standard and accepted definition of operating earnings and there is not even universal agreement about data for past years, to say nothing of forecast data for the near future.

Since most of the differences between earnings (or "reported earnings" as some call them) and the adjusted or operating earnings reflect unusual charges and write-offs, reported earnings are usually smaller than operating earnings. In other words, if a stock analyst or a company investor relations officer wants to hype a stock, using operating earnings is a good way to inflate the profits numbers people use to evaluate the stock. The depth of the muddiness in operating earnings is seen in the historical data— there is often little agreement on what *last* year's operating earnings were. Moreover, if the company restates its recent history, all bets on what operating earnings were are off. The operating earnings concept is good, but the practice is far from perfect. Investors should be wary. Moreover, this wariness should climb if comparisons with other companies or with indexes suggest a particular company is almost too good to be true.

The second issue in looking at EPS is whether one is looking at actual data or at a forecast. Since choosing a stock to buy is basically forecasting what the stock will do in the future, it is natural to look at analysts' forecasts of earnings. Moreover, no one wants to make a decision based on old information, so if you are reviewing a stock in the middle of the year, you are likely to be using an estimate of EPS that is an average of the part of the year that is over and already reported and the part of the year that is yet to come. Earnings tend to rise over time, especially in attractive stocks. So, chances are that earnings in 2000 will be higher than earnings in 1999. That means that the p–e using actual 1999 earnings will be a larger number (smaller earnings) than the p–e using forecasted 2000 earnings. The small 2000 p–e makes the stock look more attractive.

To calculate earnings per share, divide the earnings in dollars by the number of shares. Knowing the number of shares is not that simple. Shares are counted in two ways: basic and diluted. Basic stock can be less than diluted or the same number. Diluted stock includes shares that would be issued for stock options and other securities like convertible bonds and shares held as Treasury shares. Standard & Poor's indexes use the basic number to count shares; most of the time the basic count is used to calculate the EPS. One might also think that finding out the right number of shares should be easy. Unfortunately this is not always the case. The number of shares a company has outstanding changes from time to time as companies issue stock when employee stock options are exercised or when certain other financial adjustments are made. These changes are seldom on a schedule, but are reported in various filings with the SEC. To make matters a bit more complicated, except for stock splits, changes in share counts are not widely publicized. As a result, it is possible for different data sources to have slightly different counts of shares outstanding.

In using EPS, there is no right or wrong calculation, but knowing which one is being reported is critically important. The biggest pitfalls are forecast versus actual and reported versus operating.

PRICE–EARNINGS RATIO

The price–earnings ratio is the most widely quoted financial data item for any corporation. When you buy a stock, what you buy is a share in the future earnings. The p–e tells you how much you paid for each dollar of earnings. When stocks are popular and everyone loves them, people pay more for a dollar of earnings and the p–e goes up. Therefore, hidden values have lower p–e's and can (hopefully) be bought before they become popular. If the management is skillful and can grow earnings more rapidly, then the $1 of today's (or this year's forecast) earnings you bought might grow to be $1.20 next year or $1.42 a year later. Stocks with rapidly growing earnings should have higher p–e's. One old rule of thumb was that the growth rate of earnings should be larger than p–e. As discussed next, the market's high values have shifted some of the rules. The p–e is the comparison stock shoppers' best yardstick.

How do we know if a p–e of 25 is cheap or dear? In winter time 40 degrees is warm, while in summer 50 degrees is cold. The easiest way is to compare the stock's p–e to benchmarks offered by an index. Start with the overall market measured by the S&P 500. For the S&P 500 the p–e ranges from a low of around 8 or 9 to a high of over 30 times. However, one should note that until the late 1990s, the high end of the S&P 500's p–e range was in the low 20s. Figure 3-1 in Part I showed the evolution of the S&P 500 p–e since the early 1970s. If the current p–e on the S&P 500 is near 30, one shouldn't assume that any stock with a p–e under 25 is cheap or that any stock with a p–e over 25 is overpriced. Rather, different industries and economic sectors have different patterns that show up in the p–e ratio.

One common method is to calculate a relative p–e. While this sounds complicated it is simply the p–e of the stock in question divided by the p–e of the S&P 500. If the p–e of the S&P 500 is 25 and the stock is selling at a p–e of 40, its relative p–e is 40/25 or 1.6.

So, after comparing the p–e on the stock to the overall market, one should also compare it to the index for its economic sector and industry. Technology stocks tend to be fast-growing popular stocks and are likely to have high p–e's. Some cyclical industries and old economy companies tend to have low p–e's and may appear cheap when they're not cheap at all. If a stock has a low p–e compared to its industry and its sector, score a point in favor of the stock.

Because p–e ratios move over time, people often look at how they have changed from year to year. Investors also look at the market's p–e as a way to see if it is cheap or expensive. Someone may say that in periods of low inflation and moderate interest rates, the S&P 500 often has a p–e in the low 20s, yet at the moment it is lower than that—suggesting someone should rush out and buy stocks. Here it is important to make sure that the earnings used are all consistent. Other than a few specialized databases, no one keeps old forecasts. (It might embarrass the forecasters.) The historic p–e's and the earnings used to calculate them are actual earnings, not someone's optimistic forecast. Second, the historic numbers are almost certainly reported earnings, while the current year's numbers are likely to be operating earnings. These two common errors both tend to make the current or near term forecast p–e appear lower than it really is, making the stocks look more attractive than they are.

EARNINGS GROWTH

Earnings today are nice, bigger earnings tomorrow are even nicer. In fact, most of a stock's value is based on its anticipated growth, not on its current earnings. Looking at earnings growth raises two kinds of questions for a would-be stock picker. First, how does the expected growth compare to other companies and second, is it reflected in the price. Here the best comparison is probably not a broad market index like the S&P 500 but a narrow index that covers only the specific industry that includes the stocks you are looking at. Comparing earnings growth for a computer maker and a car company is less useful than comparing the computer company to other computer companies facing similar competitive and economic issues. So, the first step is to compare the forecasted EPS growth with expected growth in an industry index, or possibly with the expected growth of the particular companies in the industry-level index.

At the same time, compare the p–e ratios among the companies in the same industry. Higher earnings growth should mean higher p–e ratios. Suppose one stock has a lower p–e but roughly the same expected earnings growth. At first glance this may look like a buy since you pay less for earnings in the cheap stock than in the others. But, look around a bit first. Consider the stock's recent history, it's consistency of growing earnings, it current size, maybe even its credit quality if there is a bond rating available. For actively traded stocks—certainly for stocks in the S&P 500—there is a lot of information available and a lot of people studying the stocks. That means that an apparent disagreement between two measures may signal a hidden bargain, or it may signal some more subtle hidden information, such as a track record of disappointing earnings reports that have pushed the price and the p–e lower.

Forecasts of earnings growth for the S&P 500 as a whole and for many stocks are readily available on the World Wide Web. Web sites from brokerage houses, other financial information companies, and companies like Yahoo all provide a variety of information. However, when dealing with forecasts, some caution may be in order. When there are 30 or 40 analysts following a stock like IBM, Microsoft, or GE it doesn't make a big difference if one of them forgets to update his estimate or had a dramatically different view. When there are three or four analysts on a less widely discussed stock, one opinion can make a huge difference. If you use earnings estimates from the Web or "Wall Street," it can pay to see who did them and when they were done. Better yet, but unrealistic for many investors, is to get the company's financials and develop your own estimates and then compare yours with the consensus. If you find a stock with a forecast of strong earnings growth and a relatively weak p–e, you should certainly try to figure out why the forecast is strong while the market seems to be ignoring it.

PEG RATIOS

As the stock market advanced in the 1990s, stock prices and p–e ratios climbed to levels that used to be considered dangerous. While some argue that these levels still are dangerous, others sought new ways to make high prices seem comfortable. In doing so, they seized on the idea of comparing the p–e to the expected growth in earnings. An old rule of thumb, possibly due to Peter Lynch, the famed manager of the Fidelity Magellan fund, was to look for stocks where the p–e ratio is less than the growth rate projected for earnings. After the market's 1990s rise, these kinds of stocks are getting very hard to find. So, analysts began to calculate the ratio of the p–e to expected earnings growth and then let the numbers gradually expand. Under the old approach, the upper limit for buying a stock was a PEG ratio of 1.0. Now it is common to see people talk about PEG ratios of 1.5 or 2, or higher. In the process, a rule of thumb that had a strict value—PEG of 1.0—has been converted into a sliding scale.

If there are no absolute values, at least there are chances for relative values. The PEG on a stock can be compared to the PEG for the market, by using the S&P 500, or for the PEG for a particular industry, by using a sector or industry index. The market's PEG suggests how confident investors are about the current level of prices and the current consensus forecast. If the market PEG falls from 1.5 to 1, it suggests that investors are getting a bit nervous about high p–e's or about the level of optimism incorporated in earnings projections. The same can be said for a particular sector or industry. If you look at a stock with a PEG much larger than the PEG for an index of that industry, you need some reason *in addition* to strong expected earnings growth to buy the stock. Earnings growth is incorporated into the PEG. In some other cases a stock with a high p–e may have very strong earnings growth and may be rescued from the reject pile by a PEG ratio that is not stratospherically out of sight.

PRICE-TO-BOOK RATIOS

We met the price-to-book ratio earlier when we discussed how stocks are split into growth and value portions in the Standard & Poor's indexes. Other than the work on the three-factor model and the division of growth and value, this is a measure that has lost a lot of its old popularity over time. Like some others there are some accounting pitfalls here as well. Some databases define book value as only the tangible or real assets a company owns, while others will include some intangible assets like goodwill. Real or tangible assets means buildings, factories, offices, inventories, and other things one can see or touch. The original idea was that if the company collapsed into bankruptcy, these were the assets that could be sold. Whether they could be sold for a value even close to the tangible book value was never discussed. More recently, other assets have become important. One of the key ones is goodwill. Suppose Acquisitions, Inc., buys the Merged Again Corporation and pays a price of $50 per share, but Merged Again Corporation only has a tangible book value of $12 per share. The difference, $38 per share, is called *goodwill*. Without the goodwill number, there is no way for the accountants at Acquisitions, Inc., to explain why they paid $50 for $12 worth of assets. Goodwill becomes an intangible asset. (Only the accountants seem to be able to touch it.) The goodwill does fade away— it is depreciated over a long period, usually 40 years for bookkeeping purposes.

In most mergers, the value of what is being acquired is much more than just a few buildings and some inventory. The real value is in the business, its reputation and customer relations. So, there tends to be a lot of goodwill in acquisitions. This, plus the number of acquisitions in the last two decades, means that there is a lot of goodwill floating around and a lot of intangible assets. Using the wrong definition of book value can lead to some surprising results.

These definitional pitfalls also point out the general problem with book value. When the dominant companies on Wall Street were manufacturing companies with huge factories, counting book value made sense. Today, more and more of a company's value depends on its value as a business— its reputation and customer relations. That means that book values are less useful. However, comparing price-to-book ratios across companies in the same industry by using an index can give you an idea of how much of the value of the stock you are considering is on the balance sheet and how much is in the mind of the market.

If all stocks in the industry have price-to-book ratios of 8 to 1, suggesting that seventh-eighths of the value is in the market's mind and not on the balance sheet, a ratio of 8 to 1 won't look too frightening. But, if the index has a ratio of 5 to 1, then 8 to 1 may be a bit too high.

PRICE-TO-SALES RATIOS

Price-to-sales may epitomize fads and fashions in finance and stock selecting. When it is hot, everyone talks about it as the latest great discovery. At other times, no one really seems to care. A recent supporter of price-to-sales was James O'Shaughnessy in a study that tested various different financial ratios for choosing stocks. In his tests, price-to-sales was the best.[35]

Comparisons to other companies in the same sector and industry are critically important here. What is meant by sales can vary from sector to sector or industry to industry. Lower price-to-sales are preferred to high ones. In effect, the ratio is an indication of how much you pay for each dollar of sales if you buy the stock: it is similar to the price–earnings ratio. Moreover, the range varies across wide margins from one sector of the market to another. In health care or technology, price-to-sales ratios of four or five times are found for sector indexes. In other areas, such as consumer cyclicals, the ratio is less than one. One could calculate a ratio of price to sales to sales growth similar to the PEG ratio. No one seems to use such an approach, possibly because price to sales is not that widely followed.

Because some industries and sectors have very different definitions, price-to-sales is sometimes not calculated. In the financial sector, it is rare for banks to list a figure comparable to the idea of sales or revenues for an industrial company. As a result, price-to-sales does not easily have universal applicability. But it can be useful for comparing companies in an industry or a sector.

DIVIDEND YIELD

There was once a time when any company that wanted to be considered an established business paid dividends. Those days seem to be long gone and even some well-known and well-established blue-chip companies don't pay any dividends at all. Both corporations' dividend practices and the way financial analysts use dividend information are in the process of changing. Nevertheless, dividends and dividend yields are still calculated and watched. The dividend yield is the indicated annual dividend divided by the price. *Indicated annual dividend* means how much the company will pay if it doesn't raise or cut its dividend between now and the end of the year.

Companies' practices are shifting. While reducing or skipping a dividend is still likely to push a company's stock price sharply lower, there seems to be less concern about keeping the ratio of dividends to earnings per share, the payout ratio, stable over time. In the last decade or so, the payout ratios for the S&P 500 has slowly but surely declined. Companies in the index are paying out less of their earnings to shareholders and reinvesting more in their businesses. Given how well the index has done, the companies are making the right choice. The funds earn more invested in the companies than they might in many other investments.

Dividends are a mixed blessing for shareholders. Certainly everyone likes getting the dividend check in the mail, but no one likes paying taxes on the dividends. Academic research has long argued that it would make more sense for companies to use the funds now paid as dividends to buy back stock on the open market. The buybacks would support the stock price and give shareholders a chance to earn a return on their investments by selling a portion of their holdings back to the company. Of course, if investors preferred not to sell, they could hold their stock. Those who did sell some stock to the company would get the same income, but it would be taxed as capital gains, not income. In recent years these arguments have been recognized and more and more companies are announcing programs to buy back their stock rather than raising their dividends.

For analyzing stocks, these programs can present some difficulties. First, there is no readily available stock buyback data for any index to use as a benchmark. Nor is there enough experience with buybacks to be able to categorize programs as large or small. One could compare the funds pledged for the buyback to the funds that would have been used to pay dividends, but here there is also a problem. Many buyback programs are not completed as announced and oftentimes buyback programs do not result in a net reduction in shares outstanding.

If one is looking at a company and an industry where dividends are common, then comparisons between the dividend yield on the stock and a sector or market index can be helpful. In some sectors, such as technology, the data are of little help. Where dividends are paid, higher dividend yields are preferred—more money paid out and relatively lower stock prices are preferable. However, a stock with an outrageously high dividend yield may be about to cut or eliminate the dividend. Often the price will reflect rumors of a coming dividend cut before it happens, signaling the possibility of a further fall after the news hits.

Dividend yields used to be widely cited as a market measure that would warn of impending doom. Until the mid-1950s, the dividend yield on stocks, as measured by the Standard & Poor's Composite, was higher than the yield on bonds. Investors, remembering the crash of 1929 and seeing stocks as risky, felt that dividend yields should be higher than bond yields. Subsequently, the potential for growth in dividends was recognized and the pattern shifted. To some extent, these shifts are still going on. Figure 16-1 shows the evolution of dividend yield of the S&P 500. Over time the "danger point" for which level of the dividend yield signals a market about to collapse has fallen from 3 percent on down to 2 percent or even less.

MOMENTUM AND RELATIVE STRENGTH

The measures discussed so far all reflect the financial condition of a stock and compare it to the average defined by an index for either the market or a portion of the market. However, a stock's value depends on its popularity as well its financials. Popularity is usually gauged by how it is trading, whether the price is rising faster or slower than other prices. Two measures that have gained some popularity for gauging both stocks and the overall market are momentum and relative strength.

Momentum refers to the stock's recent past performance. Research suggests that over time periods of a few months stocks tend to keep moving in the same direction. In the short term, stocks that are rising are likely to keep rising and those that are falling are likely to keep falling. In contrast,

FIGURE 16-1   The evolution of the dividend yield of the S&P 500 from 1960 to 1999.

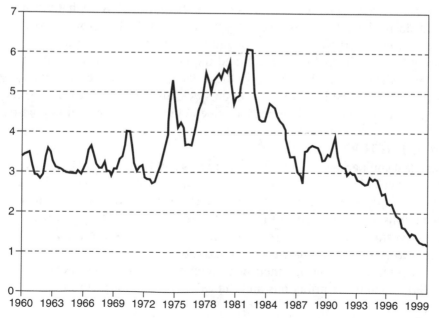

there is also some evidence that over a period of a few years stocks exhibit *mean reversion*—they move back toward the averages. If you review a stock and see that its price has climbed 15 percent in three months, it appears to be on a strong up trend that may well continue. However, if the whole market is up 20 percent in the same period, the stock may look like a laggard to be avoided. The same is probably true of a particular industry or sector. Even if the 15 percent gain by the stock beat the overall market, it could still be lagging compared to similar stocks in the same industry, as shown by an industry index that moves up faster than the stock does.

Relative strength puts this comparison of a stock with an index into a ratio. To measure the relative strength of a stock against the S&P 500, one takes price data for the stock and the index over a period of time and divides the stock price by the index value. Then, divide the ratio just calculated for each day (or week) by the ratio on the first day. The relative strength for the first day is 1.0. If the figures are above one, then the stock has risen more in percentage terms than the index has; if the relative strength is less than 1, then the stock is lagging the index. One can repeat the same calculation to compare a sector index to the market as a whole. If this seems like a lot of calculations, you can pick up a copy of a newspaper like *Investor's Business Daily,* which caters to people who follow technical analysis, or try a Web site that provides the calculations already completed.

Both momentum and relative strength will give you an idea of whether people are buying or selling the stock. Neither will tell you what the stock will do in the future. However, if you are looking at a growth stock—a stock where everyone expects strong growth and has bid the price up—you might wonder if relative strength and momentum suggest it is not a very popular investment. Likewise, if these technical measures appear very strong, but you believe this is a value stock that has not been discovered, you might wonder why it appears to be enjoying such technical popularity.

TOTAL RETURN

The last comparison is total return. For indexes and mutual funds, it is common to calculate the total return an investor earns before taxes and trading costs. *Total return* means that any dividend, income, or capital gains contributions are reinvested in the fund or the index when they are received. An investor can achieve essentially these results by asking the fund company to automatically reinvest the distributions.

Few investors manage their own stock portfolios this way; that is, they seldom take the distributions and immediately reinvest them in their portfolio, spreading the distribution across all their holdings. Moreover, many investors do pay taxes and often adjust their buying and selling plans to limit their tax liabilities. However, even though you may not run your portfolio exactly the way the total return calculations for the S&P 500 are done, you can still make some useful comparisons between the index and your own results. At the beginning of Part III we noted that a majority of mutual funds doesn't do as well as the S&P 500 in most years. As daring as it may sound, some investors should probably compare their results to the index. If they consistently lag the index, they might make more money by moving some of their investments to an index fund instead of choosing stocks. Certainly running your own portfolio has some entertainment value as well as investment returns, but you might want to see how much the entertainment is really costing. You may also want to compare the volatility and risk of your portfolio with the volatility of the S&P 500.

COMPARABLES, CURRENCIES, AND OTHER ANGLES

In a lot of investment analyses one needs to find similar companies to use as benchmark comparisons. *Comparables* is the name given to these benchmarks chosen to gauge how well a particular company is doing. Indexes are a good source of comparables. Take broad market indexes like the S&P 500, S&P MidCap 400, or S&P SmallCap 600 that are divided into sectors and industry groups. The list of companies in the same industry group as the company being analyzed is a good place to start looking for some comparable companies.

Investing is increasingly international, but often patterns and values are local. If you review foreign companies, there may be some special pitfalls. First, all the analysis should be done in your home currency. The company may look wonderful in euros but be a disappointment in dollars if the euro keeps sliding. However, be careful because a company with a low p–e compared to the S&P 500 might have a sky-high p–e in its home market if the home market faces different factors. In general, market comparisons should be made in the market where most of the stock's trading takes place and then the expected returns should be translated into dollars to see if the foreign exchange markets are threatening your hard-won gains.

Table 16-1 summarizes the discussion on using some common measures for selecting stocks and using indexes as benchmark comparisons. In all of these, the measures are simply starting points to choosing stocks to invest in. You should go far beyond a list of numbers. Read the annual report to see whether the management's discussion makes sense and they

TABLE 16-1   Investment Measures and Index Benchmarks

Measure	Index to Use	What to Look For	Comments
p–e ratio	S&P 500, then sector index	Low p–e's are better	
Earnings growth	Sector or industry	Faster is better	If another stock has faster earnings growth, why not buy it?
PEG ratio	Sector or Industry	Lower preferred	Over 3 is pretty dangerous territory.
Price to book	Market or sector	Lower preferred	Confirm if it is growth or value.
Price to sales	Sector or industry	Lower preferred	Marketwide measures are not useful.
Dividend yield	Sector and market	Higher preferred	Be wary if it is too high.
Momentum	Sector first	Recent gains preferred	Only a popularity contest.
Relative strength	S&P 500	Above one	Another popularity contest.
Total return	S&P 500	Higher preferred	Can you beat the market?

seem to know what they're doing. Look for other information about the company's business and the prospects for its industry. It is much easier to choose winning stocks in booming industries than in slumping backwaters. After you buy it, check on it from time to time. See if the stock is up, if it is doing better than its industry, its sector, and the market overall.

17

THE MARKET'S PROSPECTS

The last few chapters have discussed how to use indexes in evaluating stocks being considered for investment. They covered lessons from the success of index funds, themes in the market—including buying stocks in an index— and ways to use indexes as benchmarks for fundamental equity measures. However, one of the largest factors in how well a particular stock will do is how well the market will do. Stocks tend to move together. When the market rises, most stocks rise and when the market falls, most stocks fall. So, for an investor picking stocks, some idea of what the overall market feels like or may do is very useful. This chapter extends some of the in- dex-based measures to a discussion of the overall stock market. Entire books have been written about the stock market, so a chapter isn't likely to reveal the absolute and complete hidden truth. It can give you some insights into the market and some tools to decide whether you should worry more about getting and losing some money or about missing the chance to buy at the bottom.

There are two kinds of forces pushing and pulling the stock market. One kind is linked to the economy, to what can be done with the capital represented by the stocks, the capital raised in the stock market and put to work in the economy. These forces can be quantified, measured, and re- lated to what's happening in the economy. These are usually called market fundamentals. The analysis of market fundamentals is based on estimating and adding up the value of the stocks in the market and trying to forecast those values using economics and finance. One of the most fundamental ideas is that any asset is worth the present value of the future returns it generates. These ideas, which are discussed and related to indexes in this chapter, form the basis of much of modern finance and economics. There is one large difficulty: the stock market seems to fluctuate much more than can be justified by changes in market fundamentals.[36]

The fluctuations lead to another second group of forces affecting the market—mass psychology, extraordinary popular delusions, and the madness of crowds.[37] *Market psychology*, a catchall term for market movements that can't be explained by economics, is the second group of forces driving the market higher or lower. Both the fundamentals and the psychology can be observed and measured with the help of stock indexes. Unfortunately, neither can be predicted with complete reliability.

FUNDAMENTALS

The essential idea behind the fundamental values in the stock market or of a single stock is that a stock value is the discounted present value of future dividends. After all, there are three reasons to buy a stock—the dividend income you might receive, the hope that you can sell it for more money in the future, and bragging rights that you knew which stock to buy. Fundamental values deal with the first two; bragging rights fall into psychology. A dollar today is worth more than a dollar next year. Why? If you have the dollar today you can invest it and earn a return on it. Why wait for next year to come around? Or, you can spend it now and enjoy whatever you buy with it today. If neither of those concepts is appealing, consider that a dollar today is a sure thing while a dollar next year includes the risk you may not get the dollar or that inflation or some other economic events will make next year's dollar worth less than you expect. If this year's dollar has the same value to you as $1.08 next year, an 8 percent difference, then your discount rate is 8 percent. In simple language, it will take an 8 percent return to get you to wait until next year instead of taking the money now.

Usually in financial analyses one assumes that the discount rate is the same amount per year no matter how many years. This means that if the rate is 8 percent for one year, it is 8 percent per year, compounded, for however many years one is talking about. Eight percent may sound small, but it can add up. A dollar this year is the equivalent of $2.16 ten years from now.[38] Alternatively, a dollar 10 years from now is not that large today, about 46 cents at 8 percent. If one goes far enough into the future, the present value of a distant dollar becomes very small. After 80 years, at 8 percent, the future dollar is worth about one penny today. So, one aspect of the value of a stock is to calculate and add up all the future payments of the stock.

The second part of the puzzle is the payments. The payments are dividends. Many stocks pay dividends, although some may not. This doesn't mean that stocks that don't pay dividends are worthless. It merely means that the fundamental value must be based on what someone else might pay for the stock at some point in the future. Of course, that investor will base his value on either dividends or selling the stock. In the end, it is the expectation of dividends that gives the stock a basis for real value. While one can add up the payments far into the future, it is also possible to make a few mathematical adjustments and get a much simpler formula. If the dividend is the same year in and year out, divide the dividend by the discount rate and get the present value. For example, a $5 dividend divided by an 8 percent discount rate has a present value of $62.50 ($5 divided by 0.08). At a 4 percent discount rate a $5 dividend has a present value of $125.)

Of course, no one wants a stock that never grows. If the dividend grows at, say, 5 percent, and the discount rate is 8 percent, one can either figure each year for, say, 100 years and add it up or use a mathematical solution to find the value of $166.67 for the stock. This version of the stock valuation is usually called the Gordon model.[39] Of course, the stock market doesn't depend on your own idea of the discount rate. In the stock market, it depends on the economy's overall discount rate. If the investments can return 10 percent consistently in the economy, then the discount rate should be 10 percent since this is what the money could earn somewhere else.

There is one more angle before we can apply this to the market as a whole. What happens if the dividends grow faster than the discount rate? If you apply the Gordon model, you get a negative number—a nonsense result. But, think about the problem for a moment. If the dividends grow faster than what investments can earn in the economy, the dividend would grow faster than the economy itself. This can certainly happen for a while, but it can't happen forever because the dividend and the stock would swallow the economy. If one wants to evaluate a stock where the dividends are expected to grow by leaps and bounds for a few years and then slow down to a normal pace a bit below the best sustainable pace in the economy, one can do the arithmetic year by year. The idea of basing a stock's value on the discounted value of future dividends is called the *dividend discount model* or DDM. If one assumes a high rate of growth for a few years, followed by a growth rate less than the discount rate in later years, it is called a *two-stage DDM.*

While dividend discount models can be applied to single stocks, they are used just as much to model the entire stock market. The S&P 500 is taken to represent the stock market. This is convenient because the S&P 500 is the benchmark most money managers use and because there is a long history and extensive data on the index and the earnings and dividends paid by the stocks in the index. The data are often presented as if the index were a company with shares. Dividends are quoted as many dollars per share where the index value is the price per share. The calculations behind this are simple to describe, though involved to do. Chapter 7 discussed how indexes are built and how there is a scale factor called the divisor. This number can be used as the number of shares outstanding to calculate the per share values for earnings, dividends, or other measures. It is the basis for all the per share values (as in book value per share for price-to-book ratios, and so forth) discussed above.

So, given some data for the S&P 500 and a figure for dividend growth and the discount rate, one can estimate what the S&P 500 should be worth. Then, by comparing the answer to the closing price on the S&P 500, one can tell if the stock market is a steal or a rotten proposition. Unfortunately, the practice is not always quite so simple. Agreeing on the future growth of dividends can lead to numerous arguments, as can debates over the right number for the discount rate. Among the various people who have weighed into the debate on what the right numbers are is the Federal Reserve. As Alan Greenspan's apparent interest in the stock market increased, it was no surprise that the Fed looked at ways to analyze the market. Out of this came one of the simplest models, which worked quite well until recently.

The Fed Model looks at earnings, not dividends, and at one figure for the discount rate—the yield on 10-year Treasury notes. While dividends are the right number, over long periods of time dividends are likely to be a stable proportion of earnings. Moreover, analysts spend a good deal of time refining forecasts of earnings and very little time forecasting dividends. Finally, since an increasing number of stocks in the S&P 500 don't pay dividends, using earnings does a better job of capturing these firms. As to the discount rate, the Fed Model takes the yield on the 10-year Treasury note as a measure of what a low-risk investment in the economy could earn. Figure 17-1 shows the actual value of the S&P 500 over the last 40 years and the value that would be estimated by the Fed Model. The values, until recently, were similar. However, in the past few years the model has fallen short of the real values. As of early May 2000, the estimated earnings for

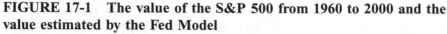

FIGURE 17-1   The value of the S&P 500 from 1960 to 2000 and the value estimated by the Fed Model

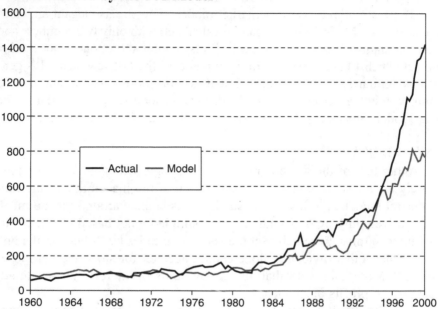

2000 were around $60 per share and the 10-year Treasury was yielding about 6 percent; this gives a Fed Model value of 1000 compared to an index value of about 1400. The market appears to be overvalued by about 40 percent. Or, as we argue in the next section, the psychological factors are adding 40 percent to the fundamental value in the market. The apparent "error" of 40 percent between what the model says the S&P 500 should be worth and what it really is worth can be seen as either a reason to reject the model or a reason to be concerned about how high stock prices are.

Take a look at the section of the chart that covers 1987, the year of the crash. When it comes to understanding stock prices in 1987, we have the advantage of hindsight (though some may argue that we still don't understand what did happen in October 1987 when the market fell about 20 percent in one day). As the chart shows, stock prices climbed from January to August 1987, leaving behind the fundamental values predicted by the Fed Model. Then the tide turned, slowly at first and then with devastatingly swift fury, and stock prices came tumbling down. They ended the year about where they began—close to the predictions from the Fed Model. If the Fed Model captured the fundamentals in the market, the impact of dividends and interest rates, then the deviations from the Fed Model should reflect psychological factors. Market psychology can easily pump stocks up to soaring heights or thrust them down into deep valleys.

There are numerous other market models. Few are as elegant and simple as the Fed Model, and few can be calculated with only two numbers and one calculation. The box at the end of this chapter shows one other market model which I have tried in various guises over the last few years. It's genesis is similar to the Fed Model, but it is a bit more versatile and can be built with either earnings or dividends. The general result is similar to the Fed Model: Stocks appear to be significantly overvalued at present.

PSYCHOLOGY

The other half of the game is market psychology. This is much more than merely an excuse or convenient explanation of the inaccuracy of the fundamental models. For one thing, stock prices bounce around far too much to be driven only by dividends or some simple model based on dividends and interest rates. Research over the last two decades by Robert Shiller and others shows that dividends alone cannot account for stock market movements.[40] More is at work than just a few shifts in interest rates or an adjustment to profits or dividends.

It is the psychological factors that give rise to the challenge of forecasting the market. It's ability to surge, collapse, run up or run down from time to time is what makes the market so fascinating and puzzling. Two ideas from economics and finance capture some key aspects of the market—efficiency and arbitrage. Most financial academic researchers describe the market as *efficient*, meaning that it already incorporates all the relevant information into the prices and there is no way to do better than the market. In fact, given inevitable trading costs, it is hard to do as well as the market. Efficiency is a very strong argument for buying a broad-based index fund or ETF and devoting your spare time to something other than stock selection.

Efficiency may come in degrees. Many people argue that the large-cap segment of the market is efficient, but that among small stocks, without a significant number of analysts following them, there are hidden gems to be discovered. This may be so, but small-cap indexes do a good job of beating small-cap funds as well. Moreover, one benefit the small-cap funds have had over the indexes lately is that some funds may have held a few large-cap stocks. Because large caps did better than small caps in the late 1990s, these out-of-style holdings probably boosted the funds' results. Another variation of efficiency is whether inside information counts or not. Inside information includes key facts that are not public and not in the market, such as an unannounced acquisition plan involving a tender offer for the stock of a public company. This kind of information can move specific stocks, and when it is revealed, it is rapidly incorporated into market prices.

Arbitrage guarantees that the markets are efficient. *Arbitrage* is buying or selling stocks when there is a riskless opportunity to make a profit. ("Risk arbitrage"—betting on pending takeovers—is something quite different and certainly not without risk.) Suppose a stock trades in both New York and London. In New York it trades in dollars, in London in British pounds. The only difference in the prices in the two cities should be the exchange rate between the dollar and the pound. If this isn't the case, a trader can buy the stock in one city and sell it in the other for a guaranteed profit. Since one can't get something for nothing, this is not likely to be the case for very long. If the stock is cheap in London compared to New York, the arbitrage buying in London will push the British price up while the arbitrage selling in New York will lower the American price. Once the correct parity is achieved, arbitrage trading will dry up.

Arbitrage and efficiency tend to drive out many small quirks in the market, leaving behind some big ones for market psychology. Periodically one hears claims about various season shifts or day-of-the-week effects. One of the more widely discussed ones is the January effect—the idea that stocks do better in January than in any other month of the year. If this were so, it would pay to buy on December 31 and sell on February 1. In some recent years there may have been some arbitrage at work. More than one commentator was heard to explain strong November stock market gains by saying that "the January effect came in November this year."

There are other similar arguments. One is to own stocks from November through May and T-bills from June through October. For more active traders there is the argument that stocks tend to fall on Mondays. Neither of these can provide any real profits, even without including trading costs. Of course, many of us dislike Mondays for other, noninvestment, reasons and may prefer not to sell stocks or do much else on the first workday of the week. Arbitrage supports market efficiency and forces the incorporation of information into the markets. If rational means that all available information, fundamental and otherwise, is incorporated into stock prices, then the markets are rational.

The key is that the information that moves the markets goes far beyond simple forecasts of dividends, earnings, and interest rates. In the summer of 1990, Iraq invaded and temporally conquered its neighbor Kuwait. The invasion came as a surprise to both American investors and the American government. Overnight the specter of a war in the Middle East loomed very

DIVIDENDS AND INTEREST RATES MODEL

The Fundamentals section of this chapter presented the simplified Fed Model of the market and suggested that far more complicated models can be developed. In building almost any statistical model for the stock market, the difficulty that confronts an investor is that he or she doesn't know all the values for the factors that affect the market. We know that earnings and interest rates matter; but, when we try to predict next year's market we don't know next year's earnings or interest rates. One leap you can take is to stick to what you do know in building the model. We don't know next year's interest rates, but we do know this year's. Further, one could argue that whatever the market knows about next year's interest rates are reflected in the current rates. (Of course, there is a lot about next year the market or any market players don't know; that's what makes investing interesting.) We can apply the same argument to dividends: We don't know next year's numbers but we do know this year's and it includes anything anyone knows about next year's dividends.

Taking this approach, we add a small wrinkle to the Fed Model, which was based on earnings divided by the yield on the 10-year Treasury note. First, go back to fundamentals and use dividends, not earnings. Second, we decide that the market's value (the level of the S&P 500) is related to or proportional

FIGURE 17-2   Model of the S&P 500

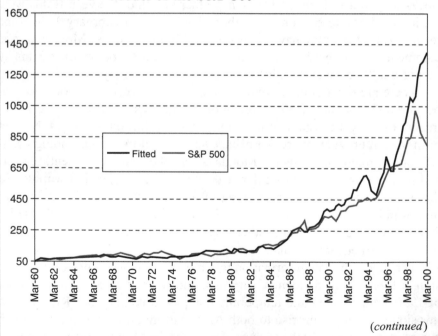

(*continued*)

to the ratio of dividends to Treasury yields. Third, we apply a little bit of statistics: We set up an equation, transform it to logarithms (where we lose most of the readers) and then fit a regression equation. The result is a formula for the fitted value of the S&P 500. Figure 17-2 shows the actual market and the results of the equation. As with the Fed Model, as of the end of the first quarter of 2000, the market is far above the model. Both the gap in 1999–2000 and in 1996 stem from the rise in interest rates. In 1996, the Fed caused havoc in the bond market but miraculously left equities alone. The Fed tightening that began in mid-1999 is also sparing equities. One reason for this lucky break is that in both cases the economy kept growing while the Fed attacked inflation.

Other than sounding fancier, is this an improvement over the Fed Model? Only a little more complexity is involved, but one can see the separate effects of interest rates and dividends. Moreover, this model is a better statistical fit than the Fed Model and is also closer to the spirit of dividend discount models and the underlying forces that determine fundamental stock values. Both are far from the psychological forces ever-present in the markets— but that would require a far more complex model.

---

large. Few American investors had much knowledge of the disagreements between Iraq and Kuwait and few knew very much about either nation or its politics and leadership. In short order the American press began to paint Sadam Hussein, the Iraqi leader, as the devil incarnate. Fears of war rose and stocks fell. This all happened too quickly—from the start of August through the end of October 1990—for the fundamentals to shift much or for any significant number of companies to alter their dividend policies. The information being incorporated into the market was not about dividends—it was about Americans' fear of a war in the Middle East that would lead to death abroad and disruption at home. Since the shooting part of the Gulf War was over in a matter of weeks in early 1991 with very few American casualties, it turned out that investors' fears were fortunately misplaced. However, this didn't make the correction of 1990 any less real or any less costly for many investors.

In the late 1990s and into 2000 there is a different kind of information driving the market. One hears stories of the new economy, soaring productivity, falling unemployment, and never-ending economic growth. These comments may seem a bit exaggerated, but they are not atypical of what investors are hearing or saying. The comments reflect a lot of optimism and high expectations about the economy and about anything related to computer technology and the Internet, the driving forces of the new economy. With the optimism in the air, is it any wonder that the stocks of many technology companies have been driven sky-high? The late 1990s may be an extreme case of this kind of euphoria—over the last six months of 1999 the technology-heavy Nasdaq index climbed 50 percent. Market psychology, reflecting mass psychology, has driven the market to levels 40 percent or more above the fundamentals based on earnings and dividends. In March 2000 some of the euphoria wore off and NASDAQ dropped sharply.

For investors the market psychology is a fact of investing life—one that should be considered and grappled with, one that often has no easy way out. By comparing the market's actual level to the price level predicted by a fundamental model, we can identify the impact of the psychological factors in the market. At present (May 2000) the psychological factors are large and have pushed prices to levels significantly higher than the fundamental values. Moreover, once we begin looking for signs of the overly optimistic, bullish psychology, they are not hard to find. Any Internet company is treated as though it will be the next Microsoft, Cisco, or GE within a few years. Price–earnings ratios are driven to levels that can only be justified if the stock grows at 50 percent annually for 10 or 20 years—by which time it will have swallowed up the entire stock market.

But, before one concludes that this kind of bullish optimism means any sane investor will sell everything and hold only Treasury bills, recognize that almost the same story could have been told in the spring of 1999, 1998, 1997, or even 1996—and the markets have not plunged yet. The psychological factors in the market often seem to follow their own rules and do not always obey what one might call common sense. One aspect of these psychological factors is that the size or extent of a reaction rarely seems comparable to the action that precipitated it. An offhand remark by a Fed official can send stocks plunging. The mere rumor of a ruling in the Microsoft antitrust proceedings managed to send stocks into a weeklong plunge in April 2000. Yet, the ruling was widely anticipated and held no real surprises. In contrast, other rulings and developments in the case—including apparent contradictions in video testimony by key witnesses—went completely unnoticed.

What should investors do when faced with the swirling, shifting sands of market psychology? Use one or another fundamental model, compare it to the market price, and see which way the psychological winds are blowing. Also consider whether they are strengthening or weakening. Now consider how much risk you want to take. If you don't like any risks and stocks are selling far above their fundamental values, reducing the portion of your financial assets in the market is probably a good idea. But, this is not a free ride. If you sell now and stock prices keep rising, you won't keep making money. Of course, if stocks fall, you will feel quite smart. The same kind of thing can be said in reverse. The best time to buy stocks in recent (maybe not-so-recent) memory was the spring and early summer of 1982. The S&P 500 offered a p–e ratio of about eight times; the economy was in a severe recession, and everyone seemed worried about interest rates and the deficit. However, a simple calculation would have suggested that stocks were drastically undervalued. Subsequent results suggest that this would have been correct—stock prices rose sharply beginning in August 1982.

An investor need not view this as an all-or-nothing proposition. It is not a case of betting everything or betting nothing. Indeed, the best use of these checks of market psychology may be to decide what portion of your investments should be in stocks now. Some analysts argue in favor of market timing—trying to get in or out of the market just before it rises or falls. This is a nice goal, but it seldom, if ever, works. A more reasonable approach is to combine one's own willingness to take risks with what one thinks is the level of risk inherent in the market to decide on a mix of stocks and cash that is comfortable. This is the beginning of asset allocation, the topic of Part IV.

IV

BUILDING PORTFOLIOS OF STOCKS AND INDEXES

This is not only the last section of the book, but also the most important. In this section we will turn all the discussion of stock indexes and investing into a series of concrete portfolios, investment plans. Because not all investors are the same, four different portfolios are offered here. Of course, there are more than four kinds of investors. However, the four shown here are a useful guide and should give most readers a head start in deciding how they want to use stock indexes to manage their own money.

Choosing a portfolio depends on two sets of decisions and two sets of information. The first, which consumed most of the book so far, involves what investments are available and how they compare. Do you want to stick with relatively less volatile large-cap stocks or do you want to plunge into small caps? If you want to invest outside the United States, will you choose developed countries like England, Germany, Australia, or Japan, or will you consider emerging markets as well? At the detailed level, which small-cap index is preferred? All these questions matter, but taken all together, they only answer half the puzzle of where to invest.

The other half involves you, the investor. It hinges on two related concerns: risk and time. If you worry about your investments all the time, if you feel that your resources are limited and you cannot afford to lose much money, you are likely to feel more comfortable with a portfolio that tends to be less volatile, less likely to plunge and wrench your stomach. On the other hand, if you feel optimistic—can always see past a rainy day or a momentary pullback in the markets—or if you are comfortable not checking your balances for long periods of time, you might prefer a more aggressive portfolio that accepts higher risks in search of higher rewards. Time also matters. The traditional advice is that the longer you have before you will need the money, the more aggressive you should be with your money. While that is a good generalization, the details are a bit more complex.

This part of the book examines all these issues and shows how to build different portfolios using indexes. We begin with the key to the puzzle, asset allocation. As explained in Chapter 18, this is the most important decision. We will see how finance and economics addresses these concerns. Then we look at some of the related tools—defining asset classes and why this matters more than anything else and how it can be approached. Next we turn to some understandings of time and risk and avoiding false myths of market timing. Finally, we bring it all together with our four portfolios and end with some comments about what to avoid.

18

THE KEY TO PERFORMANCE: ASSET ALLOCATION

ASSET ALLOCATION MATTERS

Choosing where and how to invest involves making a lot of decisions. Some are very detailed, such as whether to buy 100 or 200 shares of a particular stock or which new Internet-based B2B dot com is the most attractive right now. Other decisions are more basic and more general—how much of your money to put into U.S. stocks, foreign stocks, or bonds or to keep as cash.

For most investors, relatively little time is spent on these basic issues and a good deal of time is spent on the detailed problems. That is unfortunate, since formal research and experience show that the basic asset allocation decisions are often the most important ones. The formal studies have engendered a fair amount of debate among academics and investment professionals, but few counter arguments to the idea that asset allocations make a big difference in performance. It is usually a bigger difference than most anything else once you decide to invest.[41] For any investor asset allocation is important. For most investors it is the most important decision they make.

If you look at the stocks, bonds, and mutual funds you own, you are likely to find some stocks that collapsed and others (we hope) that soared. You may even find some bonds or mutual funds with outsize gains or losses. If you are skilled enough to always own stocks like Qualcomm, which rose 2700 percent in 1999, then you can put all your money in one stock and be happy. If you're like the rest of us (and if you're reading this book, you probably can't guarantee always picking the next Qualcomm) some of your stocks were like the 256 stocks in the S&P 500 that fell in 1999. The point of the asset allocation argument is that over time stocks tend to perform alike. Even the superstocks come back to earth after a while. However, as stocks and bonds move around, stocks tend to behave like other stocks and bonds like other bonds. Over the long haul what matters most is whether you choose stocks or bonds. More formally, stocks are called an *asset class*, a group of investments with some common characteristics and performances. Asset classes are important when we put asset allocation to work.

Asset classes do matter. Figure 18-1 shows the differing results you would have gotten from the S&P 500 and 10-year Treasuries from early 1989 to early 2000. An investment of $1000 in the S&P 500 became almost $6500 while the same investment in 10-year Treasuries would have grown to only $2300. However, these bonds were less volatile. The biggest monthly drop in these bonds was $104 while the biggest drop in the S&P 500 investment was over $700. These numbers show us the trade-off that asset allocation is concerned with: we all like bigger profits and returns, but we don't like bigger risks and losses. How much of one should we give up to get rid of the other?

FIGURE 18-1   Comparing the S&P 500 and Treasuries

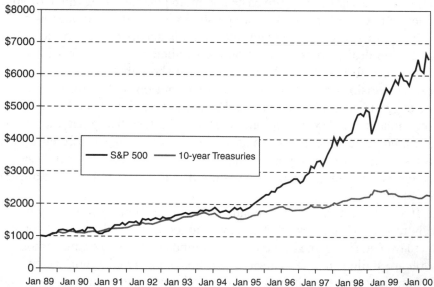

Every investment book, including this one, talks about *diversification*, spreading your money around. A hint of what this can do is seen in Table 18-1. We have a simple set of examples based on four investment options: U.S. stocks modeled by the S&P 500, foreign stocks modeled by the MSCI EAFE index, bonds modeled by the Lehman index of 10-year Treasuries, and cash (or money market funds) modeled by the Lehman index of 6-month Treasury bills. The table shows the returns and risks over the period from February 1989 to April 2000. Returns are simply monthly averages compounded to annual rates; risks are monthly standard deviations stated as annual rates.

Instead of looking at the four different options, we have mixed and matched them to create four portfolios. These are all arbitrary examples to see the power of diversification and asset allocation. Figure 18-2 plots the four asset classes and our four portfolios by comparing the returns and risks available. The returns are measured on the vertical axis and the risks on the horizontal axis. Ideally you would like to be in the upper left corner with very high returns and very low risks. That is not easy, and none of these fall in that spot. The worst case would be the lower right corner with low returns and high risks; foreign stocks don't look very attractive in the example. Table 18-2 shows the combinations used for the four portfolios. Each one is a mix of the same percentages among the four asset classes. They are named by which asset class is given the highest percentage, 40 percent. Note that this is not all the possible combinations—nor is the best or worse likely to be found here. But Figure 18-2 shows the effect of diversification.

Figure 18-2 shows the four asset classes and the four portfolios. The portfolios all have returns and risks between the best asset class (U.S. stocks) and the worst (cash). However, they tend to be closer to the hot spot of the upper left-hand corner than any of the individual asset classes. The exact mix does matter; the 40US has a better return than the 40EAFE and almost the same risk. There is something to diversification, but how can one choose the right mix?

TABLE 18-1   Return versus Risk (February 1989 to April 2000)

	Return	Risk
S&P 500	19.1	13.6
EAFE	8.3	17.2
Treasury Bond	7.9	6.7
Cash	5.8	1.9

FIGURE 18-2   Return versus Risk of Sample Portfolios and Asset Classes

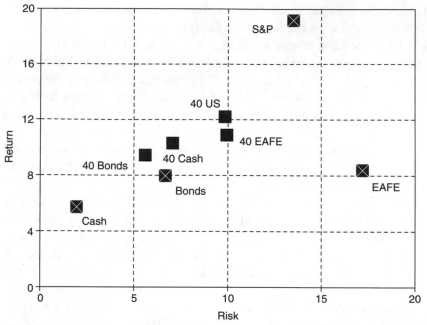

A VERY SHORT GUIDE TO MARKOWITZ

Guessing at portfolios weighted 40–30–20–10 may be one way to allocate assets, but there is a much better way based on work done in the 1950s by Harry Markowitz, a pioneer of modern portfolio theory and a Nobel Laureate. A lot of modern finance, including measures like beta as well as asset allocation, has its roots in his work.[42] Markowitz took the idea of diversification and made it the center of an approach to selecting the right asset allocation. He recognized that if we could find two assets where one rose while the other fell, we would have some automatic protection against collapse. To do this, we look at the correlation between the returns of dif-

TABLE 18-2   Composition of Sample Portfolios

	40 S&P	40 EAFE	40 Bond	40 Cash
S&P 500	40%	30%	20%	30%
EAFE	30	40	10	20
Bond	20	10	40	10
Cash	10	20	30	40

ferent assets. If the returns on stocks always rise when bonds rise and always fall when bonds fall, they are perfectly correlated—and useless for diversification. This is not the case with stocks and bonds: In August 1998, when the S&P 500 portfolio in Figure 18-1 lost $700, the bonds gained $89. But, if one looked at two technology stocks, they probably did rise and fall together most of the time.

Second, Markowitz set a specific goal for doing asset allocation. He developed the mathematical tools to identify those portfolios where the only way to get higher returns is to take on more risk. This is also the portfolios where the only way to lower the risks is to accept lower returns. These portfolios form a line on the chart of returns and risks seen in Figures 18-2 and 18-3.

Efficient is a term economists use when something is clearly preferred to something else —no matter what someone's personal opinion or taste may be. Given a choice between two investment portfolios where one has higher returns and lower risks than the other, the preferred choice is obvious. On Figure 18-3 we have added the efficient frontier for the four asset classes in the example. The points are the same points as in Figure 18-2, some of the labels were dropped to keep things readable.

FIGURE 18-3   The Efficient Frontier

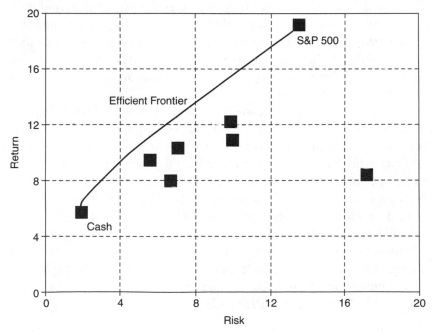

Because the efficient frontier incorporates the essence of asset allocation and diversification, it is worth a few extra words. Points above and to
the left of the frontier may be desirable, but we can't get there. We would
all like an investment as low risk as Treasury bills with a 20 percent annual return. Alas there aren't any to be had. Points below the frontier are
clearly those to be avoided, such as foreign stocks in the 1990s when Japan's
stock market crashed. On the frontier the top end is always the highest return asset available, regardless of risk, and the low end is always the lowest risk asset, regardless of return. The points along the frontier are all
equally valid and interesting; they represent a menu of efficient portfolios
that offer the best combinations of risk and return.

How do we choose where we want to be on the frontier? You, the investor, have to decide how much risk you can afford. If you have no fear,
go for the top right-hand end of the frontier. If you are nervous or if you
will need the money very soon, go for the lower left-hand end. Anyone
else, read on to the discussions on time horizons and choosing a risk level.
In the end, though, choosing how much risk is a personal decision, not one
an investment adviser or an investment book can make for you.

WHAT DOES RISK MEAN?

Of all the various elements of asset allocation and diversification, probably the most debated is the definition of risk as the standard deviation of
an asset's returns. First, for most people the last thing they confronted (but
didn't understand) in statistics was standard deviation. Second, once they
read a little about it, they discover that the mathematics seems to say that
seeing the return 10 percent too high adds as much to risk as seeing the
return come in 10 percent too low.

The standard deviation is a convenient way to measure how volatile or
dispersed a series of numbers are. Look at the returns paid by a money
market fund—month in and month out, the annual rate is likely to be very
stable. Over a few years, the highest number might be 5.5 percent and the
lowest 4.5 percent. Little variation and a lot of certainty about what you
get. Now look at a stock index like the S&P 500. There is a lot more bouncing around. While the average return (stated as an annualized number) may
be around 10 percent, some months plunge and others soar. Stocks are more
volatile than money markets. Standard deviation uses a formula that does
two things. First, it compares each monthly number to the average of all
monthly numbers and then calculates the average difference between the
monthly numbers and the average. (If there are too many averages in the

last sentence remember that statisticians call the average the *mean* and think of the standard deviation as a measure based on the average difference between a group of numbers and their mean.) Second, the calculation does treat highs and lows the same—all these differences are squared so that we don't have to worry about negative signs. A rough rule of thumb, also extracted from deep in statistics, is that two-thirds of the returns will be between the average plus one standard deviation and the average minus one standard deviation.

In very simple terms, big numbers for standard deviations mean volatility and risk. What's a big number? If given as an annual rate (the most common version), anything above 20 is big. The figure for the S&P 500, depending on the time period used for the measurement, is likely to be between 10 and 25. For T-bills and money market funds, numbers under 5 are common; for bonds, figures from 3 to as high as 8 or 10 are typical.

Why is this a good measure of risk? The risk in investing is that the unexpected happens. In the summer of 1998 your stocks—which you thought would rise forever with the coming of the new economy—collapsed in August when Russia defaulted on some bonds. The unexpected happened. A glance at the standard deviation, however, would have warned you that the unexpected often does happen with stocks.

Why does an unexpectedly high return add as much to "risk" as an unexpected low return? Ideally it shouldn't. In Markowitz's original work he discussed using a one-sided measure of standard deviation called *semivariance.* At the time (1950s) he set aside this idea because the computers couldn't handle the calculations that would have been involved. Subsequently, various economists and financial analysts have experimented with semivariance; a few people use it. However, it turns out to make relatively little difference for most investment problems. More often than not, the variation in returns of most asset classes are *symmetric.* Higher than expected values are as likely as lower than expected values. As a result, there is no difference in the results or the efficient frontier when calculated. One reason that the returns are generally symmetric is that asset allocation analyses usually use monthly or quarterly data. Daily returns tend to have other statistical quirks (including a phenomenon named "fat tails") that create some difficulties.

In short, risk is a gauge of the unexpected happening to you, and most people don't like that. Standard deviation, for all its difficulties, is the best yardstick for measuring risk that anyone has found in the last 50 or more years.

WHAT DOES RETURN MEAN?

Returns are simpler than risks, at least at first glance. Returns are what you expect to get. The numbers and the figures shown previously are all based on what happened over the past 10 or so years. We know these numbers; we don't know what will happen in the next 5, 10, or 20 years. Yet, we are investing now for the future, not in the past. Forecasting future returns is not only possible, but also essential. Relying on the average results of recent years as a guide to the future is likely to lead to missed opportunities or worse. At the end of 1981, the economy was in a recession, inflation was high and the market was falling. Over the last five years stocks had earned 9 percent annually, and inflation had consumed all of that. Real estate—always a great bet for inflationary times—looked much better. But, less than a year later the great bull market began. Of course, someone at the beginning of 2000 merely looking at recent data would assume that stocks always return 25 percent a year. We doubt it, but time will tell. In Chapter 19 we will look at asset classes and discuss plausible future returns for each one.

The same arguments about expected returns can be made about risks. We need to forecast risk as much as we need to forecast return. However, risks tend to be more consistent and stable over time than returns, and it is safer to assume that the past pattern of risks and correlations among asset classes will persist than it is to assume that returns will repeat their past patterns. It is also far more difficult to forecast risks. On balance, most analyses use risks that closely follow experience but independently forecast returns.

FINDING YOUR SPOT ON THE EFFICIENT FRONTIER

Getting to your right asset allocation requires two kinds of information. First you need information about the investments you can make. That is what most of this book covers. Second, you need information about your own situation and the risks you are willing to accept. That depends on you, not on the investments. The rest of this chapter will look at some of the questions about your own risks that are worth thinking about. We start with the relation between risks and how long you will hold the investments, then we turn to other aspects of the risks.

There is a common belief that the longer the time you are planning to hold your investments, the more risk you should take. One ancient guide to retirement planning was that the percentage of bonds in your portfolio should equal your age. If you were 25 years old, 25 percent should be in bonds; if you were 65 years old, 65 percent should be in bonds. Likewise,

TABLE 18-3   Risk and Returns over Different Time Horizons

	1 Yr	5 Yrs	10 Yrs	20 Yrs
Standard deviation	16.4	6.2	4.7	3.1
Maximum return	52.1	28.7	21.2	18.6
Minimum return	−26.5	−0.8	2.5	6.9
Range of returns	78.6	29.5	18.7	11.7

many financial advisers use time horizons as a measure of risk. While the idea that more risk is reasonable for longer time horizons generally makes sense, the details are not that simple.

A common argument about time and risk is based on calculating the average annual return for stocks over periods of 1 year, 5 years, and 10 years and looking at the range of numbers. In Table 18-3 this kind of analysis is done for the S&P 500 for investment periods ending in 1945 through 1999.

The first row shows the standard deviation of the annual returns measured over investment horizons of 1 year, 5 years, 10 years, and 20 years. The longer the horizons, the lower the standard deviations, suggesting less risk. The next two lines show the highest and lowest single figures found. As the horizon gets longer the maximum drops and the minimum rises, and the range (the last line) declines. All this suggests that the longer you invest, the less risk there is. Measured as the annual return, that is the case. However, we are not always interested in only the annual return. We are also concerned with how much money we have at the end. This is called the *terminal value*, or *terminal wealth*.

We can do the same kind of thing with terminal wealth and find some rather different results. See Table 18-4. For terminal wealth what we measure is how much we would have after 1 year or 5, 10, or 20 years for an investment of $1. For example, the best 1-year period was a return of about

TABLE 18-4   Terminal Wealth Ratios for Different Time Horizons

	1 Yr	5 Yrs	10 Yrs	20 Yrs
Standard deviation	0.2	0.5	1.4	5.9
Maximum ratio	1.5	3.5	6.1	26.8
Minimum ratio	0.7	0.9	1.1	2.0
Range ratio	0.8	2.6	5.0	24.9

50 percent giving a maximum of 1.5; the worst was a return of −30 percent for a terminal value of 0.7. As one moves from one 1 year to 5 years to 10 and 20 years, the maximum and minimum must climb because we are looking at longer and longer investment time periods. The variability of terminal wealth, as measured by its standard deviation, also rises. However, the chance of a loss—a terminal ratio less than 1—falls. Whether this makes you feel better over time depends on how you want to define risk.

The tables don't show a third view, but one that is potentially a big concern for some. The size of a small probability loss rises. In other words, if you are very pessimistic and define risk as a loss so bad there is only a 1 in 100 chance of it occurring, this devastating loss gets bigger as time increases.

Tables 18-3 and 18-4 are based on specific data—the S&P 500 annual returns from 1926 forward. One can do the same analyses using assumptions about the market's statistical properties. But, part of the answer depends on what we believe drives the market and part depends on what we are trying to measure—annual return or terminal wealth.[43]

Glib arguments that time takes care of risk should be looked at carefully, because it isn't always exactly the case. However, there are some cases where time is a very important way to control risk. First, in a long-term investment program you are not likely to set up your plan and *never* touch it again for the next 20 years. You may not day trade your retirement account, but you probably will, and certainly should, look at every it year or so. If things change, you can adjust your investment strategy. This ability to make adjustments can be a big factor in ameliorating risks. One adjustment is to change your contributions to take advantage of increased income or changes in the financial markets. Second, if worse comes to worse and your retirement account is caught in a steep market decline, there may be enough time to raise your contributions and still reach some reasonable goals. In this case, time definitely does affect risks. Finally, if you believe that the market will always come back and will, if you wait long enough, always pay a reasonable return, then enough time would control risks. Of course, enough time may be a very long time.

Taken together, there are good reasons to accept more risk when the investment time horizon is longer. Further, the time horizon is often longer than you think. Most people planning for retirement assume that they have a time horizon that ends with the day they retire. This may not be the best way to look at things. At age 65 most people have about another 20 years of life expectancy. So, if you are 55 and looking at retirement in 10 years, the truth is that you plan to start drawing down your nest egg in 10 years and make the nest egg last for another 20 years. While you will probably do a major review of your investments when you retire, the time horizon seen from today (at age 55) is more like 20 or 30 years than only 10 years to retirement. If you do well and can leave something behind to your heirs, the time horizon could be even longer. Sometimes the life of the money exceeds the life of the investor. One practical result of this is that the old rule of thumb about the percentage of bonds being equal to your age probably gives you too little in stocks.

One aspect of time and risk that won't go away is at the short end. Financial markets are volatile. If you are planning to buy a house in a year, don't invest the down payment in some hot corner of the stock market.

CONSIDERING YOUR OWN TIME HORIZON

If you are saving for retirement and need a rough figure for the time horizon in years, figure how long to your planned retirement date. Then estimate how long you may live in retirement and add half that amount to time until retirement. The reason to add half the amount is that during retirement you will consume the nest egg, so it is declining over the retirement period. Of course, you will need to take advantage of the time by periodically reviewing your situation and probably adjusting your investments. For other investments, the time considerations are probably easier. For things like college savings plans, there shouldn't be all that much uncertainty about how long the investment horizon is.

WHAT ABOUT RISK?

The question is really not risk, but how much risk are you willing to accept in hopes of more return. Will you focus all your efforts on one sector, like technology, or diversify across a wide range of different kinds of stocks? Will you bury yourself in bonds or keep all your money in equities?

Professionally managed pension funds usually prepare long detailed statements of their investment policy to describe and explain how much risk they will take. At the other extreme, some investors jump in without even a sidelong glance. Increasingly financial planners and brokers are urging individuals to consider risk as they develop comprehensive financial plans for themselves. While some customers think this is simply a gimmick to sell more mutual funds, these exercises in risk exploration can be useful.

In most risk assessment questionnaires there are three areas of interest. One, time horizons, we covered above. The others are the investor's comfort or willingness to take on risks and his or her ability to carry the risks. Ability is simple to describe. If the investments go south, will you go to the poorhouse? Someone who is already deeply in debt should not be risking their last pennies on a high-flying high-risk investment. Some of the typical questions posed to investors include how much of one's monthly income goes to pay off old credit card bills, if the investor owns his or her home, and how much equity he or she has in it. If a reversal in the market, even a rather unlikely reversal, will cause disaster, the investor is in over his head and should get out before the worst happens.

How much risk someone is willing to accept is more difficult to define. Most of the questionnaires and most planners are really trying to educate investors with a little history while scaring them enough without chasing away any potential clients. In the end, all one can say is that markets do fall—usually more than most investors expect they will. Falling markets are no fun, but only you can even guess how much of a collapse is too much. If you have read the various discussions of market history in this book, you already know as much about what has happened as most investors. If you didn't read anything here that worried you even a bit, go read some really scary tales of the bear market of 1974 or the crash of 1929. Figure out what it means to say the market fell by 80 percent from 1929 to 1932.

Of course, a short questionnaire can't teach market history, so sometimes it tries to be both plausible and a little frightening. A common question is to ask what you would do if the market fell by 20 percent—bail out and sell everything, buy more stocks, or something in between. Then, having suggested a 20 percent plunge, the next question may be, "If the market declines by an additional 15 percent, what would you do now? Look how little money is left!"

In Chapter 20 we present four sample portfolios. Think about what level of risk you think is reasonable. We also present some statistics about what these portfolios would have done in recent years. Their volatility and your thoughts about risk may be able to give you some guidance.

19

ASSET ALLOCATION FOR OURSELVES

Armed with the background about asset allocation from Chapter 18, we can begin to put together an investment plan. The key building blocks are asset classes—groups of stocks or bonds that are alike in the way they behave over time, with similar risk/return behavior that is different from other asset classes. When working with indexes, asset classes can be represented by index funds or ETFs and one doesn't have to search through actively managed funds or individual stocks for the ones that will behave as expected.

Broadly defined asset classes include domestic stocks, foreign stocks, bonds, or cash. Each of these is quite different from the others. Stocks represent hoped-for future profits from a corporation—big gains if things work out and nothing if things fail. Bonds are promises to pay agreed-upon sums of money; either you get what was promised or you don't, but there are no upside riches. Cash is, well, cash. Foreign stocks add in the additional risks of foreign exchange and different laws, regulations, and customs.

Asset classes are often defined more precisely than just stocks, bonds, cash, and foreign stocks. Most of the definitions and attention is focused on U.S. stocks. Further, for most U.S. investors, this is where they concentrate their efforts to raise returns and lower risks. Anyone who has read much about mutual funds or money management has come upon box diagrams, usually with three columns and three rows like this:

177

	Growth	Blend	Value
Large cap			
Midcap			
Small cap			

This is the common way to define asset classes for U.S. stocks. Stocks are classified by market capitalization and whether they are growth or value stocks. "Blend" or sometimes "core" covers portfolios or mutual funds that mix growth and value in roughly equal weightings. This division is based on the Fama-French three-factor model discussed in Chapters 14 and 15. The combination of these two factors produces the nine categories shown in the box diagram. There are indexes for all categories, but there are not always index funds for each category. We will focus on large-cap growth and value and on midcap and small cap. Foreign stocks don't fit in the box diagram, but they are important and merit consideration as well.

Bonds are not as simple as one might expect. First, there is a major split in tax treatment. Bonds issued by state and city governments and their agencies usually pay interest that is exempt from federal income taxes. Among taxable bonds there are also many different flavors and varieties with different risk and return patterns. For the asset allocations here, we will distinguish among four different asset classes of bonds: investment grade straight debt, junk bonds, asset-backed securities and bonds denominated in currencies other than the U.S. dollar. What follows is a brief tour of these asset classes and what they can do for you as you build a portfolio.

LARGE-CAP STOCKS OF THE S&P 500

This is the starting point of almost any long-term investment plan in the United States. For the past 75 years stocks have offered substantially better returns than bonds, with some additional risk. The long history was referred to earlier and is explained in detail in some recent studies.[44]

Large-cap stocks usually mean stocks with a market capitalization of about $4 billion or more. As a point of reference, at the end of May 2000, the largest company in the S&P 500 and the largest U.S. corporation, General Electric, had a market capitalization that was about $521 billion. Company number 354 in the S&P 500, NCR Corporation, had a market capitalization of just over $4 billion. Generally speaking, large cap refers to either the S&P 500 or to the 400 to 500 largest publicly traded companies in the U.S. markets. Of all companies in the stock market, these tend to be the most established. Further, their size and experience usually means that there is less financial risk in their stocks than in securities of smaller companies.

One can look at even narrower definitions than the S&P 500. There is the S&P 100, an index drawn from the companies in the S&P 500. This list has far less turnover and much more stability that the S&P 500. Moreover, in periods when large-cap stocks dominate the markets, as they did in 1995 to 1999, the S&P 100 can be an excellent choice. Another narrowly based large-cap list is the ever-famous Dow Jones Industrials. If you want to hold only the blue chip stocks, a simple choice is to buy the 30 stocks in the Dow Industrials.

Over the last 25 years (1975–1999 inclusive) the S&P 500 has returned about 15.7 percent before adjusting for inflation. Inflation averaged about 4.7 percent over the period, so the inflation adjusted or real rate is about 11 percent. While 25 years is certainly a long period, the comparison may be somewhat tilted to good results. 1975 followed a deep bear market in 1973–1974 which severely depressed stock prices, while 1999 was at the end of a record-breaking run of very good returns.

As we have argued numerous times before in this book, stocks are not without risk. While the risks in large-cap stocks are usually less than in small-cap stocks or foreign stocks, they are still greater than bonds. Stocks do fall. Moreover, after long periods of time when they rise unusually fast, they often stall out or fall. In short, stocks are very far from assured and should be considered as risky. However, if one were asked to build a portfolio with only two asset classes, large-cap U.S. stocks would be one of the two chosen. Further, investing in large-cap stocks with index funds or exchange traded funds offers the lowest costs of virtually any investment you are likely to consider.

GROWTH VERSUS VALUE

Chapter 14 discussed growth and value. They can and should be seen as distinct asset classes because they do have different risk and return patterns. Over the entire 25-year period, which is the history of the growth/value split of the S&P 500, value beats growth. Value returns 16.0 percent versus 15.0 percent for growth, and value has less risk: the standard deviation is 14.2 percentage points for value versus 16.2 percentage points for growth. However, growth may be catching value—growth beat value in the past 5 and 10 years. More important, or more frustrating, for investors is the fact that their performances can be very different in short time periods. In the five years through 1999, growth returned 28.2 percent per year, while value returned 18.9 percent, almost 10 percentage points less. Value did retain its low-risk edge by about a percentage point of the same five years. This huge margin of returns may have been magnified by the strong market, but being on the wrong side of the growth/value fence could be very disappointing.

Growth and value offer two key lessons for portfolio building. First, risk matters. The lower risks make value stocks attractive and have preserved their importance even in a period when they lagged growth stocks badly. Second, if one needs any reminder that the returns that matter are the ones we don't know—the future returns—growth and value offer that reminder. There is no widely accepted or easy way to forecast which one of the growth/value pair will win out in any year. About all that can be reliably said is that while any period when one beats the other will include a few months of reversal, there does seem to be some momentum and consistency over periods of a year or two or three. If you see a clear pattern that has run for a year to a year and a half, a bet that it will continue for a little while longer is probably a reasonable assumption.

SMALL CAPS

One of the most enduring debates in investment and finance is the "small-cap effect," the idea that small-cap stocks do better than large-cap stocks and that any serious long-term investor should own a lot of small-cap stocks. One thing that is clear about small caps: whether or not returns are greater than large caps, the risks are greater. The arguments about greater returns center around a debate about whether there were some occasional periods when small caps outperformed large caps or if there is a sustainable pattern. Given that returns of both large- and small-cap stocks bounce around a bit, one would expect to find periods when small caps do better than large caps. In effect, history does not make an airtight case for buying small-cap stocks; nor does history give enough solid hints about when small caps will outperform their large brethren. History does confirm that the risks tend to be larger in small caps than in large caps. Moreover, in almost any market downturn, a common complaint is that the major indexes, such as the S&P 500 and the Dow Industrials, understate the extent of the damage. The damage that is understated is the damage among small-cap stocks.

One thing small caps are probably not is the next Microsoft or Cisco. Somehow investors all have the image of small-cap stocks as being two people building Web sites in the "dotcom garage." As romantic as this may be, it is a bit of an exaggeration. The original work on small-cap stocks was based on the bottom 20 percent of the New York Stock Exchange list by size. This group certainly includes a lot of interesting companies, but few genuine garage owners. As for the dotcoms of the 1990s, most of those managed to be large caps at their initial public offerings. Moreover, their fate seems to be following a new pattern, not one based on an alleged history as a small-cap stock. As to how or where to find the next Microsoft or Cisco, unfortunately neither the theories about small-cap outperformance or anything else offers a sure bet to success.

A look through the data over the last 75 years does show that an investor who bought and stuck with small-cap stocks would suffer much greater swings in value and bigger risks, but would in the end be rewarded for his or her suffering with larger returns. These points are worth remembering when you consider how risky a portfolio you want. If you conclude you are an aggressive investor—one who will gladly take additional risks in hopes of being in the right place in one of those rare right moments when everything works together—then small-cap stocks are likely to be something worth your consideration.

Small-cap stocks raise another issue related to asset class construction for building portfolios. The proportions, or weights, assigned to each asset class are usually judged in comparison to the overall market. If we look at small caps compared to all U.S. equities, they represent a very small portion of the overall market. As a proportion of the overall U.S. equity market—excluding foreign issues, ADRs, ETFs, closed-end funds, and other nonequity instruments—small caps are slightly less than 7 percent of total capitalization even though they are about 85 percent of the number of stocks listed. Large caps are 83 percent of the market cap and 6 percent of the number of stocks listed. Midcaps make up the rest. If a portfolio holds 7 percent of its equities in small caps, it is "market weighted." An aggressive investor betting on small caps would hold more than 7 percent of his equity funds in small-cap stocks. How much more is open to debate, but a 100 percent overweighting to raise the small cap percentage to 14 percent is probably a lot by most money management standards. The real point is that the market portfolio is really a large-cap portfolio and small-cap investing requires a conscious decision to focus on this asset class.

INTERNATIONAL STOCKS

Foreign stocks, equity securities issued by companies in other countries, is an asset class of considerable interest. Terms need to be defined in this area. *International* usually means securities from any country other than the United States while *global* means securities from any country including the United States. While this may be different than the dictionary definition of these terms, that is the way they are usually used in investments, especially for mutual funds.

A second definition is the difference between emerging markets and developed or industrial countries. *Emerging markets* is the investment term for developing nations or what used to be referred to as less developed countries, or LDCs. This business of names is no small matter for the countries concerned since it affects their ability to raise capital in global markets, to borrow from banks, and—most of all—their national egos. Despite the importance of designating a country as emerging or developed, there is no universal agreement on either the factors that determine developing status or who should make the categorization. Some cases are clear: England and Japan are developed industrial nations, Malaysia is an emerging market. Others are often open to debate, especially in southern or eastern Europe. Greece is generally expected to "graduate" to developed status around the time it becomes a full member of the European Community.

For U.S.-based investors who keep their accounts in U.S. dollars, investing in any nation outside the home country raises the specter of foreign exchange risks. Investing in emerging markets raises a whole other layer of risks as well. We look at issues surrounding developed nations first and then briefly turn to the emerging markets.

Developed Nations

For investors holding stocks issued in other countries the first new concern is the foreign exchange risk. The stocks' principal markets are likely to be somewhere other than the U.S., and the trading will be in something other than the U.S. dollar. This means that aside from whether the stocks or the funds rise or fall, you also have to worry about the currency. Currency movements of 10 percent, 20 percent, or more during the course of a year are quite possible. The new common European currency, the euro, began life at about $1.17 per euro; a year later it was worth barely a dollar. An investor holding European stocks would have lost almost 15 percent during 1999 from the currency swings before even considering what the markets overseas did. Of course, the movements can go the other way and the U.S. dollar can fall, offering investors in foreign stocks a free ride up. Investors need to recognize that there are some extra risks one doesn't have at home.

There are also some extra benefits. Markets in the United States and other nations are not perfect copies of one another. Often when one is rising another may be pausing or sliding in. Therefore, investing in foreign markets offers a chance to diversify one's holdings and lower the overall risk of the portfolio. This is the biggest reason for looking outside your home country. While sudden shocks, such as Russia's debt default in the summer of 1998, often send turmoil rapidly circling the globe, most market movements that are measured over periods of weeks and months are not perfectly correlated among different countries. This means that diversification will work.

While foreign markets will offer diversification and a free ride to somewhat lower risks, they won't offer higher returns than here at home. In today's modern interconnected globe there is little reason to expect a company in one industrial country to be fundamentally more, or less, profitable than a company in another. Making cars in Europe is not a better or worse business than building cars in the United States or Japan. If it were, the car companies would pick up and move to the better market. Or, baring such a dramatic migration, prices for auto stocks in the more profitable countries would rise while those in the less profitable countries fell to rapidly offset or arbitrage the difference away. Markets work and information flows rapidly. So, getting rich by buying abroad is not likely to work among the developed markets.

It is true that Japan's market substantially outperformed U.S. markets for the 1970s and 1980s. However, other forces may have been at work. First, the exchange rate between the yen and the dollar moved sharply in the yen's favor—from 360 yen/dollar to about 100 yen/dollar. Second, at the beginning of the period, Japan was not as industrialized or as developed as the United States—at the end it was. Finally, some of these swings may take time. Japan's stock market in the 1990s has performed miserably, giving back much of the gains of the 1970s and 1980s compared to the United States.

One last comment about international investing relates to how much of a portfolio to invest outside the United States. The U.S. markets, even after their surge in the second half of the 1990s, represent a bit less than half of the world's equity markets.[45] However, most U.S. investors would feel that putting half of their equity assets outside of the United States was very risky. Even 25 percent of one's holdings in foreign stocks probably seems high to Americans. As a result, few U.S. investors come close to market weighting their international holdings.

Emerging Markets

Emerging markets offer outsize risks and outsize returns. They are also a place where index funds, if available, are often the best way to invest. Almost by definition, investment and financial information at the company level is harder to come by in emerging markets than in developed markets. The risks and the expenses of investing are likely to be greater in emerging markets as well. This means that anything that can mitigate the risk or lower the expenses is attractive. Index funds—through diversification and relatively lower costs—accomplish these goals.

Emerging markets as a group represent only a very small portion of the world's equity.[46] This means that an investor trying to market weight his portfolio will have relatively little exposure to this asset class. However, given the volatility of the asset class—the standard deviation of the S&P/IFC indexes investable index is much larger than the standard deviation of either the S&P 500 or the MSCI EAFE (a common benchmark for industrialized international markets). All this suggests that investors need to understand the risks in emerging markets and probably stay reasonably close to a market weighting unless they fancy themselves as specialists in the field.

BONDS

For most investors the fixed income asset classes are principally used to control risks. *Fixed income* is the traditional term for bonds and money market securities that pay a fixed return. If you buy a bond, things never get better than you expected—if everything goes along perfectly, you still get your interest payments on time and the principal back when the bond matures, nothing more. With a stock, if everything goes perfectly, the stock soars in price. Of course, even with a bond, if everything goes wrong, you don't get anything back at all. People like bonds because in most situations they provide steady interest payments for income. Further, while bonds can be total disasters, most people think they are a bit more stable than stocks and more likely to provide some cushion in hard times. Bonds come in various different varieties and make up a number of asset classes, some of which are best left to professional bond traders who (usually) know what they are getting into.

Bonds usually have credit ratings, and mutual fund companies should indicate what the ratings of the bonds in the fund are. Ratings are assessments of how likely it is that the bond will pay interest and principal on time. Ratings are divided into two broad categories called investment grade and junk. Within either category, there are several different rating levels. The ratings are given by companies that specialize in credit analysis, including Standard & Poor's and Moody's Investor Services.

Bonds are also distinguished by the way payments are structured and whether the payments can vary over the life of the bond. The simplest kind are called either "plain vanilla" or straight debt and offer a fixed interest payment, usually twice a year at a rate set when the bond was originally issued. If an investor wants to hold bonds in a portfolio to limit risks, investment grade straight bonds are a common choice. The risk that the company that issued the bond (and borrowed money from the bond holders) goes bankrupt is not the only risk in owing a bond. When interest rates rise, bond prices fall.[47] Movements in interest rates represent another risk to bond holders.

Some bonds are supported or backed by other financial instruments or loans. One of the most common are mortgage-backed securities, where a financial institution buys mortgages and then issues a bond backed by the mortgages. Anyone who ever read all the fine print on their mortgage knows that you can usually pay it off early if you want (or if you sell the house before 30 years go by). When mortgages that support a bond pay off early, a small part of the bond pays off early. Further, if the mortgages have adjustable interest rates, there may be other changes to the schedule of payments bond investors are expected to receive. These kinds of bonds, often called asset-backed bonds, are more complicated and carry their own risks related to how interest rates gyrate.

The last kind of bond we will mention are junk bonds. These are issued by companies of questionable credit quality which may go bankrupt long before the bonds pay off. Of course, these bonds tend to offer unusually high interest rates. Moreover, if the companies do well, the bonds may turn out to be much better risks than anyone thought. In such cases the ratings usually rise and the prices can climb sharply. Junk bonds involve risks related to the particular companies issuing the bonds. In this way, junk bonds are often more like stocks than they are like investment grade bonds.

CASH

The last asset class is the simplest, but also one of the most important: cash. In investing terms, cash includes investments like Treasury bills or money market funds which have very short maturities and relatively little or no credit risk. Cash usually earns very little interest but offers significant safety and security. For an investor cash meets two different needs. First, if one needs the money soon, cash is the only answer. Planning to make a tuition payment next week or a down payment on a house next month, keep the funds in cash rather than bonds or stocks. The chances of a big drop in stocks in only a month may be modest—but the damage of the losses would be devastating. Second, cash is one of the best ways to reduce risk. In Chapter 12 we showed how a little cash can take a lot of risk out of a portfolio.

Cash does cover a range of different investments, some of which have special aspects. First, money market funds usually come in a few distinct variations, including taxable, tax-exempt municipal bonds, and federal instruments. The interest income in the last is normally exempt from state and local, but not federal, income tax. Second, some 401(k) and other investment programs offer "stable value funds" that look a lot like cash, except the interest rates are a bit better. These are usually guaranteed investment contracts (GICs) offered by insurance companies. The guarantee is only from the insurance company, not the federal government, so treat it with some skepticism at times. The rates are not set in the markets by people trading securities; rather, they are determined by the insurance company based on its own investments and operations. One result is that rates appear to change very little because they are not set in an open market. This can be misleading. If rates in the market move sharply lower or higher, the GIC rates will follow after a while.

For each of these asset classes, there are one or several indexes and, for many of them, index-based investments through mutual funds or exchange traded funds. If the asset classes are design elements of an investment program, the funds are bricks and mortar of that investment plan. Chapter 20 assembles these into a series of four portfolios at different levels of risk. Chapters 21 and 22 consider some of the questions that usually surround long-term investment plans.

20

C H A P T E R

FOUR PORTFOLIOS FOR FOUR INVESTORS

ESTIMATING LONG-RUN RETURNS TO BUILD ALLOCATIONS

The first step in building a portfolio is to catalog the possible asset classes or indexes. If you think of an asset class without finding an index to describe it, practical investment planning will be rather difficult. Even something as far from investing as Impressionist paintings can't be seriously considered as an investment without some measure of its past performance. Of course, most people who buy, or invest, in Impressionist paintings and other fine arts don't do it only for the financial aspects. On the other hand, most mutual fund investors aren't interested in the fund's intrinsic beauty. Once the possible asset classes and indexes are identified, the second step is to estimate or project returns, risks, and correlations. To build a portfolio we need estimates of returns and risks for different asset classes or indexes.

The easiest and most practical way to estimate risks and correlations is to use a reasonably long run of historical data. Risks vary, but far less than returns do. Further, risks and correlations are more difficult to estimate either through guesswork or analytical models. A fairly long period of time should try and encompass at least one recession or market reversal as well as a number of years. In the examples shown here, we use monthly data from early 1989 to May 2000. As is often the case, the data are limited by the availability of a longer historical time series. For many asset classes, especially emerging market equities or certain kinds of bonds, more than 10 or 15 years of data are hard to come by.

Returns are more variable than risks and more important to most investors. As a result, some attention to estimating returns is important. For the portfolios here, we build returns from a series of economic assumptions, as described in Table 20-1.

The stock market doesn't exist and grow independently of the economy. Rather, the market's long-run returns are based on the fortunes of the economy, so we begin with the economy. Economic growth can be projected from growth in the labor force and changes in its productivity. Current demographic estimates for the United States suggest that the labor force will grow about 0.9 percent per year over the next 10 to 20 years. The biggest part of that number is simply people being born and reaching age 16 when they are counted in the labor force. Since everyone who will turn 16 before 2016 has already been born, this number is not that hard to figure. It is also affected by immigration, so a major change in U.S. immigration policies could affect the pace of economic growth.

The second line is productivity, how much the labor force can produce. Until recently this was an obscure number economists debated and everyone else pretty much ignored. In the last two or three years with talk of the

TABLE 20-1   Estimating Long-Run Returns (Using Data from 1989 to 2000)

Economic Element	Percentages
Labor force growth	0.9
Productivity	2.5
Real economic growth	3.4
Inflation	2.6
Nominal economic growth	6.0
Cash return	6.0
10-year government premium	1.0
10-year government	7.0
Equity risk premium	3.3
Large-cap equities	10.3
Small-caps premium	1.0
Small-cap equities	11.3
International	10.3

"new" economy, productivity has made it to page one of the newspaper. Productivity is output or product per manhour of labor. (Although the labor force is close to 50–50 male and female, the term *manhour* is still used.) Each year we get a little more productive and can do a little more in the same amount of time. How? Partly by using better tools, faster computers, easier-to-understand software, and so forth; partly by being smarter and better trained for our jobs. If this sounds like magic, it should. However, this is also the source of most human progress. Higher productivity lets us produce far more than in our parents' or grandparents' generation and often work shorter hours.

How much productivity growth should we expect. In the "golden age" of the 1960s, people talked about 3 percent; in the disappointing years of the 1970s people were relieved to get 1 percent. The pace accelerated a bit in the 1980s and early 1990s and then surged at the end of the 1990s. The figure shown here, 2.5 percent, would be scorned as too low by true believers in the new economy and would be equally scorned by the traditionalists warning of irrational exuberance.[48] However, it gives results consistent with recent comments from the Federal Reserve and some widely followed economic forecasts. Further, changing just the productivity number without adjusting some of the other data will simply push all the returns higher. For these portfolios, we will use 2.5 percent for productivity growth.

Adding 0.9 percent and 2.5 percent for labor and productivity growth gives a figure for real economic growth of 3.4 percent. "Real" growth means economic growth excluding inflation. This is better than the results of the last 20 years, but worse than the results of the last three or four years. Inflation is the next key variable. We use an estimate of 2.6 percent, again consistent with the kinds of assumptions being made by the Federal Reserve. Adding inflation to real growth gives nominal growth in the economy of 6 percent. This is also the estimate for the cash return.

Over the long term, it is hard to get a higher investment return than the overall economy unless the investor is willing to take some risk. If you could invest in the entire economy, you will still bear the risk that the whole show slips, but you would have diversified all your other risks into the general economy. One could argue that this should be a global calculation, not just for the United States. However, investing globally introduces a lot of risks that are largely absent within the United States, including currency shifts and some political upheavals. Another way to look at it is that a low-risk investment shouldn't grow faster than the source of that investment's value and return—the overall economy.

Of course, we don't want to invest just in Treasury bills or cash, and we would like to make returns greater than about 6 percent including inflation. This leads to taking on some additional risks in return for greater returns. Holding bonds instead of cash opens the door to some additional risks because the bond market changes as interest rates move up and down. Over the life of a 10-year Treasury note, there will be shifts in its value and in the returns earned on interest income that is received and reinvested. To balance these risks, investors expect higher returns. Based on performance over the last decade or more, the added return or risk premium is estimated at 1 percentage point, giving a projected return for intermediate-term Treasuries of 7 percent. Treasuries do not have any credit risk since the government could, in theory, print money to pay off its debts. (Further, as of 2000, the government is running a surplus and some politicians are actually discussing how long it will take to pay off all of the national debt.) Other kinds of bonds do have some credit risk and do earn higher returns than Treasuries to compensate for the added risks. As the risk rises, or as credit ratings decline from AAA through BBB to lower levels, returns generally rise.

Probably the most debated figure on the table is the equity risk premium, the added returns to equities over Treasury bonds because equities are riskier. There is a long literature about this and an outstanding puzzle about the historical value.[49] Over long stretches of the twentieth century the equity risk premium has been around 6 percent. At the same time, most studies of consumer behavior and the economy cannot justify a figure much above 2 or 3 percent at most. A lot of the long-term studies are affected by including periods like the Great Depression which magnifies both risks and returns. We use a figure of 3 percent here because we are assuming somewhat stronger growth and productivity than over the sweep of the twentieth century and because we are not suggesting a repeat of the Great Depression. There will be recessions, but not a significant risk of a total collapse of the economy. Investment planning for another Great Depression would be different and would include a lot of cash and possibly a larger non-U.S. position than any of the portfolios discussed here.

The equity risk premium of 3 percent added to the return on Treasury bonds give an expected return for large-cap U.S. stocks of 10.3 percent. This is much lower than the average of 1996 to 1999 when the S&P 500 returned 25 percent annually. It is, however, close to the longer period returns seen since World War II. In real terms, the return of 7.8 percent is also typical of the S&P 500 in the last 50 years. Comparing these calculations to the last few years is further evidence that the late 1990s were not typical years for the U.S. stock market. Lest you feel doomed to never seeing much wealth, recognize that 10 percent annually doubles your money in about seven years—not all that bad.

As discussed previously, small-cap stocks are accorded a small risk premium compared to large-cap stocks of 1 percentage point. This is not a free ride since small caps are riskier than large caps and don't earn this extra return month in and month out. However, large-cap stocks in other industrial nations are not expected to have any higher returns than large-cap stocks in the United States. In today's world with global communications and international competition, there is no reason to believe that a company in the United States is fundamentally more, or less, efficient and profitable than a company in Japan or Europe or Canada or any other industrialized nation. So, international equities don't have a return premium. They do offer some diversification benefits and can be useful in portfolios. This argument does not apply to emerging markets. In these newly emerging nations, conditions are very different from the United States. Economic growth can be two or three times faster than here and markets are growing rapidly. Certainly risks are greater, but so are potential returns in the emerging markets.

Table 20-1, which summarized the estimation of long-run returns, gives you the tools to develop your own estimates, if you disagree with the assumptions discussed here.

We will look at four suggested or model portfolios. All can be assembled with index funds (or in many cases exchange traded funds) or with a combination of funds and stocks. Figure 20-1 and Table 20-2 show the efficient frontier and the four model portfolios discussed here.

THE CONSERVATIVE INVESTOR

The first portfolio, "long-run conservative," is the left most of the four and therefore the lowest risk. At the same time, it is not very far left. Given the long-time horizon and the opportunity for an investor to track and adjust his positions, restricting the investments to bonds or cash would mean giving up substantial returns for no real gain. If you want an investment that is a sure thing for Rip van Winkle—one you can lock up and not look at for 20 years—this may not guarantee a peaceful nap. But, for more practical purposes over a long-term period, this is consistent with what investors have experienced in the last several decades. One thing should be clear: this is aimed at someone with a reasonably long time frame—15 or more years and a low appetite for risk. Many financial advisers would put much less than 40 percent in bonds for a time frame of 15 years or more. If the

FIGURE 20-1   The Efficient Frontier for Portfolios

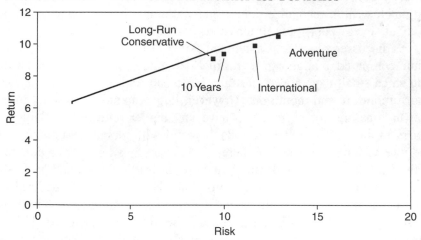

risks seem too large or your time period is shorter, the easy adjustment is
to shift more from stocks to bonds. Of course, this would lower the anticipated returns.

This portfolio puts 60 percent in large-cap stocks. This can be done
through any S&P 500 index fund or exchange traded fund. It can also be
done with other indexes, although data will be harder to find and, since
there is less competition, low-cost funds will also be harder to find than
with the S&P 500. The other 40 percent is in 10-year Treasury securities.
This can be accomplished with an intermediate-term bond index fund that
limits itself to high investment grade issues. (There are no fixed-income
exchange traded funds). If one is dealing with a large amount of money, it
may also be efficient to work with a broker to assemble a portfolio of bonds
to meet the fixed-income requirement. In this case, the bonds could be tax-
exempt municipal bonds that also help on the tax side.

This portfolio probably sounds rather boring. In one sense it is—few
stories to tell at cocktail parties about great investments. However, at moments in the last decade or two, this portfolio hit all the hot spots. The
60 percent exposure to large-cap stocks would have been brilliant in the
late 1990s while the 40 percent in government bonds would have been a
stroke of genius in 1982–1984, when bonds outperformed some stocks
as well as most of their own history. And the risks, while not zero, are
quite moderate.

This portfolio, given the estimated returns described above and the historical risks, would be expected to return about 9 percent annually with a
risk (standard deviation) of 9.4 percent. These are projections and, as the

mutual fund advertisements always say, "past performance is no guarantee of future results." The risk suggests that two-thirds of the time, the return would be between zero and 18 percent annually. This portfolio—and just about any investment—can lose money.

AN INVESTOR LOOKING FORWARD 10 YEARS

For an investor willing to take on some more risk than the first person and looking at a 10-year time horizon, the second portfolio is worth some consideration. It offers a bit more return, projected at 9.4 percent, with some additional risk and a small increase in complexity. There is also more opportunity to make adjustments and vary the details over time.

First, this portfolio adds 10 percent in non-U.S. equities. The international equity asset class is modeled with the MSCI EAFE index. This is one of a handful of widely used international equity indexes with long histories available. It is also the basis of some mutual funds. Moreover, components of EAFE are the basis of iShares MSCI series of exchange traded funds.[50] The international component doesn't add return, but it does diversify away some of the risk.

Second, this portfolio splits the S&P 500 (or large-cap stocks) into two parts: growth and value. The two segments behave differently and have different risk and return patterns. We assume that the value stocks return a bit more than the growth stocks giving the value half an expected return of 10.6 percent and the growth side an expected return of 10 percent. This is roughly consistent with their long-run experience. In contrast, in the last few years growth has done better than value. However, the history back to 1975 still puts value as the better bet over the long haul. Their risks are also different, with value having slightly lower risks, in part because they offer higher dividend yields.[51] This portfolio equally weights value and growth, so the effect is the same as using only the S&P 500. However, an investor may want to make adjustments over time to either lower risks slightly or to place modest bets on his or her ability to predict near-term winners in the value versus growth race.

This portfolio still has 30 percent in bonds. This may seem like a large position, but risk considerations do still matter if the funds are really going to be needed in 10 years. An investor who sees this as too conservative can replace the bonds with more stocks, or look to one of the next two portfolios.

AN INTERNATIONALIST

This portfolio takes a larger stake in international equities than the others. At times investors believe that the opportunities outside the United States are far better than those inside. Coming off almost a decade of outstanding economic growth and stock performance, it is hard to realize that at times the grass looks greener in the other guy's pasture. However, during the 1980s Japan was viewed as invincible with a market that would never fall. People talked about Japan as number one and how its global position would soon exceed America's. Things certainly didn't work out that way, as Japan's markets slid and the economy crumbled in a series of financial reversals at the end of the 1980s. But, memory of Japan's moment in the sun should remind us that economies and markets can rise and fall. There are certainly times when investment abroad will outperform those at home.

The internationalist puts 30 percent of his money in equities outside the United States. Since 10 percent is put in cash, the 30 percent represents a third of the equity investments for this portfolio; this is a bit below but close to the market share represented by non-U.S. equities among world equities. As before this is modeled with the MSCI EAFE index, as in the previous portfolio. However, most dedicated international investors will probably want to look at more detailed country-by-country allocations. Most of the single-country mutual funds use one or another index as a benchmark, but the majority are not managed to closely track an index. There are some index funds available, plus a number of exchange traded funds. This means that investors can use the indexes to analyze past performance and consider how they want to design their portfolio.

The internationalist differs in other ways from the 10-year portfolio. The fixed income position is 10 percent rather than 30 percent and the weighting of growth and value for U.S. equities is not equally weighted. The overall index has an anticipated return of 9.9 percent, based on the expected returns discussed at the beginning of this chapter. It has an anticipated standard deviation of 11.7 percentage points. Compared to the earlier portfolios, both risk and return are higher. This portfolio is more volatile and more likely to experience years with losses than the earlier ones. But, over the long run it is also expected to give better returns.

For U.S. equities, 35 percent is put into large-cap value stocks and 25 percent is in large-cap growth stocks. Over the period from 1975 to 1999, value outperformed growth. From 1994 through 1999, growth beat value for the longest such run on record, averaging about a 9 percentage annual margin. However, in the first five months of 2000, value beat growth by over 5 percentage points. Reflecting the better long-run performance of the value side as well as its lower risk, a slightly larger commitment to value stocks is suggested here.

While value stocks are attractive index plays, growth stocks may be a place where some investors would substitute individual securities. The focus on large-cap growth has left the top of the S&P 500 and the S&P 500/BARRA Growth index rather top heavy. With only 35 stocks representing the top 50 percent of the S&P 500's market value as of early 2000, it may be possible select a handful of leading growth stocks to get most of the impact of holding the S&P 500/BARRA Growth index through one or another mutual fund. For active stock pickers, this provides an opportunity to choose exposure to some well-known large-cap technology stocks. If you want to be overweighted in Cisco or underweighted in Microsoft, you can customize this portion of your portfolio. At the same time, you can leave areas that are harder to keep informed about, such as international investing, to the indexes.

AN ADVENTUROUS INVESTOR LOOKING FOR SOME HIDDEN OPPORTUNITIES

The hidden argument for this portfolio may be that one can be adventurous and still use indexes. We begin with a brief review of the portfolio and then turn to which parts could be based on stocks instead of indexes. Unlike the other portfolios, this one is 100 percent equities. As such, it is not a good choice if the portfolio is going to be liquidated and the funds used within a few years. The stock market is too volatile for most investors to place funds that are targeted for a specific use within a few years 100 percent in equities. No matter how good, or lucky, you are as an investor, you are asking for a guarantee against loss—a guarantee that the market simply can not give. But, for the more adventurous and longer-term investor, this is a good place to start.

Like the internationalist portfolio, there is 35 percent in large-cap value stocks and 25 percent in large-cap growth stocks. Recall that value stocks are ones where not everyone sees the value since there isn't a lot of earnings growth in evidence yet. As a group, value stocks do nicely most of the time; as individual stocks, they sometimes require strong commitments and strong stomachs. The 25 percent in large-cap growth will assure some exposure to the popular spots of the moment.

The more adventurous part comes with 20 percent in small caps and 20 percent in international stocks. The 20 percent in small caps is roughly double the market weight of this sector and represents a large bet. It is also an area where stock pickers can shine if they are careful. There are two widely used small-cap indexes tracked by mutual funds: the S&P Small-Cap 600 and the Russell 2000. The Russell 2000 is the more often quoted of the two.

While both indexes focus on small-cap stocks, there are some differences between the two indexes beyond the number of stocks in each. The Russell 2000 is reconstituted once a year at the end of June. It represents the 1001st through 3000th largest stocks traded in the United States. There is a big cap index, the Russell 1000 represents the first 1000 stocks. During the year some stocks drop out. Once a year the entire list is redone. This causes a huge spate of trading at the end of June as stocks shift in and out. Before the annual rebalancing, the index may contain some high fliers that will be "promoted" to the Russell 1000 index—meaning that some of the stocks may not be very small by the time they leave the index. Given the large number of stocks in the Russell 2000, it is likely that some index funds do not hold all the stocks. Rather, they use statistical models to select a smaller sample and hope that this will mimic the overall index.

The S&P SmallCap 600 is run differently from the Russell 2000. First, there are about a third as many stocks. Second, instead of an annual rebalancing when 20 percent of the stocks may turn over, the stocks are monitored all the time and replaced as necessary. Generally, this means the index can stay closer to small-cap stocks rather than be pushed around by the market. Over the period since January 1995, the S&P SmallCap 600 outperformed the Russell 2000 by a narrow margin. The S&P SmallCap 600 also enjoyed slightly lower risk. If you end up choosing between two index funds—one based on one index and the other on the other—you should look at returns, risks, and expenses. Returns are an obvious thing to look at. Here it is important to look at the fund's returns, not the index. They can vary due to expenses, trading costs, and strategies about how many of the stocks in the index to actually own.

Second, look at expenses. In a boom year when stocks rise 20 percent, no one cares whether the fund expenses are a half percentage point or 2 percentage points. In a so-so year when stocks rise only 2 percent, the expense ratio may be the difference between profit and loss. You should also look at risk. While we wouldn't expect to see major differences since the risks of the two indexes are close, it is worth watching. One way to compare two funds for risk and return is to calculate the Sharpe ratio, defined as the return less the risk-free return and then divided by risk. The risk-free rate is usually taken to be Treasury bills. The higher the Sharpe ratio, the more return beyond T-bills you are getting for each unit of risk you take. This can also be done with individual stocks, although the data are much harder to come by and the risks tend to be a lot larger so it may not be too practical. The last part of the Adventurous portfolio is international;

the same comments about considering some country-by-country bets discussed above apply here.

The biggest difference in this portfolio is certainly the 20 percent in small-cap stocks. While this sounds modest, it is about twice the market weighting so it represents a substantial position. It is also an area where some investors will want to skip indexes and choose some individual stocks. This is an interesting idea if you have access to some good analysts and stock pickers, but it can also result in sharply higher risks than expected. For many investors, small caps are thought to be synonymous with dotcom start-ups in Silicon Valley. This is not the case if one looks at either the Russell 2000 or the S&P SmallCap 600. Both indexes have much broader representation and probably no more than a third of the market capitalization in technology. There is nothing wrong with technology, but you could end with a portfolio that is overweighted in technology if you're not careful. The growth–value portions of the S&P 500 will probably be about 25 percent technology; if all your "small caps" are really small technology stocks (and probably growth stocks as well) you will have a portfolio that is 45 percent in technology as well as 45 percent in growth. This is not the mix you were probably aiming for and certainly not the risk level implied in the example. If you pick stocks, check the balance between growth and value and among economic sectors with some care so as to realize when you are betting on an odd corner of the market.

TABLE 20-2   Index Asset Classes, Returns, and Risks for Suggested Portfolios

	Long-Run Conservative	10 Years	International	Adventurous
Expected Return	9.0%	9.4%	9.9%	10.5%
Expected Risk	9.4%	10.0%	11.7%	12.9%
Cash	—	—	10%	—
10-Year Treasuries	40%	30%	—	—
S&P 500 Value	30%	30%	35%	35%
S&P 500 Growth	30%	30%	25%	25%
Small-Cap Stocks	—	—	—	20%
International (EAFE)	—	10%	30%	20%

Table 20-2 summarizes the portfolios giving the positions in each of the indexes/asset classes and the expected returns and risks. The returns and risks are expected—not assured or in any way guaranteed; further they are based on long-term patterns so any single year or a few years is almost certainly going to give different results.

21

MARKET TIMING AND OTHER MYTHS

The hardest part of investing is probably what to do after you build the portfolio. Doubts creep in: should you take more risk? Is this really the *right* moment to get into the market? Maybe I need a bit more weight in midcap growth stocks? Am I too light on technology? For many of us the doubts about decisions morph into an urge to trade; or worse, to a panic to pull out. Still others correctly anticipate these doubts and never invest at all. One of the lessons of index funds is that buy-and-hold investing works best for most people. Index funds may seem like the slow way to wealth, but they have been demonstrated to be the successful way to wealth. This chapter examines some of the ideas that can distract us from buy and hold or drive us toward more active trading. Some of these strategies do work, and there may well be tactics that are theoretically more profitable than buying index funds. There are certainly approaches that are more enter-taining than index funds. So, separating the entertainment value from the investing values is important. Neither entertainment nor investment are bad, and both are worth pursuing; just put a (big) piece of the nest egg in the index nest before the show starts.

MARKET TIMING

Market timing is the idea—the wish—that we can buy when the market is low and sell when it is high. It is also an eternal hope. More questions and fewer reliable answers from Wall Street deal with timing, what the stock market will do next, and how much of your money to put in the market than anything else. Virtually every major investment house and Wall Street institution has a recommended asset allocation[52] that claims to time the market. Few if any consistently beat a buy-and-hold strategy of never making such bets.

Market timing is very difficult because one must be consistently right to reap any gains and because it holds the seeds of its own destruction. Consistently right because one needs to know both when to get out of the market and when to get back in the market. One of the most famous market calls of the last decade was Alan Greenspan's speech about irrational exuberance. On December 5, 1996, Federal Reserve Chairman Alan Greenspan, giving the Francis Boyer Lecture of The American Enterprise Institute for Public Policy Research described the then-current state of the stock market as "irrationally exuberant" and strongly hinted that the market would pull back. It didn't. Rather, it was only the beginning of what proved to be the strongest five consecutive years on record. Greenspan is no amateur when it comes to economics, finance, or forecasting. His track record as Chairman of the Federal Reserve, and before that as an economic forecaster, is one of the best. (His record as an investor is not a fair target since as Fed Chairman he has chosen to avoid any possible hints of conflicts of interest by keeping most of his money in U.S. Treasury securities.) Moreover, Greenspan has as much data, as much computer power, and as many skilled analysts and economists available as any investor. So, it's not easy to get the timing right even once. Getting it right more than once seems to be even harder.

Timing, like some other strategies, tends to lead to its own downfall. Suppose someone identified an indicator that did accurately foretell when the market was near a peak. Once word got around that a particular strategy worked, investors would begin to watch it carefully in anticipation of a key signal. As the indicator got closer and closer to its critical level, some would start to sell to avoid the anticipated rush to get out. This selling would grow in volume and would depress the market. Pretty soon, by the time the much anticipated sell signal was seen, the selling would be over and done with. The indicator's apparent past success would have eliminated its value for market forecasting.

One market anomaly is the January effect—the idea that stocks perform better in January than in any other month. This has been widely written about, debated, and researched. It has also led to such comments as "this year the January effect came in November" to explain a rise in stocks around Thanksgiving. Timing does strange things for language as well.

We do know that stocks fluctuate and that not all shifts in the stock market can be explained by changes in economic fundamentals such as economic growth, corporate profits, or dividends. So far no one has found an enduring way to time these fluctuations closely enough to profit from them. Most attempts miss because they are based on poor information. A small portion may seem to be on target but don't give signals that are early enough or strong enough to cover the trading costs (and tax liabilities) involved. An even smaller portion of these timing systems appear to work.

The focus should be on "appear" because there are enough people trying to time the market that some of them will be right some of the time, just by random events. A question in many securities licensing examinations relates the tale of a stock picker who sent out several thousand letters predicting the market would rise and an equal number predicting it would fall. A few months later, he sent out two more sets of letters, but only to those who got the "correct" letter the first time. He dropped the fortunate people who got the wrong letter the last time around. This process of elimination continued until he was left with a modest number of people who had seen him correctly call the market's next move several times in a row. He offered them a chance to give him their money to manage. With enough people trying to time the market, the surprise would be if no one got it right.

Can market timing ever work? It is rather doubtful. Paying some attention to overall trends is helpful, as is understanding the broad sweep of market history. History does suggest that long-term buy-and-hold investors in the stock market do well, but also warns that there are long periods where the market makes little progress or barely beats inflation. But, identifying these periods in advance is not easy. Moreover, when stocks do poorly, bonds rarely do better, so there may not be much to escape to.

One should add, in both fairness and completeness, that the current moment (midyear 2000) is certainly a period when some analysts question whether the stock market can continue to perform superbly well in the next decade or so. By most measures, the market is richly valued. Further, it has grown faster and farther than most other parts of the economy and sometimes seems ready to pause for other parts to catch up. However, with interest rates and inflation low, relative to the experience of the last two or three decades, it is unlikely that bonds would do much better in coming years. For those who are concerned about stock prices and who doubt the "new economy" stories, raising the non-U.S. portion of one's portfolio beyond the levels suggested in the last chapter might be the best hedge against a disappointing decade here at home.

SEASONALITY STORIES

On Wall Street the coming of summer is marked with stories about the summer rally, the fall is heralded by laments about October being the worst month for stocks (statistically it is actually September), and the turn of the year is celebrated with the January effect—which may not always arrive but rarely comes in November. Mark Twain's comments about the stock market may have said it best, "October, This is one of the peculiarly dangerous months to speculate in stocks in. The others are July, January, September, April, November, May, March, June, December, August and February."[53]

Despite Mark Twain, the idea of season patterns in the market doesn't die. There are probably some seasonal patterns in the stock market, just as there are in most economic phenomena. However, the seasonal patterns are not stable, very hard to predict, and very fast to change as investors recognize them. This all raises the key point of what can be discovered versus what can be profited from.

To make money from any kind of predictable and nonrandom behavior in the stock market we need to discover it, find enough supporting information to convince ourselves it is not just a random quirk, do this all fast enough so that everyone else doesn't eliminate the pattern with their arbitrage trading, and still have enough of a market move left to make some profits. Even in today's Internet world, trading stocks is not free. There are (usually) commissions, and there are also bid–ask spreads and market movements. Seasonal patterns fall prey to all these concerns very quickly.

If, despite all these comments, you still want to try to play the seasons, what should you do? The January effect does have a few hints amidst all the comments about it. It seems to be most pronounced among small-cap stocks, suggesting that seasonal patterns may be more pronounced in some parts of the market than others. They are also less likely to be arbitraged away overnight if they are localized to only a few spots in the market. Look for different sectors of the market or industries that may show some seasonal shifts. Retailing stocks tend to depend on Christmas sales for a large portion of their annual profits. Moreover, most retailers use a fiscal year that ends in January so that their inventories are at a post-Christmas seasonal low in their annual results. This means they report out of synchronization with most of the market, increasing the chances for strange seasonal patterns. Other industries where analysts often claim to detect seasonal patterns are semiconductors or producers of seasonal items. Christmas is the granddaddy of all seasonal shifts, and few sectors of the stock market, or anything else, are completely immune to Christmas-based seasonality.

ANOMALIES

There are a number of market anomalies that do hold up statistically and suggest that to some extent one can predict returns in some corners of the stock market.[54] Some of these are probably too small to trade on profitably and others are probably arbitraged away and replaced by different versions all the time. Nevertheless, a few are worth mentioning. It would not be prudent to bet the farm on any of these, but some people will both follow the research and make some bets on some of these.

We look at two kinds of developments: low prices and momentum. Low prices mean that prices compared to dividends, earnings, or book values are lower than usual, or lower for these stocks than for others. These are value stocks. They tend to have price-to-book, price-to-dividend, or price-earnings ratios that are lower than average. Note that all these ratios are sometimes inverted and reported the other way around. Rather than price-to-dividend, it is more common to discuss the dividend yield which is the dividend divided by the price. Because either book values or earnings can be zero, it is often easier to use book-to-price or earnings–price ratios in statistical analyses. Low prices mean high returns.

These are long-term bets. One shouldn't buy low-price stocks and expect them to outperform their high-priced brethren overnight. As the last few years have shown, there are times when low price doesn't win, even over five years. However, over the long run value has beaten growth, and the low-price strategy does seem to have statistical validity. For index fund players, this is a very easy strategy to consider and to use because the number of growth and value indexes has grown in recent years. In the portfolios in Chapter 20 we recommended having more in value than in growth in the international and adventurous portfolios. When value is out of fashion, as in the last few years, it is also easier to use indexes for value plays because it may be hard to find a lot of analysts following and recommending value stocks. Before you skip value as too unfashionable, remember that some great fortunes have been built on value plays, including Warren Buffett's.

Momentum is based on the idea that yesterday's action has something to say about today's action. The counterargument is that the market is random and what happened yesterday has no effect on what might happen today. Momentum argues that over short time periods of a year or so, stocks that are rising will keep rising and stocks that are falling will keep falling. A closely related idea is reversals—that stocks that were rising will reverse and decline. Studies find both patterns with momentum typical over periods of a year or a bit longer and reversals over periods of around five years. Reversal may also be a variation on value stocks. If a stock or a group of stocks fall, they end up with prices that are low compared to their earnings, dividends, or book values; in other words, they are value stocks.

However, the momentum and reversal patterns do not seem robust enough to offer easy profits or even any profits at all. The studies of these effects typically form portfolios of hundreds of stocks and trade them on a monthly basis to generate returns of around 1 percent per month above the total market. (Remember that the total market can fall, so some months the best momentum/reversal strategies still lose money.) Moreover, the returns are often concentrated in small stocks where the bid–ask spreads and the effects of trading, which are not included in the theoretical studies, can be large.

MEAN REVERSION

When you flip a coin several times, you often find a string of all heads or all tails. Imagine you have what a statistician calls a "fair" coin, meaning that there is a 50–50 chance of getting heads (and the same for tails; ignore stands on edge as a possible result). Should you, after a long string of heads, expect the next flip to be tails?

With coins the answer is no. Each flip is separate and independent of each other flip. What the last flip, or the last 100 flips, turned out to be tells us nothing about the next result. Does the stock market behave like coin flipping? In statistical terms, we call the market a random walk, meaning there is no method to its madness and the past has nothing to tell us about the future. Under this approach, the fact that the years 1995–1999 were the best five consecutive years on record doesn't suggest anything about how 2000 or 2000–2004 will turn out.

With the stock market there is an alternative view, mean reversion. This is the idea that there is some long-run average or mean behavior and the market will return (revert) to it over time. The reversion need not be very fast to make a difference in the long run. Since we have 75 years of history for the S&P 500 and, combining that with other data, around 200 years of U.S. stock market history, it might seem easy to settle this debate with the numbers. Unfortunately, it's not. For any empirical demonstration for (or against) mean reversion, one can find an equally erudite objection. The jury is still out.

However, the debate over mean reversion is more than just a curiosity for investors. If you believe the market will revert to some long-term normal pattern, and if you enjoyed big gains in the 1995–1999 run-up, then mean reversion argues that you should take some money off the table now, before the market reverts toward its mean. Of course, if you really were a believer in mean reversion, you would have taken some money off the table in 1997, more in 1998, and even more in 1999; you might be completely out of the market by now.

DIVIDEND PRICE MODELS AND THE LONG RUN
Concerns similar to worries about mean reversion also show up in different models of the market that suggest it is poised for a big fall and a long period of disappointing performance. These kinds of things are not hard to generate. Simply calculate the average price–earnings or dividend yield over the last 20 or 30 years and compare it to the current levels. In either case, today's values are at, or close to, the most extreme ever seen. One of the longest data sets is the one used by Robert Shiller that extends back to 1871.[55] These all suggest that the stock market is at very high levels and should soon return to earth.

We do know that 2000 is different from 1871 and different from many of the years that came between 1871 and 2000. However, if we want to completely set aside not only the market of 129 years ago, but also the markets before roughly 1980, we must accept some different views. Arguing that today's valuations should not be a cause for concern, that today's low dividend yields and high p–e's don't count, requires some aggressive views of risk, volatility, and economic growth.

The risk in stocks shifts over time. Certainly, with the power of hindsight we can say that stocks in the 1980s were less risky than in the early 1930s. Stocks were less risky in 1987, when they recovered from the crash in less than a year, than in 1929, when they didn't even hit bottom for three years and then didn't recover for another 21 years. However, the question really is what kinds of risk the future holds and how we perceive it. If stocks are truly becoming less risky, then their prices will rise and stay up to reflect this risk reduction. (Consider the stock of a company with a record of volatile earnings that average 15 percent growth over 10 years. If a new CEO comes in and delivers the same 15 percent growth with more stable and predictable earnings, the stock will rise because the risk of a rotten year—and a price dive—is less.) If the arrival of the Internet and the new economy in recent years has reduced the risks of business and the volatility of earnings, then stocks should be able to support higher prices.

There is another aspect of this picture, though. If the risks inherent in stocks are less now than 20 years ago, stocks are likely to return less going forward. After all, returns are partly a reward for risks and if the risks are less, so will be the returns. This is usually seen in the equity risk premium, the difference between the return on bonds and stocks. If stocks are less risky, then this spread narrows and, in the future, stocks won't earn as much as in the past.

The other aspect of wanting to set aside the historically high valuations of today's market is economic growth. Most of the debates around the new economy center on the idea that productivity and economic growth are stronger now and in the future than in the past. As with the mean reversion question, one would like to answer this with some data. Unfortunately, the data are still scanty and the argument is far from resolved. Early evidence suggests there is something to the new economy story, but how much and how long-lasting no one knows as yet.

Where does this leave us? We do know that the last few years have pushed stocks to very high levels and that these same years have seen very strong economic growth. We also know that while the future is bright for the economy, markets have a way of getting a bit carried away and overshooting their reasonable values. So, while a lot of the new economy story and at least some of the lower-risk ideas are probably true, the stock market may have gained a fair amount of hype and hot air in the last five years. We would not be slaves to history that says the dividend yield must return to 5 percent or that the price–earnings ratio must drop to 14 times. But we would be wary of some pullback as some of the hottest air and highest hopes are squeezed out of the market in coming years. We would also remember that most of the alternatives, such as bonds, aren't likely to see extraordinarily good times if stocks do slow a bit.

CHAPTER

22

PUTTING IT TOGETHER AND KEEPING IT SIMPLE

WHAT TO DO FIRST

Investing and investing successfully seems to be shrouded in mystery at times. As you venture into investment books or talk to friends about investing, you hear about arcane theories, war stories of brilliant stock picks, and tales of exemplary investors, ranging from Warren Buffett to Internet chat room experts to the friendly stockbroker. Through the last two hundred pages we have argued that with a sense of financial history and a general understanding of what a stock index is, one can be a reasonably successful investor without decades of experience or several advanced degrees. One of the secrets of index investing is that anyone can do it; it requires a lot of patience, but not much higher math.

Probably the major drawback of indexing as an investment strategy is that it lacks entertainment value most of the time. Today investing is not just something one sets aside a couple of hours a week to do as part of an effort to ensure retirement funds. Rather, investing rivals professional sports as an all-consuming avocation, major topic of television and radio, and the preferred conversation topic for every initial meeting or ice breaking—business or romantic. Index investing is a preferred route to investment success, but it is not likely to grip your audience at a summer picnic or help meet members of the opposite sex at the local singles bar. This last chapter offers some closing comments about planning and investing for retire-

ment, about how to manage investments with indexes, and why it sometimes seems not to work as well as you hoped. Of course, the most difficult part of investing, as with many other things, is getting started. Taking
that step is the most important—and also one that indexes can't help with.

RETIREMENT . . . DON'T JUST SETTLE, INVEST!

Most sessions or discussions about retirement planning begin with a ser-
mon about setting goals and then lead to a statement about retiring on
75 percent of your current income. Until the advent of business casual dress,
comments that after retirement your dry-cleaning bills will be lower used
to be included. Retiring on 75 percent of your current income might sound
like a reasonable idea. But, retiring on 500 percent of your income is certainly a better idea. In fact, if you can do it on 1500 percent, that is better
still. A reasonable minimum is probably around 100 percent of what you
expect your income to be shortly *before* you retire.

If you are setting a goal, the answer should be as much as possible.
Having too big an estate to leave behind is a problem we would all love to
have. Wanting as much as possible doesn't mean that you should take out-
rageous retirement risks or swing for the fences when you choose stocks.
It doesn't mean never owning a bond or buying only a small-cap stock index. But, when you develop your own retirement investing program, or
when you look at the model portfolios described in Chapter 20, don't think
about merely reaching some nearby goal. Rather, think about how much
you want to invest and how much risk you are comfortable with. Then develop a program using some index funds.

If you want to scare yourself a bit, consider a simple rule of thumb.
Take whatever annual withdrawal amount you want your retirement nest
egg to support and multiply it by 25 to get an idea of how much money
you need. Want to retire on $100,000 per year? Then you need about $2.5
million in your portfolio. Both simulation analyses and historical reviews
suggest that this is a good place to start.

Second, unless you are within a few years of retiring, you should assume that your income will rise between now and then and so will your
appetite for spending your income. We all read sad stories of people at age
62 with no retirement nest egg. There is little one can do about saving it
all in only a few years. Equally disturbing are stories of people at age 22
who think they can save for retirement with only a savings account paying
3 percent—they forget that their salaries will be much higher after 40 years
of working life, and so will their retirement needs. In simple terms, don't
settle—seek some more.

INFLATION'S NASTY IMPACT

If you remember the high inflation days of the 1970s or have read a few tales of woe, you know that inflation has a way of raising all the targets to very high levels. Even with the recent lower inflation, a rough or prudent number to use in long-term planning is probably 3 percent or 4 percent inflation. At this rate, your money loses half its value in less than 20 years. If you are 25 years old now, the dollar you put aside today is worth less than a quarter when you finally retire. The two best defenses against inflation are holding stocks and having more wealth. The first is part of achieving the second. Again, more money is better. A little greed rather than agreeing to settle for less is important in planning your retirement.

If you are worrying about sending children to college, recognize that the time frames are probably shorter and the inflation rates are probably higher. Otherwise, everything else is little changed from the retirement puzzle.

DOES INDEXING ALWAYS WORK?

If the goal of investing is to seek high returns with risks you can manage in investments that you understand, indexing works. Moreover, experience shows it is low cost and usually outperforms other approaches quite handily. Moreover, it is simple and easy and leaves time for other activities you may like better.

There are two caveats: if you want the entertainment value, and what to do if all the active managers seem to be beating the indexes.

If you want entertainment with your investing, that's fine. Set some of the money aside in an index portfolio and actively manage the rest. Compare the results of the two portfolios every year or so and see which is doing better. If you turn out to be an investment genius, you can move money from the index portfolio to your stock picking. (And, you will also appreciate indexing even more.) If you turn out to be a rotten stock picker, or you're just getting bored and want to take up golf, then put the active-managed money into the index portfolio.

What if indexing seems to be slipping? Chances are indexing is doing fine, you're in a less-than-favored asset class. If you're in large-cap stocks and using the S&P 500 and you find that a higher than normal number of active managers and mutual funds are beating the index, compare the returns of large-cap and small-cap indexes. What is usually happening is that the small-cap index is outperforming the large-cap index. The active managers aren't holding pure large-cap portfolios the way the index is. If they are lucky to be overweighted in small caps, they are getting an extra ride from small caps and outperforming the large-cap index. The answer may be to shift your balance of large-cap and small-cap indexes.

Think the active managers always know where to be? Doubtful, since in most years two-thirds of them underperform the index. Moreover, many of those active managers don't have pure portfolios when their asset class is in favor. In other words, in the years when large caps beat small caps, the large-cap index funds will clean up compared with the large-cap actively managed funds. Indexing does work.

Notes

1. Data from Standard & Poor's/Micropal AIM databases.
2. Based on data in the 1999 *Annual Report* for Berkshire Hathaway, a dollar invested in 1965 in Berkshire's book value would have appreciated over 1900 times by the end of 1999; the same dollar invested in the S&P 500 would have appreciated only about 60 times. No wonder Warren Buffett is respected as an investment genius. The rest of us may be better off with the index.
3. *Flow of Funds Accounts of the United States, Release Z-1,* Board of Governors of the Federal Reserve System, Washington, DC, various dates.
4. See Profit Sharing Council of America Web site, http://www.PSCA.org/grow-401k.html. Data for the 1999 study are being collected in early 2000.
5. *Flow of Funds Accounts of the United States, Release Z-1,* Board of Governors of the Federal Reserve System, Washington, DC, March 10, 2000.
6. *Flow of Funds Accounts of the United States, Release Z-1,* Board of Governors of the Federal Reserve System, Washington, DC, June 2000, Table L9.
7. Jeremy Siegel, *Stocks for the Long Run,* Second Edition, McGraw-Hill, 1998, chapter 7.
8. Alfred Cowles, III and Associates, *Common Stock Indexes,* Principia Press, Bloomington, Indiana, 1939, Table P-1.
9. Alfred Cowles, III and Associates, *Common Stock Indexes,* Principia Press, Bloomington, Indiana, 1939.
10. James K. Glassman and Kevin A. Hassett, *Dow 36000: The New Strategy for Profiting from the Coming Rise in the Stock Market,* Times Books, 1999.
11. Earnings forecasts can be found at various Web sites or in newspapers. Standard & Poor's publishes forecasts at www.spglobal.com and www.personalwealth.com.
12. Data from Standard & Poor's/Published Image ChartSource data.
13. As discussed in the introduction, the author is directly involved in the work on the S&P 500.
14. William F. Sharpe, "The Simple Arithmetic of Active Management," *Financial Analysts Journal* 47(1), pp. 7–9 or www.wfsharpe.com.
15. Some investors—not the ones in the fund—may want to sell stock short. To do this they are required to borrow the securities. The interest paid on these loans provides

some income to funds that partially offsets the costs of the fund. Not all index funds lend securities and some actively managed funds may also lend securities.

16. Henry Shilling, "Investing in Index Funds" in Frank Fabozzi and Robert P. Molay, *Perspectives on Equity Indexing,* Fabozzi Associates, 2000.

17. See Jeremy Siegel, *Stocks in the Long Run,* McGraw-Hill, 1998, Chapter 6.

18. Ibbotson Associates, *Stocks, Bonds, Bills and Inflation,* Ibbotson Associates, Chicago, Ill., various annual editions.

19. see www.dfafunds.com.

20. Eugene Fama and Kenneth French, "Size and Book to Market Factors in Earnings and Returns," *Journal of Finance*, vol. 50, no. 1, March 1995, and other papers by the same authors.

21. Readers may want to refer to discussion about the author's position at Standard & Poor's in the introduction.

22. "Stocks, Bonds, Bills, and Inflation: Year-by-Year Historical Returns (1926–74)," *Journal of Business* 49, January 1976, pp. 11–43.

23. Eugene Fama and Kenneth French, "Size and Book to Market Factors in Earnings and Returns," *Journal of Finance*, vol. 50, no. 1, March 1995, and other papers by the same authors.

24. See www.Barra.com; www.dfafunds.com; www.russell.com; www.spglobal.com.

25. The easiest reference for a lot of data and detail is www.msci.com.

26. The reference for the FTSE World Actuaries is www.ftse.com.

27. Further information can be found at www.ishares.com or at www.indexfunds.com.

28. Sharpe, "Simple Arithmetic of Active Management," *Financial Analysts Journal,* 47(1) pp. 7–9 or www.wfsharpe.com; John C. Bogle, *Common Sense on Mutual Funds*, Wiley, 1999.

29. Terrance Odean, "Do Investors Trade Too Much," *American Economic Review,* December 1999.

30. Any good finance text will discuss the capital asset pricing model, Sharpe's work, and the three-factor model developed by Fama and French.

31. Probably the most dedicated value stock adherent is Robert Haugen, *The New Finance: The Case Against Efficient Markets*, Prentice Hall, 1995.

32. Jeremy J. Siegel, *Stocks for the Long Run*, Second Edition, McGraw-Hill, 1998, p. 95.

33. See Siegel and R. Banz, "The Relationship Between Return and Market Value of Common Stocks," *Journal of Financial Economics*, 9(1981), pp. 3–18.

34. A major popularizer of these arguments is Harry Dent, *The Roaring 2000's*, Touchstone Books, 1998.

35. James P. O'Shaughnessy, *What Works on Wall Street*, McGraw-Hill, 1997.

36. Robert Shiller, "Do Stock Prices Move Too Much to Be Justified by Subsequent Changes in Dividends?" *American Economic Review,* 71, 1981.

37. The text is stealing from the title of Charles McKay's classic, *Extraordinary Popular Delusions and the Madness of Crowds*, 1841, which described the tulip bulb mania of the 1600s, the South Sea Bubble, and other famous market events.

38. Time value of money calculations are explained in most introductory finance books. For 8 percent, the dollar in 10 years is $(1.00) \times (1.08^{10})$.

39. Mathematically, if D is the dividend, r is the discount rate and g is the dividend growth rate then the stock's value is $D/(r - g)$.

40. Shiller's earliest work in the area is "Do Stock Prices Move Too Much to Be Justified by Subsequent Movements in Dividends," *American Economic Review*, 71(3), 1981.

More recently, he has provided a review of his research in *Irrational Exuberance*, Princeton University Press, 2000.

41. See Roger G. Ibbotson and Paul D. Kaplan, "Does Asset Allocation Policy Explain 40%, 90%, or 100% of Performance," Ibbotson Associates at www.Ibbotson.com, April 1999.

42. Harry Markowitz, *Portfolio Selection*, Yale University Press, 1959, summarizes the asset allocation work. Despite the importance of mathematics in finance, much of the book can be easily understood with little more than high school algebra.

43. See Mark P. Kritzman, *Puzzles in Finance*, John Wiley & Sons, 2000, Chapter 3.

44. The leading modern soon-to-be classics include Jeremy Siegel's *Stocks for the Long Run*, McGraw-Hill, 1998, Robert Shiller's recent *Irrational Exuberance*, Princeton University Press, 2000, and the annual yearbook published by Ibbotson Associates, Chicago, Ill. All these offer discussions of long-term results in the U.S. stock market.

45. *Emerging Stock Markets Factbook 1999,* International Finance Corporation, Washington, D.C., 1999.

46. All emerging markets are about 7 percent of global market capitalization according to the *Emerging Markets Factbook 1999.*

47. This is probably the most counterintuitive fact in all of finance. Suppose you buy a bond paying 6 percent interest. A week later interest rates all rise and the same kind of bond now pays 7 percent. Isn't your old 6 percent bond worth less?

48. See "Productivity on Stilts," *The Economist,* June 12, 2000.

49. For a recent and comprehensive review of the issues, see Bradford Cornell, *The Equity Risk Premium*, Wiley, 1999.

50. Information of most exchange traded funds can be found on the AMEX Web site, www.AMEX.com or www.ishares.com.

51. Robert Haugen has argued that value stocks are a much better bet. See *The Inefficient Stock Market,* Prentice Hall, 1999.

52. That includes Standard & Poor's Investment Policy Committee.

53. Mark Twain, *Puddn'head Wilson,* 1893.

54. This section draws on John H. Cochrane, "New Facts in Finance," *Economic Perspectives,* Third Quarter 1999, Federal Reserve Bank of Chicago.

55. Reference is Shiller's Web site: www.econ.yale.edu/~shiller/

Index

ABOUT THE AUTHOR

David M. Blitzer, Ph.D., is managing director, chief investment strategist, and chairman of the S&P 500 Index Committee for Standard & Poor's. Dr. Blitzer wrote *What's the Economy Trying to Tell You? Everyone's Guide to Understanding and Profiting from the Economy.* He currently writes *Trends & Projections,* a Standard & Poor's monthly review of the U.S. economy, and regularly contributes analyses to *Credit Week* and other S&P publications. A regular guest on CNBC, CNN, and *Nightly Business Report,* Dr. Blitzer is often quoted in the national business press, including *The New York Times, The Wall Street Journal, USA Today,* and other publications.